Professional Examinations

Certificate in Business Accounting

Paper C1

Management Accounting Fundamentals

CIMA Study Text

KAPLAN

PUBLISHING

FOULKS LYNCH

British Library Cataloguing-in-Publication Data

A catalogue record for this book is available from the British Library.

Kaplan Publishing Foulks Lynch
Swift House
Market Place
Wokingham
Berkshire RG40 1AP

ISBN 1 84390 653 8

© FTC Kaplan Limited, 2004

Printed and bound in Great Britain.

Acknowledgements

We are grateful to the Chartered Institute of Management Accountants, the Association of Chartered Certified Accountants and the Institute of Chartered Accountants in England and Wales for permission to reproduce past examination questions. The answers have been prepared by Kaplan Publishing Foulks Lynch.

INTRODUCTION

Working closely with experienced CIMA tutors, we have developed a range of comprehensive and easy-to-use Study Texts.

Fully updated for the new CIMA exams, this Study Text forms an excellent resource for your exam preparation. It covers all syllabus topics to the required depth, and contains a wealth of exam-style and practice questions.

Throughout the text you will find plenty of relevant examples, activities, tables and diagrams. These will put the subject matter in context and help you absorb the material easily.

The following points explain some of the concepts we had in mind when developing the layout of this book:

DEFINITION

- **Definitions.** The text defines key words and concepts, placing them in the margin, with a clear heading, as on the left. The purpose of including these definitions is to focus your attention on the point being covered.

KEY POINT

- **Key points**. Also, in the margin, you will see key points at regular intervals. The purpose of these is to summarise concisely the key material being covered.

- **Activities**. The text involves you in the learning process with a series of activities designed to catch your attention and make you concentrate and respond. The feedback to activities is at the end of each chapter.

- **Self-test questions**. At the end of each chapter there is a series of self-test questions. The purpose of these is to help you revise some of the key elements of the chapter. All the answers to these questions can be found in the text.

- **End of chapter questions**. At the end of each chapter we include examination-type questions. These will give you a very good idea of the sort of thing the examiner will ask and will test your understanding of what has been covered.

Good luck with your studies!

CONTENTS

SYLLABUS AND LEARNING OUTCOMES

Learning aims

This syllabus aims to test the student's ability to:

- explain the basic concepts and processes used to determine product and service costs

- explain absorption cost, marginal cost, opportunity cost, notional cost and relevant cost concepts

- apply CVP analysis and interpret the results

- apply a range of costing and accounting systems

- explain the role of budgets and standard costing within organisations

- prepare and interpret budgets, standard costs and variance statements.

Below we reproduce the learning outcomes and syllabus content. The numbers in brackets denote the chapters in which each topic is covered.

Learning outcomes and syllabus content

Cost determination - 30%

Learning outcomes

On completion of their studies students should be able to:

- explain why organisations use costing systems (1)

- explain raw material accounting and control procedures (5)

- explain and calculate re-order quantity, re-order level, maximum stock, minimum stock and economic order quantity (6)

- explain FIFO, LIFO and weighted average stock valuation methods (5)

- calculate stock, cost of sales and gross profit under LIFO, FIFO and weighted average (5)

- explain labour accounting and control procedures (7)

- discuss and calculate factory incentive schemes for individuals and groups (7)

- explain absorption costing (3, 4)

- prepare cost statements for allocation and apportionment of overheads including reciprocal service departments (3)

- calculate and discuss overhead absorption rates (3, 4)

- calculate under/over recovery of overheads (3, 4)

- calculate product costs under absorption and marginal costing (3, 4)

- compare and contrast absorption and marginal costing. (4)

Syllabus content

- Classification of costs (1)

- Materials: accounting and control procedures (5)

- Labour: accounting and control procedures (7)

- Factory incentive schemes for individuals and groups (7)

- Overhead costs: allocation, apportionment, re-apportionment and absorption of overhead costs. Note: The repeated distribution method only will be used for reciprocal service department costs (3)

- Absorption costing (3, 4)

- Marginal costing (4)

- Materials: re-order quantity, re-order level, maximum stock, minimum stock, economic order quantity (6)

Standard costing - 15%

Learning outcomes

On completion of their studies students should be able to:

- explain the principles of standard costing (14)

- prepare the standard cost for a product/service (14)

- calculate and interpret variances for sales, materials; labour; variable overheads and fixed overheads (15, 16, 17)

- prepare a report reconciling budget gross profit/contribution with actual profit. (17)

Syllabus content

- Principles of standard costing (14)

- Preparation of standard costs under absorption and marginal costing (14)

- Variances: materials: total, price and usage; labour: total, rate and efficiency; variable overhead: total, expenditure and efficiency; fixed overhead: total, expenditure and volume (absorption costing); fixed overhead: expenditure (marginal costing); sales: total sales margin variance. (15, 16, 17)

Costing and accounting systems - 20%

Learning outcomes

On completion of their studies students should be able to:

- compare and contrast job, batch, contract and process costing systems (18)

- prepare ledger accounts for job, batch, contract (in accordance with SSAP 9) and process costing systems NB: the average cost method will only be used for process costing and students must be able to calculate normal losses and abnormal loss/gains and deal with opening and closing stocks (18, 19, 20)

KAPLAN PUBLISHING

- prepare and contrast cost statements for service and manufacturing organisations (19)
- prepare profit and loss accounts from the same data under absorption and marginal costing and reconcile and explain the differences in reported profits (4)
- prepare accounting entries for an integrated accounting system using standard costs (21)
- explain the difference between integrated and interlocking accounting systems. (21)

Syllabus content
- Job, batch, contract and process costing (18, 19, 20)
- Cost accounting statements for services and service industries (19)
- Marginal and absorption costing profit and loss accounts (4)
- Accounting entries for an integrated accounting system (21)
- Interlocking accounting (21)

Marginal costing and decision making - 15%

Learning outcomes
On completion of their studies students should be able to:
- identify relevant costs and revenues (8)
- identify cost behaviour (2)
- explain the contribution concept (9)
- calculate and interpret the break even point, profit target, margin of safety and profit/volume ratio for a single product (9)
- prepare break even charts and profit/volume graphs for a single product (9)
- calculate the profit-maximising sales mix for a company with a single resource constraint which has total freedom of action (10)
- discuss CVP analysis. (9)

Syllabus content
- Relevant cost concepts, including sunk costs, committed costs and opportunity costs (8)
- Fixed, variable and semi-variable costs (2)
- Contribution concept (9)
- Break even charts, profit volume graphs, break even point, profit target, margin of safety, contribution/sales ratio (9)
- Limiting factor analysis (10)

Budgeting - 20%

Learning outcomes
On completion of their studies students should be able to:
- explain why organisations prepare budgets (11)
- explain how organisations prepare budgets (11)
- explain the use of IT in the budget process (12)
- prepare functional budgets, profit and loss account, balance sheet and a simple cash budget (11, 12)
- calculate simple cost estimates using high-low method and line of best fit (2)
- prepare simple reports showing actual and budgeted results (13)
- explain the differences between fixed and flexible budgets (13)
- prepare a fixed and flexible budget (13)
- calculate expenditure, volume and total budget variances. (13)

Syllabus content
- Budget theory (11)
- Budget preparation (11, 12)
- IT and budgeting (12)
- Cost estimation and estimating techniques (2)
- Reporting of actual against budget (13)
- Fixed and flexible budgeting (13)

HELPING YOU WITH YOUR STUDIES

Take control

Create favourable conditions and a positive attitude.

- Plan to study at specific times each week. Devise a schedule and set goals.

- Choose a location where you can concentrate.

- Ask questions to be an active learner and to generate interest.

- Continually challenge yourself.

Study

Develop good learning techniques

- Use the **SQR3** method – it works with reading accountancy and management subjects. **Survey** (get an overall picture before studying in detail), **Question** (important things to learn are usually answers to questions), **Read** actively (to answer your questions), **Recite** (recall what you have read and connect topics) and **Review** (what you have covered and accomplished).

- Use the **MURDER** method – **Mood** (set the right mood), **Understand** (issues covered and make note of any uncertain bits), **Recall** (stop and put what you have learned into your own words), **Digest** (go back and reconsider the information), **Expand** (read relevant articles and newspapers), **Review** (go over the material you covered to consolidate the knowledge)

- Use **repetition** to increase remembering.

- Create **associations** and analogies to relate new ideas to what you already know and to improve understanding.

Practise

Practise under exam conditions

- **Practise** as much as possible – go through exam style and standard questions under exam conditions.

Prepare for the exam

Develop exam technique

- Be familiar with the structure of your exam and know how to approach and answer the questions.

KAPLAN PUBLISHING

EXAMINATION

Format of the examination:

This examination is computer-based and must be sat at a CBA centre.

40 objective testing questions with one or more parts
Total time allowed: 90 minutes

100 marks

Computer-based assessment (CBA)

When sitting a CBA make sure that you are fully familiar with the software before you start answering the questions. If in doubt, ask the assessment centre staff to explain it to you.

With CBAs the questions are displayed on the screen and answers are entered using the keyboard and mouse. All the questions are of objective testing type, the most common of which being multiple choice. Other types of objective testing questions include true/false, matching pairs of text and graphic, sequencing and ranking, labelling diagrams and numeric entry. Answer every question – if you do not know the answer, you do not lose anything by guessing. Don't panic if you realise you answered a question incorrectly you can always go back and change the answer. At the end of the assessment, if you are successful, you will be given a 'certificate of achievement' and your exam status will automatically be updated to reflect your success. If you are unsuccessful, you will receive performance feedback to help you identify areas of the syllabus where you need better understanding.

You can take a CBA at any time during the year - you do not need to wait for May and November exam sessions. However, do not attempt a CBA until you have completed all the study material relating to it. Do not skip parts of the syllabus.

For a CBA demo and the list of CIMA accredited CBA centres, see the CIMA website at www.cimaglobal.com.

MATHEMATICAL FORMULAE

Inventory control

EOQ basic model $\sqrt{\dfrac{2CoD}{Ch}}$

Where Co = cost of placing an order

Ch = stock carrying cost

D = annual demand

Chapter 1

INTRODUCTION TO MANAGEMENT ACCOUNTING

Syllabus content

Classification of costs.

- In this chapter we introduce management accounting and, in particular, the role of cost accounting. We consider why such systems are needed, the basic principles under which they operate, and how they link in with financial accounting systems. We also introduce some costing terminology that you will use throughout your management accounting studies, including the different ways in which costs may be classified.

Contents

1   Accounting

2   Cost units

3   Classification of costs

1 Accounting

1.1 Financial, cost and management accounting

DEFINITION

Financial accounting – The classification and recording of the monetary transactions of an entity in accordance with established concepts, principles, accounting standards and legal requirements and their presentation, by means of profit and loss accounts, balance sheets and cash flow statements, during and at the end of an accounting period.

The financial accounts record transactions between the business and its customers, suppliers, employees and owners, e.g. shareholders. The managers of the business must account to outsiders for the way in which funds entrusted to them have been used and, therefore, records of assets and liabilities are required, as well as a statement of any increase in the total wealth of the business. This is done by presenting a balance sheet, profit and loss account, and cash flow statement at least once every year. The law requires that accounts of certain businesses shall be presented in a specific way and particular details of transactions may be required by the Inspector of Taxes.

- Financial accounting is the classification and recording of the monetary transactions of an entity in accordance with established concepts, principles, accounting standards and legal requirements and their presentation, by means of profit and loss accounts, balance sheets and cash flow statements, during and at the end of an accounting period. (CIMA Official Terminology, 2000)

However, in performing their job, managers will need to know a great deal about the detailed working of the business. This knowledge must embrace production methods and the cost of processes, products, etc. It is not the function of financial accounting to provide such detail and therefore the managers require additional accounting information geared to their own needs.

DEFINITION

Cost accounting – The establishment of budgets, standard costs and actual costs of operations, processes, activities or products; and the analysis of variances, profitability or the social use of funds.

- Cost accounting is 'the establishment of budgets, standard costs and actual costs of operations, processes, activities or products; and the analysis of variances, profitability or the social use of funds'. (*CIMA Official Terminology*, 2000)

- Management accounting is the application of the principles of accounting and enterprises, both public and private. (*CIMA Official Terminology*, 2000) financial management to create, protect, preserve and increase value so as to deliver that value to the stakeholders of profit and not-for-profit

DEFINITION

Management accounting – The application of the principles of accounting and financial management to create, protect, preserve and increase value so as to deliver that value to the stakeholders of profit and not-for-profit enterprises, both public and private.

Management accounting is a wider concept involving professional knowledge and skill in the preparation and particularly the presentation of information to all levels of management in the organisation structure. The source of such information is the financial and cost accounts. The information is intended to assist management in its policy and decision-making, planning and control activities.

The particular concern of this text is with the **cost accounting** branch of management accounting.

1.2 Management accounting

This involves participation in management to ensure that there is effective:

- formulation of plans to meet objectives (strategic planning)

- formulation of short-term operational plans (budgeting/profit planning)

- acquisition and use of finance (financial management) and recording of actual transactions (financial accounting and cost accounting)

- communication of financial and operating information

- corrective action to bring plans and results into line (financial control)

- reviewing and reporting on systems and operations (internal audit, management audit).

1.3 Profit statements

It may be helpful at this stage to examine a simple trading and profit and loss account to consider the work of the management accountant:

XYZ Company
Trading and profit and loss account for the year ended . . .

		£	£
Sales			200,000
Cost of sales:	Materials consumed	80,000	
	Wages	40,000	
	Production expenses	15,000	135,000
Gross profit			65,000
Marketing expenses		15,000	
General administrative expenses		10,000	
Financing costs		4,000	
			29,000
Net profit before tax			36,000

The above statement may be adequate to provide outsiders with an overview of the trading results of the business, but managers would need much more detail to answer questions such as:

- What are our major products or services and which are most profitable?
- How much has our stock of raw materials increased?
- How does our labour cost per unit compare with last period?
- Are our personnel department expenses more than we expected?

The management accountant will aim to maintain a system that will provide the answers to those (and many other) questions on a regular and ad-hoc basis. In addition, the cost accounts will contain detailed information concerning stocks of raw materials, work-in-progress and finished goods as a basis for the valuation necessary to prepare the financial accounts.

Activity 1

(a) Distinguish between financial accounting, cost accounting and management accounting.

(b) What is the work of the management accountant likely to include in a typical manufacturing situation?

Feedback to this activity is at the end of the chapter.

1.4 Benefits of cost accounting

Cost accounting systems are primarily designed to determine costs: costs of operating identifiable sections of the business and the cost of output products or units or service. The system thus represents a data bank that can be referred to and adapted to suit the needs of people throughout the organisation.

The overriding benefit is the provision of information that can be used specifically to:

- disclose profitable and unprofitable activities

- identify waste and inefficiency
- support cost reduction programmes
- analyse movements in profit
- estimate and fix selling prices
- value stocks
- develop budgets and standards to assist planning and control
- evaluate the cost effects of policy decisions.

2 Cost units

2.1 What is a cost unit?

At this stage, it is helpful to consider cost accounting procedures in relation to a single aim:

determining the cost of the output/product of the business

DEFINITION

A cost unit is a unit of product or service in relation to which costs are ascertained.

A cost unit is a unit of product or service in relation to which costs are ascertained. For a paint manufacturer, a single cost unit might be a thousand litres of paint; for a paint retailer the cost unit is more likely to be one litre of paint.

2.2 Why do we need cost units?

The determination of the cost per cost unit is important for a variety of reasons:

- making decisions about pricing, acceptance of orders, and so on
- measuring changes in costs and relative levels of efficiency
- inventory valuation for financial reporting
- planning future costs (budgeting and standard costs).

The process of determining unit costs involves analysis, classification and grouping of costs, as discussed in the next section of this chapter.

2.3 Examples of cost units

Industry or activity	Cost unit	
Manufacturing industries		
Brewers	Hectolitre	
Brick-making	1,000 bricks	
Coal mining	Tonne	
Paper	Ream	
Ready Mix concrete	Cubic metre	
Service industries		
Hospital	(a)	Bed occupied
	(b)	Out-patient
Professional service, e.g. accountants	Chargeable man-hour	
Individual departments		
Personnel departments and welfare	Employee	
Materials storage/handling	(a)	Requisition units issued/received
	(b)	Material movement values issued/received

3 Classification of costs

3.1 How and why are costs classified?

Classification is a means of analysing costs into logical groups so that they may be summarised into meaningful information for management.

Management will require information concerning a variety of issues, each of which may require different cost summaries. For example costs may be required for a particular department, or for a product and costs will need to be classified differently for each of these purposes. For this reason there are many different classifications of cost that may be used. The main classifications are explained below.

3.2 Elements of cost

The initial classification of costs is according to the elements upon which expenditure is incurred:

- materials
- labour
- expenses.

Within cost elements, costs can be further classified according to the nature of expenditure. For example material costs may be further classified according to whether they are raw materials, components, cleaning materials, maintenance materials, etc.

3.3 Direct and indirect costs

Direct costs are 'expenditure which can be economically identified with and specifically measured in respect to a relevant cost object.' (CIMA). The aggregate of direct materials, direct wages and direct expenses is known as **prime cost**.

Indirect costs are 'expenditure on labour, materials or services which cannot be economically identified with a specific saleable cost unit.' (CIMA) The total of indirect materials, indirect wages and indirect expenses represents **overheads**.

The definitions shown are taken from the CIMA *Official Terminology,* 2000.

Summary

Direct materials
Direct labour } Prime cost
Direct expenses }
} Total cost
Indirect materials
Indirect labour } Overhead
Indirect expenses }

Whether costs are direct or indirect depends on the individual circumstances.

Activity 2

Consider direct and indirect costs and note down in particular the types of factors that are likely to influence whether a particular cost is treated as direct or indirect in relation to a cost unit.

Feedback to this activity is at the end of the chapter.

3.4 Functional analysis of cost

Overheads are usually categorised into the principal activity groups:

- manufacturing/production
- administration
- selling
- distribution
- research.

3.5 Classification by behaviour

Another way in which costs may be classified is by their behaviour – how the total cost varies with changes in levels of activity (units produced or sold, labour hours worked, etc.). This is a fundamental area of cost accounting, and is dealt with in the next chapter.

3.6 Other ways in which costs may be classified

The four classifications mentioned so far – between elements of cost, direct/indirect costs, by function or by behaviour, are the most important for you to understand at this stage. However, there are other terms associated with classifying costs of which you should be aware:

- **Normal and abnormal** – An important feature of management reporting is that it should emphasise the areas of the business that require management attention and possible action.

  Normal costs are those that are expected; abnormal costs are those that are unusual, either by nature or size and are those to which management's attention should be drawn.

- **Controllable and non-controllable** – A cost is deemed controllable by a manager if they are responsible for it being incurred, i.e. they authorised the expenditure. Clearly, all costs are controllable at some management level.

  When preparing performance reports for appraisal of managers it is vital that costs are classified as controllable or non-controllable. Managers will become disillusioned with cost control if their performance is evaluated on items outside their control.

- **Relevant and irrelevant** – Managers need information to assist them in making the correct choice between alternatives. For these purposes and to ensure that valuable management time is not wasted only those costs that increase or decrease as a result of management's decision are important. These are classified as relevant costs. Costs that would not be affected by the decision are non relevant or irrelevant costs.

- **Notional costs and real costs** – A notional cost is a cost that will not result in an outflow of cash either now or in the future. This compares to other 'real' costs that will cause cash outflows. Notional costs are sometimes used when comparing performances of two or more operating units. For example when comparing the profitability of two shops, one that is owned and one that is rented, the management accountant might include a notional rent charge in the cost accounts of the shop that is owned.

Activity 3

Classify the following cost:

Wages of an employee who supervises the machine operators within a production process which makes engines.

Feedback to this activity is at the end of the chapter.

3.7   Cost centres

A **cost centre** is a production or service location, function, activity or item of equipment for which costs are accumulated (CIMA). A cost centre may be a whole department or merely a sub-division of a department. A number of departments together would comprise a function.

It is important to recognise that the ascertainment of cost centre costs, apart from the aspect of calculating unit costs, is necessary for control purposes.

The terms direct cost and indirect cost may be used in relation to a cost centre. For example, a supervisor's salary would be a direct cost of the cost centre in which he is employed, whereas rent would need to be shared between a number of cost centres and so is an indirect cost of any particular cost centre. Both of these costs are, of course, indirect as regards specific cost units.

Summary

This chapter was an important introduction to much of the terminology involved in dealing with costs and cost accounting. In order to understand cost accounting processes it is vital that an understanding is gained of the different types of costs and the different possible classifications and groupings of those costs.

By the time you have finished this chapter you should be able to:

*   explain why organisations use costing systems.

Self-test questions

Accounting

1   What is management accounting? (1.1)

2   What is cost accounting? (1.1)

3   Describe the inadequacies of trading and profit and loss accounts as a source of management information. (1.3)

4   State three ways in which information derived from a cost accounting system may be used by management. (1.4)

Cost units

5   What is a cost unit? (2.1)

6   Give an example of a cost unit that may be used by (i) a hospital and (ii) a brick manufacturer. (2.3)

Classification of costs

7   What are indirect costs? (3.3)

8   What are the principal activity groups into which overheads are usually categorised? (3.4)

9   What is a cost centre? Give an example. (3.7)

Exam-type questions

Question 1

Prime cost is:

A   all costs incurred in manufacturing a product

B   the total of direct costs

C   the material cost of a product

D   the cost of operating a department

Question 2

When comparing the profitability of different branches, a firm charges rent as an expense in all the branch operating statements even when the particular branch premises are owned and not rented. In these circumstances the rent is:

A   an avoidable cost

B   a relevant cost

C   a notional cost

D   a fixed cost

Question 3

Which of the following would be classed as indirect labour?

A   Assembly workers in a company manufacturing televisions.

B   A stores assistant in a factory store.

C   Plasterers in a construction company.

D   An audit clerk in a firm of auditors.

Question 4

Cost centres are:

A   units of product or service for which costs are ascertained

B   amounts of expenditure attributable to various activities

C   functions or locations for which costs are ascertained and related to cost units

D   a section of an organisation for which budgets are prepared and control exercised

Question 5

Direct costs are:

A   costs which can be economically identified with a single cost unit

B   costs which can be identified with a single cost unit, but it is not economic to do so

C   costs incurred as a direct result of a particular decision

D   costs incurred which can be attributed to a particular accounting period

Question 6

Which of the following might be a suitable cost unit for a college of further education? (tick all that apply)

Lecture room   ☐

Full time student   ☐

Lecture hour   ☐

Personnel department   ☐

Lecturer fees   ☐

For the answers to these questions, see the 'Answers' section at the end of the book.

Practice question

Classify

A company manufactures and retails clothing. Group the costs that are listed as (1) – (10) below into the following classifications (each cost is intended to belong to only one classification):

(i)   direct materials

(ii)   direct labour

(iii)   direct expenses

(iv)   indirect production overhead

(v)   research and development costs

(vi)   selling and distribution costs

(vii)   administration costs

(viii) finance costs.

(1)   lubricant for sewing machines

(2)   floppy discs for general office computer

(3)   wages of operatives in the cutting department

(4)   telephone rental plus metered calls

(5)   interest on bank overdraft

(6)   Performing Rights Society charge for music broadcast throughout the factory

(7)   market research undertaken prior to a new product launch

(8)   wages of security guards for factory

(9)   carriage on purchases of basic raw material

(10)   royalty paid on number of units of product XY produced.

For the answer to this question, see the 'Answers' section at the end of the book.

Feedback to activities

Activity 1

(a) In modern business, the three functions of financial, cost and management accounting merge together in many ways. It will be very difficult clearly to define the three terms. However, a generalised definition could be:

  (i) **Financial accounting**

  The recording of the financial transactions of an enterprise firm and their summary in periodic financial statements for the use of persons outside the organisation who wish to analyse and interpret the enteprise's financial position.

  (ii) **Cost accounting**

  Involves a careful evaluation of the resources used within the enterprise. The techniques employed are designed to provide financial information about the performance of an enterprise and possibly the direction that future operations should take.

  (iii) **Management accounting**

  • has accounting as its essential foundation

  • is essentially concerned with offering advice to management based upon information collected

  • may include involvement in:

  decision-making

  planning (budgetary)

  controlling the business.

(b) The management accountant's work may include the following:

  (i) The application of accounting principles and costing principles, methods and techniques in the ascertainment of costs.

  (ii) The analysis of savings and excesses as compared with previous experience or with standards.

  (iii) Operating costing systems to provide the following information:

  • details of product or service profitability

  • stock valuation records (raw materials, work-in-progress, finished goods)

  • labour cost records

  • overhead control records

  • bases for evaluation of selling prices.

Activity 2

Direct costs are all costs that are 'physically traceable to the finished goods in an economically feasible manner' (CT Horngren). All other costs are indirect. There are several factors that will affect whether a cost is direct or whether it is treated as being indirect. For example, as the definition suggests, certain costs may be traceable to finished goods but it may not be economically worthwhile to do so.

If the cost unit is very large, for example the cost of building a motorway bridge, then the majority of costs, including depreciation of plant and machinery and the supervisor's salary will be direct costs for this unit. For 'small' cost units where for example, several cost units are processed on a machine, the depreciation of the machine is not traceable to individual cost units. It would, therefore, be treated as an indirect production overhead.

Another cost which may be direct or indirect is overtime premium. This is the extra amount paid to employees, over and above their normal hourly rate, in return for working more than their normal contracted hours. It may be possible to trace which jobs are carried out during overtime hours, and charge the premium to those jobs. However, if overtime is worked to increase the overall volume of production it would not be equitable to charge the premium to certain units simply because they happen to be worked on during overtime hours. The premium would therefore be treated as an indirect production overhead unless the overtime is worked at the specific request of a customer. In this case it would be possible to trace the overtime premium to a specific cost unit and it would be classified as a direct labour cost of that unit.

Activity 3

The wages cost cannot be traced directly to individual cost units therefore it is a production overhead (indirect labour cost).

PAPER C1 : MANAGEMENT ACCOUNTING FUNDAMENTALS

Chapter 2

COST BEHAVIOUR

Syllabus content

Cost estimation and estimating techniques.

- In chapter 1, we looked at the different ways in which costs may be classified. Here we consider one of the most important methods for cost planning and control – classification by behaviour. This looks at the way in which costs are expected to change, if at all, as the level of activity changes. This is essential information for management, who will use it in setting budgets, carrying out variance analysis, and decision-making.

- If a cost is identified as having both fixed and variable elements, we may use various techniques to quantify these two elements for the purpose of cost estimation; two of these are specified in your syllabus, and will be covered here.

Contents

1   Analysis of costs

2   Cost estimation (prediction)

1 Analysis of costs

1.1 Total cost

Let's look at the way costs behave in response to changes in the volume of sales.

Example

	500 units	1,000 units
	£	£
Sales (@ £3 per unit)	1,500	3,000
Total costs	1,000	1,500
Profit	500	1,500
Average unit cost	£2.00	£1.50
Average unit profit	£1.00	£1.50

Sales are higher – they have doubled – but costs have only increased by 50%. This is because some costs will not rise in relation to the increase in the volume of sales.

1.2 The two cost components

A **fixed cost** is a cost that is incurred for an accounting period, and that, within certain output or turnover limits, tends to be unaffected by fluctuations in the levels of activity (output or turnover).

A **variable cost** is a cost that varies with a measure of activity.

Suppose in the example above the product is widgets and the only costs are:

(a) rental of a fully equipped factory, £500 pa

(b) raw materials, £1 per widget.

Then the behaviour of these two costs in response to producing varying numbers of widgets is as follows.

(a) **Factory rental – a fixed cost**

Although production rises, the same rent is payable.

Graph showing relationship between total fixed cost (rent) and output

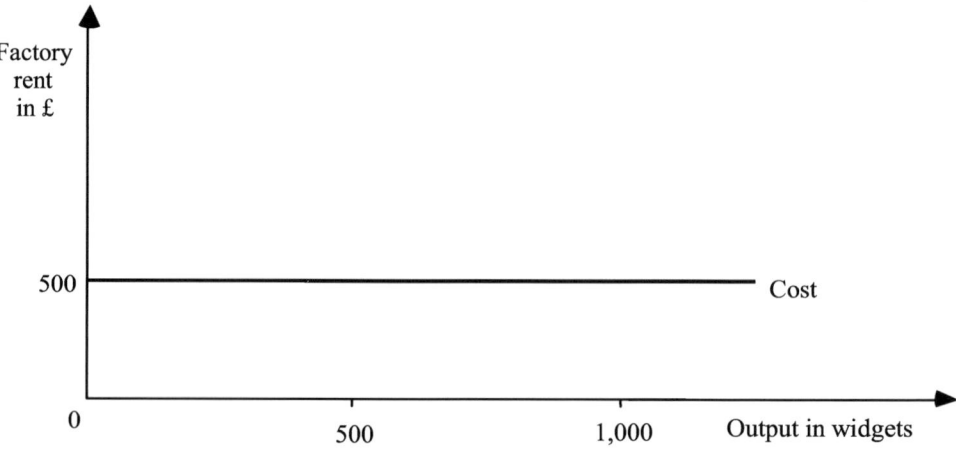

This may be shown by plotting the average fixed cost per unit on a graph.

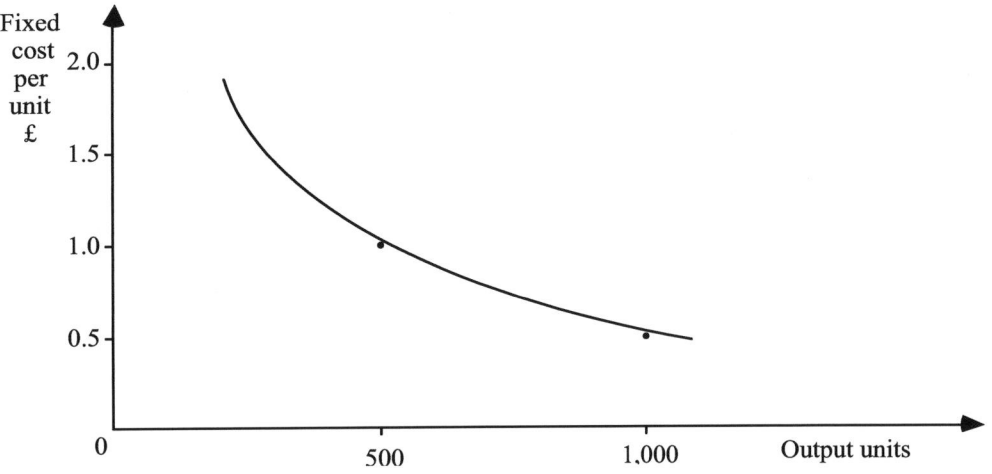

As output increases, the fixed cost per unit reduces. The total rent cost only changes if a new or larger factory is rented.

(b)   **Raw materials – a variable cost**

Every widget has a raw material cost of £1. Therefore the cost varies directly with the level of production.

Graph showing relationship between total variable cost (raw materials) and output

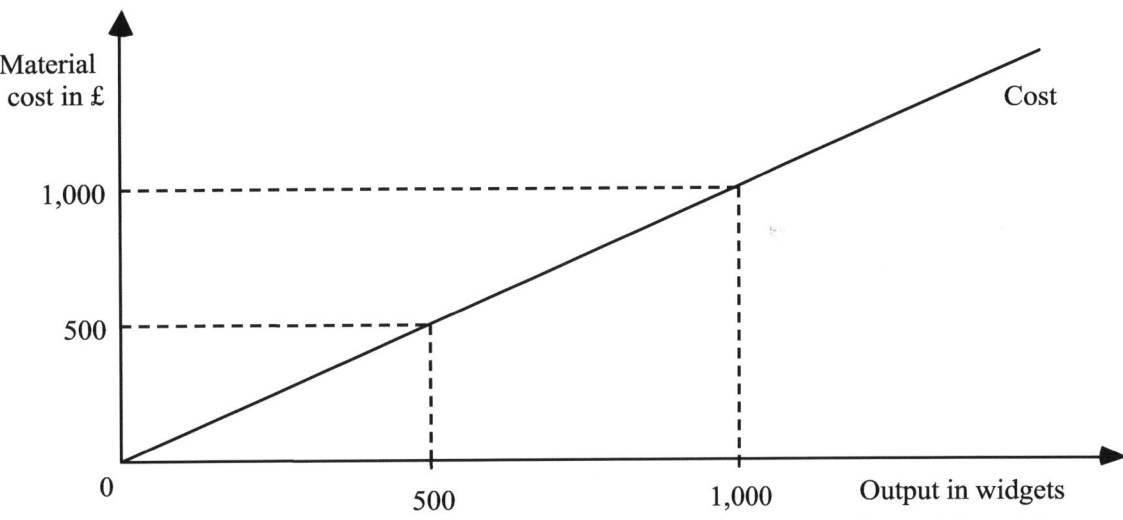

In the case of variable costs, the cost per unit remains constant irrespective of the level of output (provided that there are no discounts for bulk purchase).

KEY POINT

In the case of variable costs, the cost per unit remains constant irrespective of the level of output (provided that there are no discounts for bulk purchase).

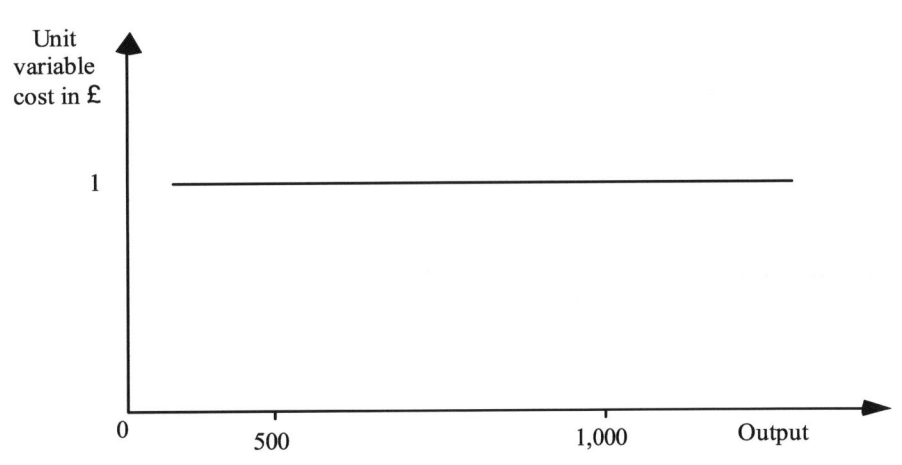

1.3 Relevant range of activity

The cost behaviour assumptions so far have been very simple. They are that fixed costs remain at a constant total amount over a period, and that variable costs per unit are constant over the period, regardless of the activity level in the period.

These assumptions will usually be valid provided that only relatively small changes in activity level are considered. The range of activity levels over which the cost behaviour assumptions are valid is called the relevant range.

Once outside the relevant range of activity, changes may occur. Two common examples are:

(a) **Bulk discounts** – where variable costs are not constant per unit.

When buying materials, it is normal to obtain discounts for larger orders. Thus, the more, e.g. tyres, ordered by a car manufacturer, the lower the price paid for each tyre. The total cost of tyres will increase as activity increases, but the gradient of the graph will reduce as discounts are received at higher levels of purchases.

**Graph showing relationship between
the total cost of tyres and the output of cars**

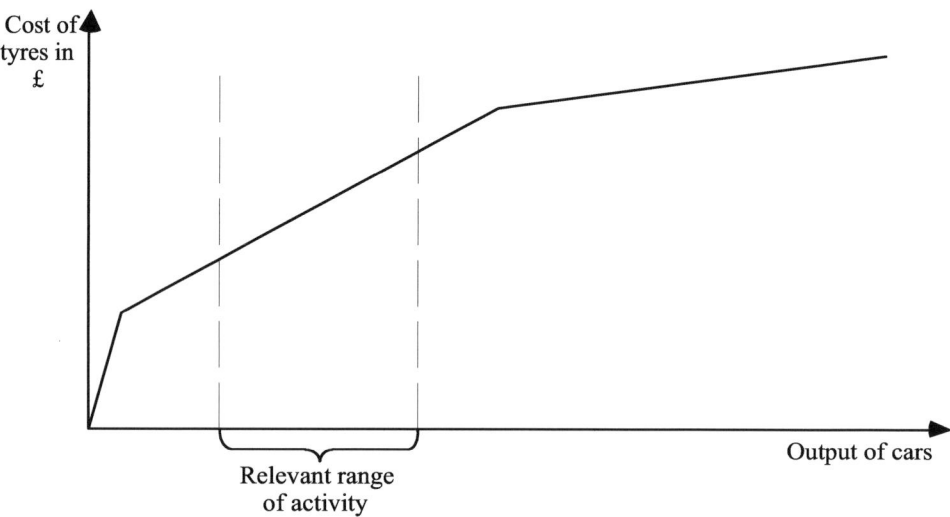

This behaviour pattern is known as curvilinear.

(b) **Step costs** – where fixed costs do not remain constant in total

Some costs rise in a series of steps. Large steps (renting a second factory) or small steps (renting a second photocopier) may occur.

- If the steps are large, the concept of the relevant range of activity usually applies, i.e. only occasionally is a new factory considered and therefore one can assume the rental cost to be fixed for the relevant range.

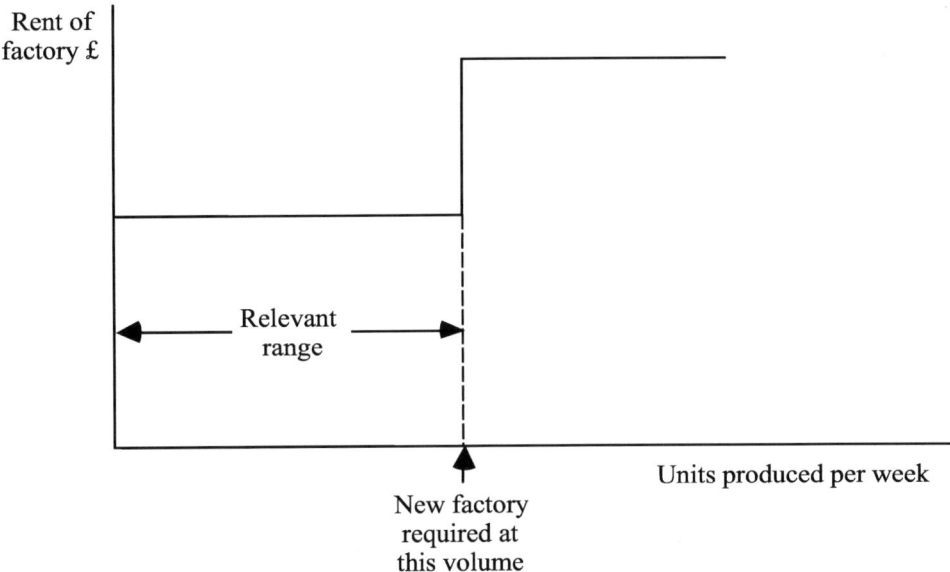

**Graph showing relationship between
factory rental cost and weekly output**

- If the steps are small they may be ignored, i.e. the cost may be treated as a linear variable cost.

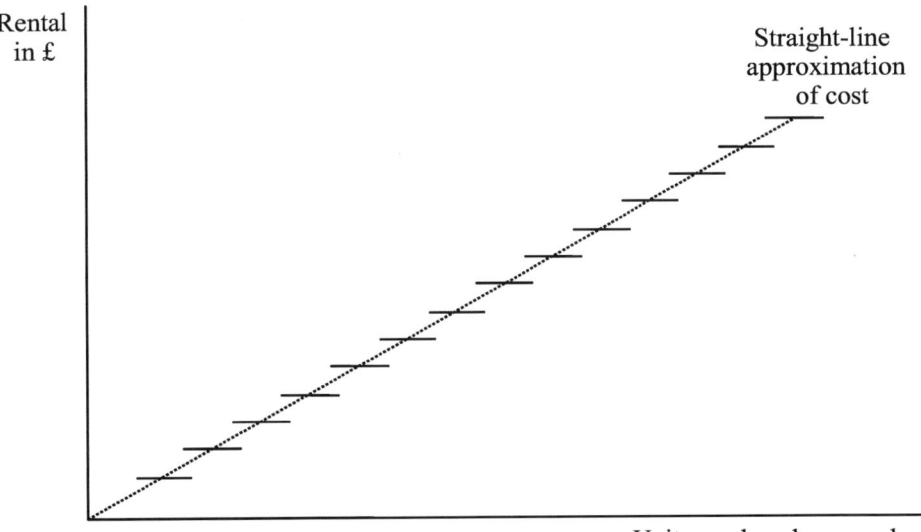

**Graph showing relationship between
total rent of photocopier and output**

1.4 Semi-variable costs

Some costs exhibit the characteristics of both variable and fixed costs, in that while they increase with output they never fall to zero, even at zero output. A semi-variable cost is a cost containing both fixed and variable components and which is partly affected by a change in the level of activity. A semi-variable cost may also be referred to as a semi-fixed cost or a mixed cost.

An example is maintenance costs: even at zero output standby maintenance costs are incurred. As output rises so do maintenance costs.

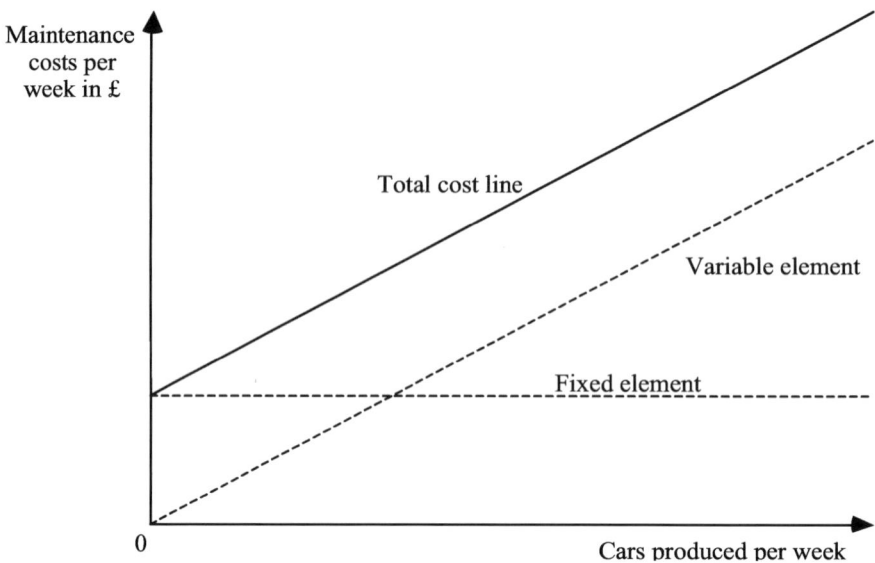

Graph showing relationship between machine maintenance costs and output

This problem can be dealt with within the basic analysis by saying that the cost consists of two components, a fixed cost and a variable cost, and by treating these separately. We shall examine this further in the next section.

Activity 1

Make a list of your personal expenditure items each month, classifying them into fixed, variable and semi-variable items

Feedback to this activity is at the end of the chapter.

2 Cost estimation (prediction)

2.1 Introduction

Observed cost behaviour patterns may be used as a basis to estimate the cost to be incurred at a given level of activity. In this process historical information provides valuable guidance, but it must be recognised that the environment is not static, and what was relevant in the past may not be relevant in the future.

A number of methods exist for analysing cost behaviour patterns and preparing cost estimates. You need to know about two of these for your Management Accounting Fundamentals syllabus.

- High low method
- Line of best fit.

In both of these approaches the assumption is made that the cost is potentially semi-variable, and that the linear model of cost behaviour is valid. The relationship between costs, y, and activity, x, is therefore of the form:

$$y = a + bx$$

Where			
	y	=	total costs
	x	=	activity level
	a	=	fixed costs
	b	=	variable cost per unit

2.2 High low (or range) method

This method is based on an analysis of historical information about costs at different activity levels.

Example

The data for the six months to 31 December 20X8 is as follows:

Month	Units	Inspection Costs
		£
July	340	2,240
August	300	2,160
September	380	2,320
October	420	2,400
November	400	2,360
December	360	2,280

The variable element of a cost item may be estimated by calculating the unit cost between high and low volumes during a period.

Six months to 31/12/X8	Units produced	Inspection Costs
		£
Highest month	420	2,400
Lowest month	300	2,160
Range	120	240

The additional cost per unit between high and low is $\dfrac{£240}{120 \text{ units}} = £2$ per unit

which is used as an estimate of the variable content of inspection costs. Fixed inspection costs are, therefore:

$$£2,400 - (420 \text{ units} \times £2) = £1,560 \text{ per month}$$

or $\qquad £2,160 - (300 \text{ units} \times £2) = £1,560 \text{ per month.}$

i.e. the relationship is of the form y $\qquad = £1,560 + £2x.$

Activity 2

Using the data from the last example, estimate the total inspection costs to be incurred in January 20X9, when it is forecast that 350 units will be produced.

Feedback to this activity is at the end of the chapter.

The limitations of the high low method are:

- It assumes that activity is the only factor affecting costs
- It assumes that historical costs reliably predict future costs
- It uses only two values, the highest and the lowest, so the results may be distorted due to random variations in these values.

Activity 3

Use the high low points method to calculate the fixed and variable elements of the following cost:

	Activity	£
January	400	1,050
February	600	1,700

March	550	1,600
April	800	2,100
May	750	2,000
June	900	2,300

Feedback to this activity is at the end of the chapter.

2.3 Scatter charts

If the data from the example was plotted on a chart, the result would be a scattergraph or scatter chart of inspection costs.

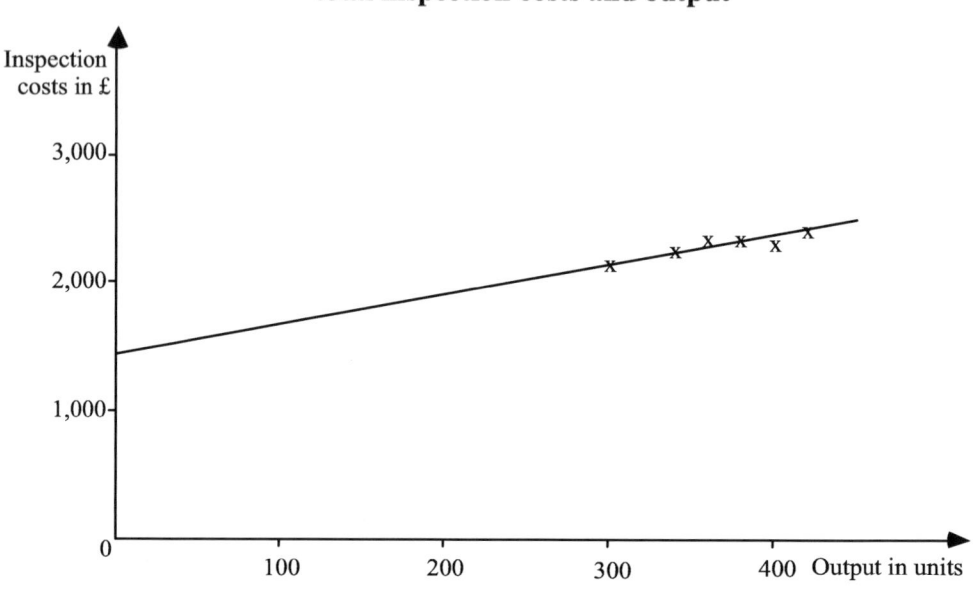

Scatter chart showing the relationship between total inspection costs and output

The line of best fit (a line which passes through the plotted points to roughly equalise the number of points on each side and minimise the aggregate vertical distance from the line) may be drawn as accurately as possible by inspection. The point at which that line cuts the vertical axis indicates the fixed cost (about £1,460 in the illustration).

Scatter charts suffer from the general limitations of using historical data referred to above. In addition, their problem is that the estimate of the best linear relationship between the data is subjective. Finally, it should be noted that this can only be converted into a mathematical relationship by actual measurement.

Activity 4

Plot the data points from the previous activity on a scatter chart and draw a line of best fit to find the fixed cost. Measure the gradient of the line to determine the variable cost.

Feedback to this activity is at the end of the chapter.

2.4 Limitations of using historical costs

The cost accountant must be careful when using analysis of historical costs as a basis for predicting future costs. This is true even if the accountant is fully satisfied with the accuracy of the analysis. The reasons are:

- It is difficult and costly to obtain sufficient data to be confident that a representative sample is used.

- Prediction implies a continuing relationship of costs to activity. In practice, methods and efficiency may change.

- The relationship between costs and activity may be obscured by time lags, e.g. recruiting trainee labour in anticipation of increased production.

- Factors other than the level of activity can influence costs, e.g. purchasing in small lots could increase handling and incidental material costs.

- Prices of the input factors may change, e.g. due to inflation or technical change.

- The high low method and scattergraph methods are based on the assumption that the cost/activity relationship is linear.

Summary

This chapter has looked at the basic types of cost behaviour – fixed, variable and semi-variable – and some variations, such as stepped fixed costs and curvilinear costs. If a cost is identified as being potentially linearly semi-variable, its two elements may be split out using one of the cost estimation techniques studied, the high low method or line of best fit. These are both based upon historical cost data, and the resulting limitations on the validity of any predictions of future costs based upon the cost estimation model must be recognised.

By the time you have finished this chapter you should be able to:

- identify cost behaviour

- calculate simple cost estimates using high low method and line of best fit.

Self-test questions

Analysis of costs

1   Distinguish between a fixed cost and a variable cost. (1.2)

2   Explain the 'relevant range'. (1.3)

3   What is a curvilinear cost? (1.3)

4   What is a step cost? (1.3)

Cost estimation (prediction)

5   Write down the relationship between total costs (y) and activity level (x) that is assumed in cost estimation. (2.1)

6   State three limitations of the high low method. (2.2)

7   State the limitations of using historical costs as the basis of predicting future costs. (2.4)

Exam-type questions

Question 1

A company's weekly costs (£C) were plotted in a scatter graph against production level in units (P) for the last 50 weeks and a cost relationship was estimated to be C = 1,000 + 250P. Which statements about weekly costs are true?

A   Fixed costs are £1,000   Variable costs per unit are £5.

B   Fixed costs are £250   Variable costs per unit are £1,000.

C   Fixed costs are £1,000   Variable costs per unit are £250.

D   Fixed costs are £20   Variable costs per unit are £5.

Question 2

The following data relate to two recent periods:

Machine hours	17,000	18,500
Overheads	£246,500	£251,750

The variable overhead rate per hour is £3.50.

The amount of fixed overheads per period is £ ⬚

Question 3

The following data have been collected for four cost types – W, X, Y, Z – at two activity levels:

Cost type	Cost @ 100 units £	Cost @ 140 units £
W	8,000	10,560
X	5,000	5,000
Y	6,500	9,100
Z	6,700	8,580

Where V = variable, SV = semi-variable and F = fixed, assuming linearity, the four cost types W, X, Y and Z are respectively

	W	X	Y	Z
A	V	F	SV	V
B	SV	F	V	SV
C	V	F	V	V
D	SV	F	SV	SV

Question 4

The following data relate to the overhead expenditure of a contract cleaners at two activity levels:

Square metres cleaned	12,750	15,100
Overheads	£73,950	£83,585

The estimated overhead cost if 16,200 square metres are to be cleaned £ ⬚

Question 5

The diagram below represents the behaviour of a cost item as the level of output changes.

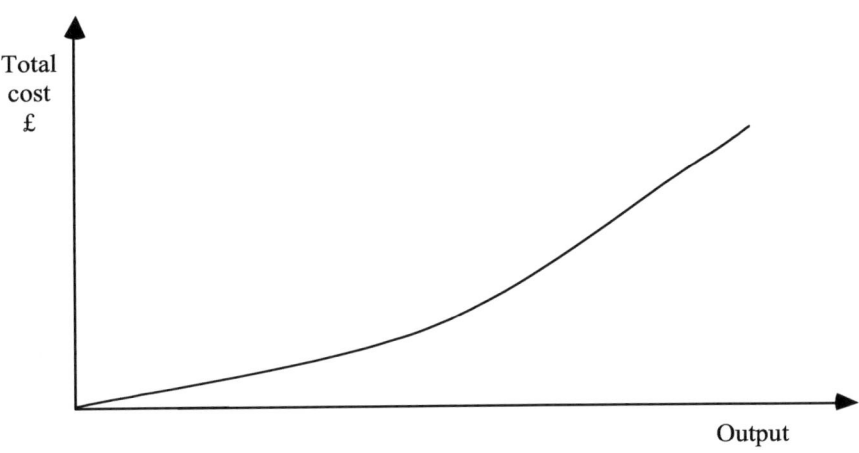

Which **one** of the following costs does this graph depict?. Tick the relevant boxes.

- The cost of direct materials, where a discount is received for higher levels of purchases.

- The cost of salaried supervisors, where additional supervisors are needed as output increases.

- The cost of direct labour, where increased hourly rates are paid for achieving higher levels of output.

For the answers to these questions, see the 'Answers' section at the end of the book.

Practice question

D & E Ltd

D & E Ltd produces brakes for the motor industry. Its management accountant is investigating the relationship between electricity costs and volume of production. The following data for the last ten quarters has been derived, the cost figures having been adjusted (i.e. deflated) to take into account price changes.

Quarter	1	2	3	4	5	6	7	8	9	10
Production X, ('000 units)	30	20	10	60	40	25	13	50	44	28
Electricity costs, Y, (£'000)	10	11	6	18	13	10	10	20	17	15

(Source: Internal company records of D & E Ltd.)

Your are required:

(a)   to draw a scatter chart of the data on squared paper

(b)   to use your scatter chart to estimate the fixed electricity cost and the variable cost per unit of production.

(c)   to predict the electricity costs of D & E ltd for quarter 11 and quarter 12, in which production is planned to be 15,000 and 55,000 units respectively.

(d)   to assess the likely reliability of these forecasts.

For the answer to this question see the 'Answers' section at the end of the book.

Feedback to activities

Activity 1

Rent – fixed

Rates – fixed

Bank loan – fixed

Petrol – variable

Electricity – semi-variable

Telephone - semi-variable

Activity 2

An activity level of 350 units is within the relevant range, i.e. it is within the range of activity levels over which the cost behaviour pattern has been observed. Therefore it is valid to apply our calculated figures for fixed costs and variable costs per unit.

Forecast inspection cost for 350 units = £1,560 + (350 units × £2) = £2,260

Activity 3

	Activity	£
High	900	2,300
Low	(400)	(1,050)
	500	1,250

Variable cost = £1,250/500 = £2.50/unit

Fixed cost = £1,050 – (400 × £2.50) = £50.

Activity 4

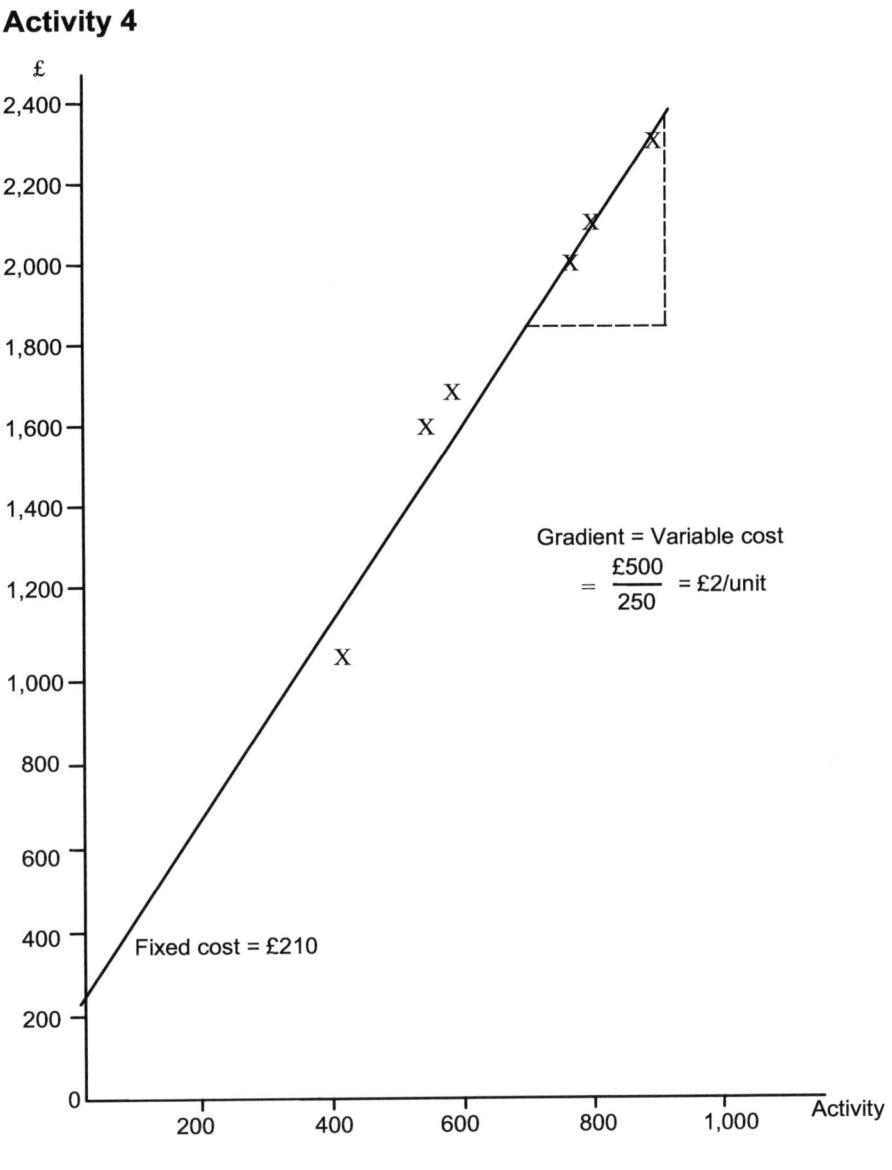

Chapter 3

OVERHEAD COSTS: ALLOCATION, APPORTIONMENT AND ABSORPTION

Syllabus content

- Overheads costs: allocation, apportionment, reapportionment and absorption of overhead costs.

- Absorption costing

  Overhead is the general term used to describe costs that are not directly related to production. They are also known as indirect costs. When a cost accountant is trying to ascertain the cost of a product there are two possible approaches available.

- Firstly he can use only direct costs and leave indirect costs as a general overhead not related to units of output. This approach is generally known as marginal costing.

- The alternative approach is where allocation and apportionment of all production overheads is used to arrive at a 'full' cost per unit. This is known as absorption costing.

  In this chapter we shall study the techniques of overhead allocation, apportionment and absorption. The following chapter explains marginal costing and then compares the two approaches.

Contents

1 Overheads

2 Overview of accounting for overheads

3 Allocation and apportionment

4 Absorption

5 Under and over absorption

1 Overheads

1.1 Introduction

Take a look at an object on your desk – your calculator say. How would you assign a cost to it?

You can probably see that it consists of various plastic parts and you can imagine that it has a bit of circuitry inside it: these are the materials and they could be weighed or measured to find out their exact cost. Presumably it was assembled on some sort of production line, and no doubt this incurred costs of running and operating the machinery: again you could measure these things precisely in terms of time taken, wages paid, power consumed and so on.

But what about costs such as heating and lighting the factory (so that people can see what they are doing and don't freeze), maintaining the machines, or moving materials from the stores to the factory? What about rental of the factory space? How much of the cost of these necessary items of expenditure did the manufacturers attribute to your particular calculator when they worked out its cost and decided how much to charge you?

There is no indisputably correct way of calculating such costs on a per unit basis, but the cost accountant has to find some solution because financial accounting regulations require it (SSAP 9/IAS 2) and because the costs of heat and light and similar overheads have to be paid and need to be reflected in the final price of the object.

For these reasons accountants have devised methods for allocation, apportionment and absorption of overhead costs into individual cost units.

1.2 Overhead cost classification and analysis

Overhead costs are those costs incurred which cannot be economically attributed to a specific cost unit. They may be incurred in many different parts of the organisation.

Overhead costs are classified by function, for example production, selling, and administration. As we'll see, this then enables them to be attributed to individual unit costs, in the case of production overhead, or dealt with separately in the case of other overheads.

1.3 Production overhead

DEFINITION

Overhead is expenditure on labour, materials or services which cannot be economically identified with a specific saleable cost unit.

Production overhead represents indirect materials, indirect wages and indirect expenses attributable to production, and also the service activities associated with production.

Indirect production costs are incurred in three main ways:

- **Production activities** – costs arising in production departments such as fuel, protective clothing, depreciation and supervision.

- **Service activities** – the cost of operating non-producing departments or sections within the factory, e.g. materials handling, production control, canteen.

- **Establishment costs** – general production overhead such as factory rent/rates, heating and lighting and production management salaries.

We will now look at the mechanics of attribution of overheads into cost units.

2 Overview of accounting for overheads

2.1 Introduction

To attribute overhead costs to cost units, a sequence of procedures is undertaken:

Step 1 Collecting production overhead costs by item.

Step 2 Establishing cost centres.

Step 3 Allocating and apportioning overhead costs to cost centres.

Step 4 Apportioning service cost centre costs to production cost centres.

Step 5 Absorbing production cost centre costs into cost units.

The procedure is illustrated diagrammatically below.

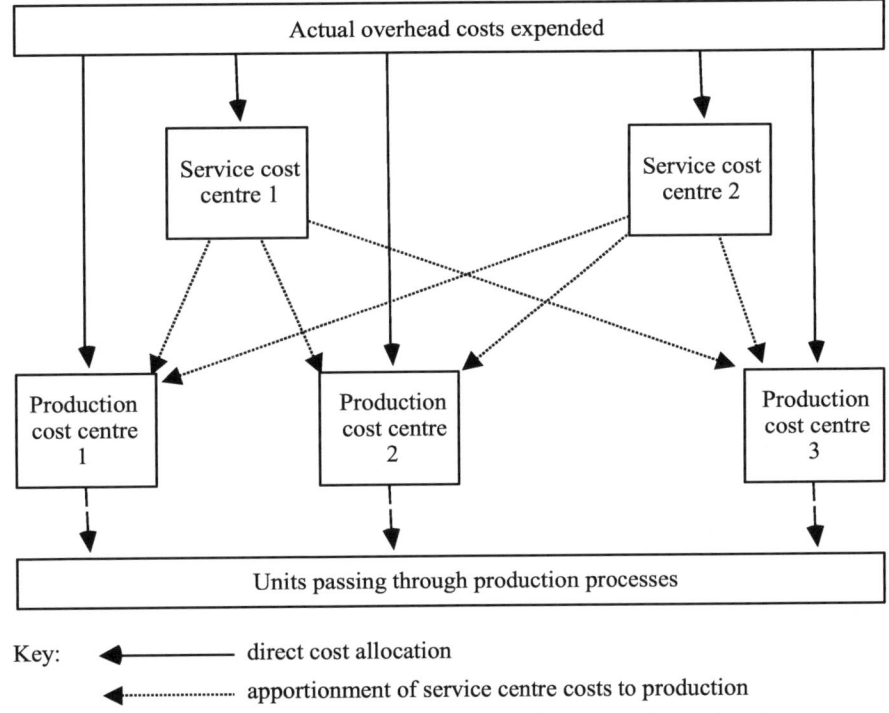

2.2 Five steps

Step 1: Collecting costs by item

As we'll see in Chapters 5 and 7, indirect materials costs can be obtained by analysing materials requisitions; indirect wages cost can be derived from an analysis of the payroll. Indirect expenses are recorded from invoices, petty cash vouchers and journal entries (e.g. for depreciation).

Step 2: Establishment of cost centres

The cost centres established should ideally combine an identifiable activity with a specific person responsible. For example, if Department A comprises three machine groups – I, II and III – under the overall supervision of a departmental supervisor, then it would be helpful for responsibility accounting to have only one cost centre for Department A. The three machine groups may, however, perform entirely different production activities, in which case three separate cost centres may be necessary for costing purposes.

Service cost centres are usually set up to represent individual service departments such as stores, but in a large factory a department may combine a number of cost centres related to the responsibility of section heads within the department: for example each substore would be a separate cost centre.

Step 3: Cost allocation and apportionment

The total cost of production overhead needs to be distributed among specific cost centres.

- Some items can be **allocated** immediately, e.g. the salary of a cost centre supervisor or indirect materials issued to a cost centre

- Other items need to be **apportioned** between a number of centres, e.g. factory rent and rates or the salary of the overall factory manager. The basis for apportioning a total amount will be selected so that the charge to a specific centre will reflect, with reasonable accuracy, the benefit obtained by that centre from the cost incurred.

Step 4: Apportioning service cost centre costs to production cost centres

Part of the total factory overhead will be allotted to cost centres which do not actually produce the saleable output. In order to reflect the cost of services in **unit** costs, service cost centre costs must be re-apportioned to production cost centres, so that the total cost of the production cost centre can be related to the units that pass through it.

Once again the basis of apportionment should reflect the benefit derived.

Step 5: Absorption into cost units

Finally, the production cost centres will have been allotted the total amount of factory overhead, representing:

- allocated costs

- apportioned costs

- share of service department costs.

The overhead to be absorbed by a particular cost unit will be calculated by dividing the production cost centre overhead for a period by an appropriate measure of the volume of production in the period.

If a cost centre produces dissimilar units the volume of production must be expressed in a common measurement, e.g. direct labour hours: if product X takes workers twice as long to make as product Y it is reasonable that it should bear twice the overhead. When a cost unit passes through several centres, the overhead absorbed should be calculated separately for each centre.

2.3 More detail

In the remainder of this chapter we will expand upon these steps by working through a series of examples.

3 Allocation and apportionment

3.1 *Example*

The ABC Washing Machine Company produces a standard washing machine in three production departments (Machining, Assembling and Finishing) and two service departments (Materials handling and Production control).

Budgeted costs for the next year are as follows:

Materials:

Machining	£240,000
Assembly	£160,000
Finishing	£40,000
Materials handling	£3,742

Wages:

Machining	£65,000
Assembly	£27,500
Finishing	£15,000
Materials handling	£8,000
Production control	£11,200

Other costs:

Machining	£21,922
Assembly	£12,960
Finishing	£7,920
Materials handling	£27,998
Production control	£2,400

It is estimated that the benefit derived from the service departments is as follows:

Materials handling:

Machining	60%
Assembly	30%
Finishing	10%

Production control:

Machining	40%
Assembly	30%
Finishing	20%
Materials handling	10%

You are required to prepare a statement showing the overhead allocated and apportioned to each of the production departments.

Solution

Overhead allocation and apportionment

Materials and wages incurred by the production departments may be assumed to be direct costs and are therefore excluded from the overhead analysis. We are only concerned with 'Materials handling', 'Production control' and 'Other costs'.

Allocation

Allocation is simply a matter of extracting the data given in the question and putting it under (i.e. allocating it to) the appropriate headings. In effect, in this example, the allocation has already been done: you just need to rearrange the information.

	Machining £	Assembly £	Finishing £	Materials handling £	Production control £	Total £
Indirect materials	–	–	–	3,742	–	3,742
Indirect wages	–	–	–	8,000	11,200	19,200
Other	21,922	12,960	7,920	27,998	2,400	73,200
	21,922	12,960	7,920	39,740	13,600	96,142

Apportionment

Service department costs (Materials handling and Production control) now have to be **re-apportioned** to production departments. The 'portions' are the percentages shown in the question.

As 10% of the production control overhead is to be charged to materials handling this must be done first, so we know the total amount of materials handling overhead to apportion.

The apportionment is shown below. (In practice of course you would simply continue the table shown above: there is no need to split them.)

	Machining	Assembly	Finishing	Materials handling	Production control	Total
	£	£	£	£	£	£
Allocated costs as above	21,922	12,960	7,920	39,740	13,600	96,142
Production control: £13,600, apportioned in the ratio 40:30:20:10:0	5,440	4,080	2,720	1,360	-13,600	–
	27,362	17,040	10,640	41,100	0	96,142
Materials handling: £41,100 apportioned in the ratio 60:30:10:0:0	24,660	12,330	4,110	-41,100	–	–
	52,022	29,370	14,750	–	–	96,142

Now that all the production overhead costs have been attributed to production cost centres, the total for each cost centre can be related to the cost units worked on in that cost centre.

3.2 Bases for apportioning costs to cost centres

The guiding principle for apportionment is that each overhead cost should be apportioned to reflect, with reasonable accuracy, the relative benefit derived by particular cost centres.

Example

Suppose that in the previous example instead of being given a department-by-department allocation of 'other costs' you were told that 'other costs' had been allocated to two headings – power, and rent and rates.

Other costs

Power   £24,400

Rent and rates   £48,800

Data about power consumption and floor space is also available.

	KwH	Sq. metres
Machining	83,844	19,870
Assembly	25,920	21,600
Finishing	15,840	13,200
Materials handling	15,996	63,330
Production control	4,800	4,000
Total	146,400	122,000

You are required to apportion 'other costs' to departments on an appropriate basis.

Solution

Power is most appropriately apportioned on the basis of kilowatt hours (KwH). The total is 146,400 hours and the proportion used in, for example, Machining is therefore 83,844/146,400. Applying this fraction to the cost of power £24,400 gives £13,974 as the amount to be apportioned to Machining.

Rent and rates is most appropriately apportioned on the basis of floor space. The total is 122,000 m^2 so the proportion used in, for example, the Finishing department is 13,200/122,000. Applying this fraction to the cost of rent and rates gives £5,280 as a fair share for Finishing.

The same calculations should be carried out for each of the other departments giving the following results.

	Power	Rent and rates	Total
	£	£	£
Machining	13,974	7,948	21,922
Assembly	4,320	8,640	12,960
Finishing	2,640	5,280	7,920
Materials handling	2,666	25,332	27,998
Production control	800	1,600	2,400
Total	24,400	48,800	73,200

The total column is the same as in the original question, so the overall answer is unchanged.

In selecting a basis for apportioning an overhead item, the cost of obtaining a high degree of accuracy must be considered. For example, the charge for heat and light could be shared on the basis of a complex formula incorporating power points, light bulbs and wattage but you should be aware that the end result would still be open to question.

Activity 1

The overhead budget for the month together with data relating to cost centres is as follows:

	£
Supervision	7,525
Indirect workers	6,000
Holiday pay and National Insurance	6,200
Tooling cost	9,400
Machine maintenance labour cost	4,500
Power	1,944
Small tools and supplies	1,171
Insurance of machinery	185
Insurance of building	150
Rent and rates	2,500
Depreciation of machinery	9,250
	48,825

| | Machine groups | | | | |
	Q	R	S	T	Total
Floor space (sq metres)	1,800	1,500	800	900	5,000
Kilowatt hours	270,000	66,000	85,000	65,000	486,000
Capital cost of machines (£)	30,000	20,000	8,000	16,000	74,000
Indirect workers (persons)	3	3	1	1	8
Total workers (persons)	19	24	12	7	62
Machine maintenance hours	3,000	2,000	3,000	1,000	9,000
Tooling costs (£)	3,500	4,300	1,000	600	9,400
Supervision costs (£)	2,050	2,200	1,775	1,500	7,525
Small tools and supplies (£)	491	441	66	173	1,171
Machine running hours	30,000	36,000	19,000	8,000	93,000

Allocate and apportion each of the costs given to the four groups of machines on a suitable basis and then calculate a cost per machine running hour (a machine hour rate) for each of the four groups of machines.

Feedback to this activity is at the end of the chapter.

3.3 Cost control

So far we've considered how overheads might be shared out from the point of view of benefit obtained. Much of the information is only relevant, however, for cost control purposes, by segregating costs which are controllable by the cost centre manager.

The overhead distribution in Activity 1 could be adapted to achieve that objective by adding a general cost centre: items which cannot be controlled by machine group supervisors (such as rent and insurance) would be charged to the general centre as the responsibility of, say, the factory manager. Cost centres would then be allotted overhead in two stages:

- allocation of controllable costs

- apportioned costs transferred from the general cost centre.

The sub-total of allocated costs would be suitable for control information and the grand total would be used, as we'll see later, for absorption purposes.

Example

Speed Manufacturing Co Ltd has three production departments (two machine shops and one assembly shop) and three service departments, one of which – the Engineering Service Department – serves the machine shops only.

The annual budgeted overhead costs for the year are:

	Indirect wages £	Consumable supplies £
Machine shop A	23,260	6,300
Machine shop B	20,670	9,100
Assembly	8,110	2,100
Stores	4,100	1,400
Engineering service	2,670	2,100
General services	3,760	1,600
	62,570	22,600

	£
Depreciation of machinery	22,000
Insurance of machinery	4,000
Insurance of building	1,800 (Note 1)
Power	3,600
Light and heat	3,000
Rent and rates	7,050 (Note 2)

Notes:

1 Because of special fire risks, Machine shop A is responsible for a special loading of insurance on the building. This results in a total building insurance cost for Machine shop A of one-third of the annual premium.

2 The general services department is located in a building owned by the company. It is valued at £6,000 and a notional rent is charged into costs at a rate of 8% pa. This cost is additional to the rent and rates shown above.

3 The values of issues of materials to the production departments are in the same proportions as shown above for consumable supplies.

The following data is also available:

Departments	Book value of machinery £	Area (sq m)	Power consumption %	Production capacity Direct labour hours	Machine hours
Productive:					
Machine shop A	60,000	5,000	50	200,000	40,000
Machine shop B	45,000	6,000	$33\frac{1}{3}$	150,000	50,000
Assembly	15,000	8,000	$4\frac{1}{6}$	300,000	–
Service:					
Stores	6,000	2,000	–		
Engineering service	18,000	2,500	$12\frac{1}{2}$		
General services	6,000	1,500	–		
	150,000	25,000	100		

You are required:

(a) to prepare an overhead analysis sheet showing the bases of any apportionments of overhead to departments

(b) to show how the service departments' overheads will be reapportioned to the production departments ignoring the apportionment of service department costs amongst service departments.

Solution

(a) **Overhead analysis sheet**

	Machine shop A	Machine shop B	Assembly	Stores	Engineering service	General service	Total
	£	£	£	£	£	£	£
Indirect wages	23,260	20,670	8,110	4,100	2,670	3,760	62,570
Consumable supplies	6,300	9,100	2,100	1,400	2,100	1,600	22,600
	29,560	29,770	10,210	5,500	4,770	5,360	85,170

Depreciation of machinery	8,800	6,600	2,200	880	2,640	880	22,000
Insurance of machinery	1,600	1,200	400	160	480	160	4,000
Insurance of building	600	360	480	120	150	90	1,800
Power	1,800	1,200	150	–	450	–	3,600
Light and heat	600	720	960	240	300	180	3,000
Rent and rates	1,500	1,800	2,400	600	750	–	7,050
Notional rent	–	–	–	–	–	480	480
	44,460	41,650	16,800	7,500	9,540	7,150	127,100

Bases of apportionment

Depreciation and insurance of machinery :		Book value of machinery
Insurance of building	:	One-third to machine shop A, balance apportioned on area
Power	:	Power consumption
Light and heat	:	Area
Rent and rates	:	Area excluding general service
Notional rent	:	8% × £6,000

(b) **Production departments**

	Machine shop A £	Machine shop B £	Assembly £	Total £
Total from overhead analysis sheet	44,460	41,650	16,800	102,910
Apportionment of service departments:				
Stores (W1) (consumable supplies)	2,700	3,900	900	7,500
Engineering service (W2) (machine hours)	4,240	5,300	–	9,540
General services (W3) (direct labour hours)	2,200	1,650	3,300	7,150
	53,600	52,500	21,000	127,100

Workings

(W1) **Consumable supplies**

	Consumable supplies £	Stores cost apportionment
Machine shop A	6,300	63/175
Machine shop B	9,100	91/175
Assembly	2,100	21/175
	17,500	

(W2) Machine hours

	Machine hours	Engineering service apportionment
Machine shop A	40,000	40/90
Machine shop B	50,000	50/90
Assembly	-	-
	90,000	

(W3) Direct labour hours

	Direct labour hours	General service apportionment
Machine shop A	200,000	200/650
Machine shop B	150,000	150/650
Assembly	300,000	300/650
	650,000	

3.4 Reciprocal services between service centres

A particular problem arises when service centres provide reciprocal services to each other, e.g.:

In this situation, a secondary apportionment of costs arises. There are several methods of dealing with this; your syllabus requires the use of the repeated distribution method.

This involves a continuous process of reapportioning costs backwards and forwards between cost centres until amounts left in the service departments are so small that they can be ignored.

Example

A company has three production departments, A, B and C, and two service departments, maintenance (M) and payroll (P). The following table shows how costs have been allocated and the relative usage of each service department by other departments.

	Production			Service	
Department	A	B	C	M	P
Costs	£3,000	£4,000	£2,000	£2,500	£2,700
Proportion M (%)	20	30	25	–	25
Proportion P (%)	25	25	30	20	–

Required:

Re-apportion the service department costs to the production departments using the repeated distribution method.

Solution

	Production			Service	
	A	B	C	M	P
	£	£	£	£	£
Costs	3,000	4,000	2,000	2,500	2,700
Reapportion M	500 (20%)	750 (30%)	625 (25%)	(2,500)	625 (25%)
				–	3,325
Reapportion P	831 (25%)	831 (25%)	998 (30%)	665 (20%)	(3,325)
				665	
Reapportion M	133	200	166	(665)	166
					166
Reapportion P	41	42	50	33	(166)
				33	
Reapportion M	7	10	8	(33)	8
					8
Reapportion P*	3	2	3	–	(8)
	4,515	5,835	3,850		

* These have been rounded to finish off the process.

Activity 2

A company has three production departments: A, B, and C and two production service departments X and Y.

Overhead costs have been attributed to these departments as follows:

Department	£'000
A	120
B	80
C	65
X	24
Y	15

An analysis of the services provided by each service department shows the following percentages of total time spent for the benefit of each department:

Service department	Production/Service Departments				
	A	B	C	X	Y
X	30%	30%	20%	–	20%
Y	50%	10%	30%	10%	–

Show the apportionment of production service department costs to production departments using the repeated distribution method.

Feedback to this activity is at the end of the chapter.

4 Absorption

4.1 Introduction

DEFINITION

Absorption costing is a method of costing that, in addition to direct costs, assigns all, or a proportion of, production overhead costs to cost units by means of one or a number of overhead absorption rates. (CIMA Official Terminology).

The final stage in the process (Step 5, if you look back at the introduction to this chapter) is to reflect the cost of overheads in individual cost units. This is done using a **rate per unit**, just like materials or labour.

- **Absorption costing** is a method of costing that, in addition to direct costs, assigns all, or a proportion of, production overhead costs to cost units by means of one or a number of overhead absorption rates. (CIMA *Official Terminology*).

- The overhead **absorption rate** is a means of attributing overhead to a product or service based for example on direct labour hours, direct labour cost or machine hours. (CIMA *Official Terminology*).

The absorption rate may be calculated by the fraction:

$$\frac{\text{Total overhead (£)}}{\text{Total of absorption basis}}$$

DEFINITION

The overhead absorption rate is a means of attributing overhead to a product or service based for example on direct labour hours, direct labour cost or machine hours. (CIMA Official Terminology).

where the absorption basis is units, hours or whatever is appropriate for the basis being used.

4.2 Absorption bases

Overhead can be absorbed into cost units by means of:

- rate per unit

- percentage of prime cost (direct labour, direct material and direct expenses)

- percentage of direct wages

- direct labour hour rate

- machine hour rate.

Example

Returning to the example of the ABC Washing Machine Company we found the following production overhead costs.

	Machining £	Assembly £	Finishing £	Total £
Production overheads	52,022	29,370	14,750	96,142

Let's say it has been decided that a separate absorption rate for each cost centre is to be calculated as follows:

Cost centre	Absorption basis	Incurred
Machining	Machine hour rate	10,000 machine hours
Assembly	Direct labour hour rate	5,000 labour hours
Finishing	Percentage of direct wages	£15,000 direct wages

Solution

Absorption rates:

Machining $\dfrac{\text{Cost centre overhead}}{\text{Machine hours}} = \dfrac{£52,022}{10,000}$

$= £5.20$ per machine hour

Assembly $\dfrac{\text{Cost centre overhead}}{\text{Direct labour hours}} = \dfrac{£29,370}{5,000}$

$$= \quad £5.87 \text{ per labour hour}$$

Finishing $\quad \dfrac{\text{Cost centre overhead} \times 100}{\text{Direct wages}} \quad = \quad \dfrac{£14,750 \times 100}{£15,000}$

$$= \quad 98.33\% \text{ of direct wages}$$

The overhead absorbed by an individual washing machine could then be accumulated.

For example if we are told that a regular washing machine takes 5 hours machining, 2 hours assembly and incurs £7.50 wages cost in the finishing department, the total overhead absorbed by that machine is as follows.

		£
Machining	5 hours × £5.20	26.00
Assembly	2 hours × £5.87	9.38
Finishing	98.33% × £7.50	7.38
Overhead absorbed		42.76

The production overhead absorbed is then added to the direct cost of each washing machine to determine the total production cost per unit.

For example if we are told that a regular washing machine incurs a direct material cost of £220 per unit and a direct labour cost of £55 per unit, the total production cost can be built up as follows.

	£
Direct material	220.00
Direct labour	55.00
	275.00
Production overhead (as above)	42.76
Total production cost	317.76

4.3 Choosing an absorption basis

The choice of an absorption base is largely a matter of fairness. It is probably reasonable, for example, to assume that the overhead costs of a machining department will be related in some way to machine hours, and likewise that the overhead costs of a manual assembly department will be in some way related to labour hours.

If this seems somewhat arbitrary and unscientific to you … you are quite right! In recent years we have seen the rise of a costing method known as Activity Based Costing or ABC, which looks at overheads and what actually causes them to be incurred ('cost drivers') in far more detail than a traditional absorption costing system. This is not on the syllabus for Paper 2 but you will learn about it in your later studies.

ABC has found favour partly because of the changing nature of production methods in the modern manufacturing environment and partly because computerisation of data collection and processing mean that it is now feasible to collect and analyse cost and activity information in fine detail, whereas it would not have been feasible in the past.

For the purpose of your present studies you must just be patient and accept that if a question tells you that overheads are absorbed on the basis of, say, labour hours then that is what you should use in your calculations.

Activity 3

A business has the following production and fixed overhead budgets for the coming year.

Production department	1	2
Fixed overhead	£240,000	£200,000
Total direct labour cost	£2,400,000	£4,000,000
Total direct materials cost	£200,000	£400,000

Department 1 labour is paid £5 per hour and department 2 labour £4 per hour. The variable production cost of an IC is as follows:

		£
Direct labour		
Department 1 : 3 hours		15
Department 2 : 1 hour		8
Direct materials		
Department 1 : 1kg	@ £4 per kg	4
Department 2 : 2 kgs	@ £5 per kg	10
Variable overheads		7
		44

If fixed overheads are absorbed on the basis of direct labour cost, what is the fixed overhead cost per unit of IC?

Feedback to this activity is at the end of the chapter.

5 Under and over absorption

5.1 Introduction

DEFINITION

Predetermined absorption
rate =
  Budgeted overhead
  Budgeted volume

The rates used to absorb overheads into cost units will not, of course, be calculated with hindsight. They will be predetermined rates, based upon budgeted figures.

A predetermined rate is used to smooth out seasonal fluctuations in overhead costs, and to enable unit costs to be calculated quickly throughout the year.

$$\text{Predetermined absorption rate} = \frac{\text{Budgeted overhead}}{\text{Budgeted volume}}$$

'Budgeted volume' may relate to units, direct labour hours, machine hours, etc.

If either or both of the actual overhead cost or activity volume differ from budget, the use of this rate is likely to lead to what is known as **under absorption or over absorption of overheads**.

Example

In year 9 the budget for the machine shop shows:

Overhead £60,000   Volume of activity 12,000 machine hours

In January year 9 the machine shop incurred £5,400 of overhead and 1,050 machine hours were worked.

Calculate the pre-determined absorption rate and the overhead under or over absorbed in January.

Solution

$$\text{Absorption rate} = \frac{\text{Budgeted overhead}}{\text{Budgeted volume}} = \frac{£60,000}{12,000 \text{ machine hours}}$$

$$= £5.00 \text{ per machine hour.}$$

	£
Actual overhead incurred per question	5,400
Overhead absorbed (1,050 machine hours × £5.00)	5,250
Under-absorbed overhead	150

The under-absorption in this example arises from a combination of two factors:

- actual overhead costs were £400 higher than the budgeted amount of (£60,000 ÷ 12) = £5,000 for the month

- actual volume was 50 hours greater than the budgeted (12,000 hours ÷ 12) = 1,000 hours for the month.

Analysis of over/under-absorbed overhead is covered in more detail under the topic of standard costing and variances, later in this Textbook.

Activity 4

A company budgeted to produce 3,000 units of a single product in a period at a budgeted cost per unit as follows:

	£/unit
Direct costs	17
Fixed overhead	9
	26

In the period covered by the budget:

(a) Actual production was 3,200 units.

(b) Actual fixed overhead expenditure was 5% above that budgeted – all other costs were as budgeted.

What was the amount, if any, of over or under absorption of fixed overhead?

Feedback to this activity is at the end of the chapter.

5.2 Treatment of under/over absorption

The unit cost of production will include overhead at the predetermined rate and, generally, overhead under or over-absorbed will be shown as a separate item in the costing profit and loss account.

Costing profit and loss account

	£
Sales	100
Cost of sales (units sold × unit cost including absorbed overheads)	70
	30
(Under)/over absorption	(5)
Operating profit	25

A large balance in the over/under-absorbed account may indicate that unit costs are inaccurate and management should be made aware that such costs must be used with care. This situation can be avoided by undertaking regular reviews of the overhead absorption rate to ensure that it still reflects current operating conditions.

5.3 Accounting for overhead absorption

The following example will illustrate the cost accounting entries relating to overhead absorbed.

Example

The following data relates to four departments of a factory.

	Actual overhead £	Absorption rates (based on pre-determined annual estimates)
Department A	1,000	£0.10 per machine hour
Department B	4,000	£0.75 per direct labour hour
Department C	7,000	100% on direct wages
Department D	3,500	£0.25 per unit

	Machine hours worked	Direct labour hours worked	Direct wages £	Units produced
Department A	10,000	11,000	6,000	100,000
Department B	3,000	5,300	6,000	48,900
Department C	6,000	18,000	6,800	52,000
Department D	14,000	30,000	10,000	13,800

You are required to:

(a) journalise departmental overheads incurred

(b) journalise departmental overheads absorbed

(c) give the journal entry recording under or over-absorbed overhead expenditure.

Solution

(a)		Dr £	Cr £
	Department A overhead account	1,000	
	Department B overhead account	4,000	
	Department C overhead account	7,000	
	Department D overhead account	3,500	
	Factory overhead control account		15,500
	Transfer of actual departmental overhead for period	15,500	15,500

(b)		Dr £	Cr £
	Work-in-progress account (W)	15,225	
	Department A overhead account		1,000
	Department B overhead account		3,975
	Department C overhead account		6,800
	Department D overhead account		3,450
	Transfer of absorbed departmental expenses for period	15,225	15,225

	Dr £	Cr £
(c)		
Profit and loss account	275	
Department B overhead account		25
Department C overhead account		200
Department D overhead account		50
Transfer of under-absorbed departmental expenses for period	275	275

Working

Absorbed overhead £

Department A	10,000 machine hours × £0.10	1,000
Department B	5,300 labour hours × £0.75	3,975
Department C	100% of £6,800	6,800
Department D	13,800 units × £0.25	3,450
		15,225

5.4 Absorption costing v marginal costing

The problem of under/over-absorption of overheads arises because absorption costing tries to treat a fixed cost as variable. A unit cost based on absorption costing principles can be misleading – if one extra unit is made then total direct costs (materials and labour) will increase by the amounts included in the unit cost, but fixed costs will not.

The alternative approach is called marginal costing and we shall look at that in the next chapter.

Summary

In order for management to take many decisions about their products, such as stock valuations, pricing decisions and production decisions, they must be given information on the cost of the items that are being produced. Cost will include not only the direct costs of production such as direct materials and direct labour but also indirect costs or overhead.

In this chapter much thought has been given to the process of collecting all of the overhead relevant to a cost centre and cost unit and then allocating those overheads to the cost centres. The allocation of these overheads may be done by means of an apportionment of the overhead to a number of departments on a common sense basis.

Service department costs will need to be reapportioned to production departments using a method based on the relative benefit derived. If service departments provide reciprocal service between themselves, the repeated distribution method can be used.

Finally the costs allocated and apportioned to the cost centres must be absorbed into the cost units in an appropriate manner.

The total absorption costing approach is to absorb all production overheads, fixed and variable, into cost units at a predetermined rate. This may lead to the necessity for an adjustment for over/under absorption.

By the time you have finished this chapter you should be able to:

- explain absorption costing

- prepare cost statements for allocation and apportionment of overheads including reciprocal service departments

- calculate and discuss overhead absorption rates

- calculate under/over recovery of overheads.

- calculate product costs under absorption costing.

Self-test questions

Overheads

1   What is overhead? (1.2)

2   What are the three ways in which indirect production costs are incurred? (1.3)

Overview of accounting for overheads

3   What are the five steps in the attribution of indirect costs to cost units? (2.1)

Allocation and apportionment

4   How would the depreciation of machines normally be apportioned to cost centres? (3.2)

5   What is the problem with apportioning the overheads of reciprocal service departments? (3.4)

Absorption

6   How is the overhead absorption rate calculated? (4.1)

7   State five possible absorption bases that may be used (4.2)

Under and over absorption

8   Why are predetermined rates used to absorb production overheads into production costs?

9   How is a predetermined absorption rate calculated? (5.1)

10   How does an over under or absorption of overhead arise? (5.1)

11   How is the overhead actually absorbed calculated? (5.1)

12   What is the usual treatment of an under or over absorption of overhead? (5.2)

Exam-type questions

Question 1

The following data relate to department X for the latest period.

Budgeted overheads	£349,780
Budgeted machine hours	87,445
Actual overheads	£437,225
Actual machine hours	72,785

(a)   Overheads for period were: ☐   under absorbed

☐   over absorbed

(b)   The amount of the under/over absorption was £   ☐

Question 2

Y Ltd absorbs overheads on the basis of direct labour hours. Budgeted overheads for last period were £310,000 and overheads were under absorbed by £15,000. Actual direct labour houses were 21,000 and actual overheads incurred amounted to £330,000.

The budgeted overhead absorption rate was (to the nearest penny) £   ☐   per direct labour hour.

Question 3

A company uses the repeated distribution method to reapportion service department costs. The use of this method suggests:

A   the company's overhead rates are based on estimates of cost and activity levels, rather than actual amounts

B   there are more service departments than production cost centres

C   the company wishes to avoid under or over absorption of overheads in its production cost centres

D   the service departments carry out work for each other.

Question 4

A method of dealing with overheads involves spreading common costs over cost centres on the basis of benefit received. This is known as:

A   overhead absorption

B   overhead apportionment

C   overhead allocation

D   overhead analysis

Question 5

An overhead absorption rate is used to:

A   share out common costs over benefiting cost centres

B   find the total overheads for a cost centre

C   charge overheads to products

D   control overheads

For the answers to these questions, see the 'Answers' section at the end of the book.

Practice question

Fibrex Ltd

Shown below are next year's budgeted operating costs for Fibrex Ltd, a company with three production and two service departments.

	Production departments			Service departments		Total
	Weaving dept	Proofing dept	Finishing dept	Personnel dept	Equipment maintenance	
	£'000	£'000	£'000	£'000	£'000	£'000
Direct materials	7,000	2,000	1,500	–	–	10,500
Direct wages	6,000	9,900	3,000	–	–	18,900
Indirect materials and wages	1,100	900	300	1,500	3,800	7,600
Power	5,200	1,000	200	100	800	7,300
Rent and rates						8,000
Factory administration and supervision						10,000
Machine Insurance						2,400

Additional data extracted from next year's budget is shown below:

	Weaving dept	Proofing dept	Finishing dept	Personnel dept	Equipment maintenance	Total
Floor area, square metres	12,000	27,000	6,000	12,000	3,000	60,000
Machine hours	1,600,000	400,000	400,000	–	–	2,400,000
Direct labour hours	1,200,000	1,800,000	600,000	–	–	3,600,000
Number of employees	600	1,000	400	100	400	2,500
Gross book value of equipment	£4.0m	£1.0m	£1.0m	–	–	£6.0m

Required:

(a)   Calculate the budgeted overhead absorption rates for each production department using the following methods:

   (i)   a machine hour rate in the weaving department

   (ii)   a direct labour hour rate in the proofing department

   (iii)   another suitable method in the finishing department.

   It may be assumed that the equipment maintenance department does not service the personnel department.

   All workings should be clearly shown.

(b)   It has been suggested that, instead of calculating department overhead absorption rates, one blanket rate for a factory may be adequate. Identify the circumstances where such a blanket rate may be suitable.

For the answer to this question see the 'Answers' section at the end of the book.

Feedback to activities

Activity 1

	Basis (see below for code)	Q £	R £	S £	T £	Total £
		Machine groups				
Supervision	A	2,050	2,200	1,775	1,500	7,525
Indirect workers	4	2,250	2,250	750	750	6,000
Holiday pay and NI	5	1,900	2,400	1,200	700	6,200
Tooling cost	A	3,500	4,300	1,000	600	9,400
Machine maintenance labour	6	1,500	1,000	1,500	500	4,500
Power	2	1,080	264	340	260	1,944
Small tools, etc.	A	491	441	66	173	1,171
Insurance of machines	3	75	50	20	40	185
Insurance of buildings	1	54	45	24	27	150
Rent and rates	1	900	750	400	450	2,500
Depreciation of machinery	3	3,750	2,500	1,000	2,000	9,250
		17,550	16,200	8,075	7,000	48,825
Machine running hours		30,000	36,000	19,000	8,000	
Machine hour rate		£0.585	£0.450	£0.425	£0.875	

Bases of apportionment:

1	Floor space	5	Total workers
2	Kilowatt hours	6	Machine maintenance hours
3	Capital cost of machines	A	Direct – allocated
4	No of indirect workers		

Note that depreciation is apportioned on the basis of capital cost. The usage of machines will be reflected in the machine hour rate.

Activity 2

	Production (£000)			Service (£000)	
	A	B	C	X	Y
	£	£	£	£	£
Costs	120.0	80.0	65.0	24.0	15.0
Reapportion X	7.2	7.2	4.8	(24.0)	4.8
Reapportion Y	9.9	2.0	5.9	2.0	(19.8)
Reapportion X	0.6	0.6	0.4	(2.0)	0.4
Reapportion Y (rounded)	0.2	0.1	0.1		(0.4)
	137.9	89.9	76.2		

Activity 3

Department 1 absorption rate = £240,000 ÷ £2,400,000 = 10% of direct labour cost

Department 2 absorption rate = £200,000 ÷ £4,000,000 = 5% of direct labour cost

Fixed over head cost per unit of IC:

		£ per unit
Department 1	£15 × 10%	1.50
Department 2	£8 × 5%	0.40
Fixed overhead cost per unit		1.90

Activity 4

Over/(under) absorption = Absorbed overheads − Incurred overheads

Budgeted fixed overhead = 3,000 units × £9 = £27,000.

	£
Fixed overhead absorbed (3,200 units × £9)	28,800
Fixed overhead incurred (£27,000 × 1.05)	28,350
Over-absorbed fixed overheads	450

Chapter 4

MARGINAL COSTING AND ABSORPTION COSTING

Syllabus content

- Absorption costing.
- Marginal costing.
- Marginal and absorption costing profit and loss accounts.

We now move on to marginal costing which is of fundamental importance throughout your syllabus, particularly in relation to decision making.

It is a common exam requirement to compare marginal and absorption costing, both in terms of their principles and the profit and stock valuation figures resulting from each.

Contents

1   Marginal costing

2   Marginal and absorption costing compared

1 Marginal costing

1.1 Introduction

Marginal costing is the accounting system in which variable costs are charged to cost units and fixed costs of the period are written off in full against the aggregate contribution. (CIMA, *Official Terminology*).

Marginal cost is the part of the cost of one unit of product or service which would be avoided if that unit were not produced, or which would increase if one extra unit were produced. (CIMA, *Official Terminology*).

1.2 Marginal costing as an alternative to absorption costing

The fundamental difference between marginal and absorption costing is one of timing. In marginal costing fixed costs are written off in the period incurred. In absorption costing fixed production costs are absorbed into units and written off in the period in which the units are sold.

Example

Company A produces a single product with the following budget:

Selling price	£10
Direct materials	£3 per unit
Direct wages	£2 per unit
Variable production overhead	£1 per unit
Fixed production overhead	£10,000 per month.

The fixed overhead absorption rate is based on volume of 5,000 units per month. Show the operating statement for the month, when 4,800 units were produced and sold under:

(a) marginal costing

(b) absorption costing.

Assume that costs were as budget.

Solution

(a) **Marginal costing**

The variable cost of sales is simply £3 + £2 + £1 = £6 per week.

	£
Sales (4,800 × £10)	48,000
Variable cost of sales (4,800 × £6)	28,800
	———
Contribution	19,200
Fixed overhead	10,000
	———
Operating profit	9,200
	———

The difference between sales value and variable cost is known as **contribution**: this only appears in the marginal costing statement.

(b) **Absorption costing**

In the absorption costing statement we have to adjust for under-absorbed fixed production overhead; no such adjustment was necessary in the marginal costing statement as fixed production overheads are not absorbed in the first place.

	£
Sales (4,800 units)	48,000
Cost of sales (4,800 × £8) (W1)	38,400
	———
Operating margin	9,600
Under-absorbed overhead (W2)	(400)
	———
Operating profit	9,200
	———

Workings

(W1) Unit cost is materials (£3) + wages (£2) + variable overhead (£1) +
fixed overhead absorbed £10,000/5,000 = £2 per unit, giving a cost
per unit of £8

(W2)	£
Fixed overhead incurred	10,000
Fixed overhead absorbed (4,800 units × £2)	9,600
	———
	400
	———

1.3   Marginal costing and stock valuation

In the above example operating profit is the same under both methods. That will
not be so, however, when production is more or less than sales, i.e. if stocks
increase or decrease.

Stock valuation under marginal costing is based on variable production costs
only. This is in contrast to absorption costing where fixed production overhead
costs are included in stock valuations using the predetermined absorption rate.

The following example illustrates the effects of the different stock valuations on
profit.

Activity 1

Suppose that in the previous example (Company A) production was in fact
6,000 units, i.e. 4,800 units sold and 1,200 units left in closing stock.

Prepare the profit statement for the month under absorption costing principles.

Feedback to this activity is at the end of the chapter.

Activity 2

Now show the profit statement for the month under marginal costing principles.

Feedback to this activity is at the end of the chapter.

1.4   Reconciliation of total absorption cost (TAC) profit and marginal cost (MC) profit

The difference in profit under the two methods in Activities 1 and 2 (£11,600 –
£9,200 = £2,400) arises because of the difference in the amount of fixed
production overhead included in stock under the absorption costing system.

The closing stock of 1,200 units includes in its absorption cost valuation £2 per
unit of fixed costs. This £2,400 is therefore being carried forward to the next
accounting period rather than being charged in this accounting period, giving a
profit figure in this period £2,400 higher under absorption costing compared
with marginal costing.

This can be summarised as follows:

	£	£
Profit under MC		9,200
Stock valuation (TAC) 1,200 × £8	9,600	
Stock valuation (MC) 1,200 × £6	7,200	
Difference (1,200 × £2)		2,400
Profit under TAC		11,600

1.5 Marginal costing and decision making

Marginal costing emphasises variable costs per unit and fixed costs in total whereas absorption costing unitises all production costs.

Marginal costing therefore reflects the behaviour of costs in relation to activity. Since most decision-making problems involve changes to activity, marginal costing is more appropriate for short-run decision-making than absorption costing.

1.6 Product comparison

It is considered more informative to present comparison statements on a contribution basis.

The term contribution describes the amount which a product provides or contributes towards a fund out of which fixed overhead may be paid, the balance being net profit. Where two or more products are manufactured in a factory and share all production facilities, the fixed overhead can only be apportioned on an arbitrary basis.

Example

A factory manufactures three components – X, Y and Z – and the budgeted production for the year is 1,000 units, 1,500 units and 2,000 units respectively. Fixed overhead amounts to £6,750 and has been apportioned on the basis of budgeted units: £1,500 to X, £2,250 to Y and £3,000 to Z. Sales and variable costs are as follows:

	Component X	Component Y	Component Z
Selling price per unit	£4	£6	£5
Variable cost per unit	£1	£4	£4

Solution

The budgeted profit and loss account based on the above is as follows:

	Component X		Component Y		Component Z		Total	
Sales units	1,000		1,500		2,000		4,500	
	£	£	£	£	£	£	£	£
Sales value		4,000		9,000		10,000		23,000
Variable cost	1,000		6,000		8,000		15,000	
Fixed overhead	1,500		2,250		3,000		6,750	
		2,500		8,250		11,000		21,750
Net profit/(loss)		1,500		750		(1,000)		1,250

Clearly, there is little value in comparing products in this way. If the fixed overhead is common to all three products, there is no point in apportioning it.

A better presentation is as follows:

	Component X	Component Y	Component Z	Total
Sales units	1,000	1,500	2,000	4,500
	£	£	£	£
Sales value	4,000	9,000	10,000	23,000
Variable cost	1,000	6,000	8,000	15,000
Contribution	3,000	3,000	2,000	8,000
Fixed overhead				6,750
Net profit				1,250

Analysis may show, however, that certain fixed costs may be associated with a specific product and the statement can be amended to differentiate specific fixed costs (under products) from general fixed costs (under total).

2 Marginal and absorption costing compared

2.1 Introduction

We have identified the following differences between the TAC and MC approaches to costing units:

- **Profit statement layout** – TAC deducts fixed production overheads as part of cost of sales to get to **gross profit**; MC only includes variable costs in cost of sales to get to contribution; with fixed overhead costs deducted as a period cost.

- **Over/under absorption** adjustment is necessary only for TAC.

- **Changes in stock levels** will lead to differing reported profits under the two approaches.

Make sure you understand these points by working this example and trying the activity that follows.

Example

A company sells a product for £10 per unit, and incurs £4 per unit for variable costs in its manufacture. The fixed costs are £900 per month and are absorbed on the basis of the normal production volume of 250 units per month. The activity levels for the last four months, when no expenditure variances arose, were as follows:

	1st month units	2nd month units	3rd month units	4th month units	Total units
Opening stock	–	200	300	300	–
Production	300	250	200	200	950
	300	450	500	500	950
Closing stock	200	300	300	200	200
Sales	100	150	200	300	750

Solution

The profit statement using absorption costing would be as follows:

	1st month £	*2nd month* £	*3rd month* £	*4th month* £	*5th month* £
Sales value	1,000	1,500	2,000	3,000	7,500
	£	£	£	£	£
Opening stock @ £7.60	–	1,520	2,280	2,280	–
Variable costs of production @ £4	1,200	1,000	800	800	3,800
Fixed costs @ $\frac{£900}{250}$ = £3.60	1,080	900	720	720	3,420
	2,280	3,420	3,800	3,800	7,220
Closing stock @ £7.60	1,520	2,280	2,280	1,520	1,520
Cost of sales	(760)	(1,140)	(1,520)	(2,280)	(5,700)
(Under)/over absorption (W)	180	Nil	(180)	(180)	(180)
Net profit	420	360	300	540	1,620

Working

Calculation of over/under absorption

Month	Incurred £	Produced (units)	Absorbed @ £3.60 £	(Under)over absorbed £
1	900	300	1,080	180
2	900	250	900	–
3	900	200	720	(180)
4	900	200	720	(180)

If marginal costing had been used instead of absorption, the results would have been shown as:

Item	*1st month* £	*2nd month* £	*3rd month* £	*4th month* £	*Total* £
Sales	1,000	1,500	2,000	3,000	7,500
Variable cost of sales (@ £4)	400	600	800	1,200	3,000
Contribution	600	900	1,200	1,800	4,500
Fixed costs	900	900	900	900	3,600
Net profit/(loss)	(300)	–	300	900	900

The total profit for the four months is £720 less under marginal costing principles. This is because the closing stock at the end of the fourth month is valued at £800 (£4 × 200 units) compared with £1,520 under absorption costing. Therefore £720 of the fixed production costs are carried forward in stock under absorption costing, to be charged against the sales of a later month.

The profit figures for each month can be reconciled as follows:

	Month 1 £	Month 2 £	Month 3 £	Month 4 £
Profit/(loss) under marginal costing	(300)	–	300	900
Stock units (decrease)/increase × £3.60 per unit	720	360	–	(360)
Profit/(loss) under absorption costing	420	360	300	540

If marginal costing is adopted, then stocks of work-in-progress and finished products will be valued at variable production costs only. Where production and sales levels are not in sympathy and stock levels are fluctuating, the net profit will be different from that disclosed by an absorption method of costing.

Activity 3

A company that manufactures one product has calculated its cost on a quarterly production budget of 10,000 units. The selling price was £5 per unit.

Sales in the four successive quarters of the last year were:

Quarter 1	10,000 units
Quarter 2	9,000 units
Quarter 3	7,000 units
Quarter 4	5,500 units

The level of stock at the beginning of the year was 1,000 units and the company maintained its stock of finished products at the same level at the end of each of the four quarters.

Based on its quarterly production budget, the cost per unit was:

	£
Prime cost	3.50
Production overhead	0.75
Selling and administration overhead	0.30
Total	4.55

Fixed production overhead, which has been taken into account in calculating the above figures, was £5,000 per quarter. Selling and administration overhead was treated as fixed, and was charged against sales in the period in which it was incurred.

You are required to present a tabular statement to bring out the effect on net profit of the declining volume of sales over the four quarters given, assuming in respect of fixed production overhead that the company:

(a) absorbs it at the budgeted rate per unit (i.e. absorption costing);

(b) does not absorb it into the product cost, but charges it against sales in each quarter (i.e. marginal costing).

Feedback to this activity is at the end of the chapter.

2.2 Marginal costing – advantages compared with absorption costing

Preparation of routine operating statements using absorption costing is considered less informative because:

- profit per unit is a misleading figure because it is based on an arbitrary absorption of fixed production overhead.

- build-up or run-down of stocks of finished goods can distort the comparison of period operating statements and obscure the effect of increasing or decreasing sales.

- comparison between products can be misleading because of the effect of arbitrary apportionment of fixed costs.

2.3 Defence of absorption costing

Absorption costing is widely used and you must understand both principles. Defenders of the absorption principle point out that:

- it is necessary to include fixed overhead in stock values for financial statements; routine cost accounting using absorption costing produces stock values which include a share of fixed overhead

- for a small jobbing business, overhead absorption is the only practicable way of obtaining job costs for estimating and profit analysis

- analysis of under/over-absorbed overhead is useful to identify inefficient utilisation of production resources.

Summary

Under marginal costing principles, only the variable costs are charged against turnover to give contribution for the period. These variable costs will include direct materials, labour and expenses as well as variable production overhead and any variable selling costs. All of the fixed costs of the business, including fixed production overhead, is then charged against contribution for the period in order to give net profit.

This also means that the closing stocks carried forward are valued at their variable production cost only. The whole of the period's fixed costs are charged to the profit and loss account for the period and none carried forward to later periods.

When stock levels change, profits reported under the TAC and MC approaches will differ as the TAC approach will carry forward fixed production overheads in its stock value.

By the time you have finished this chapter you should be able to:

- calculate product costs under marginal costing

- compare and contrast absorption and marginal costing

- prepare profit and loss accounts from the same data under absorption and marginal costing and reconcile and explain the differences in reported profits.

Self-test questions

Marginal costing

1   What is marginal costing? (1.2)

2   What is the difference between marginal costing and absorption costing? (1.2)

3   What is contribution? (1.2)

4   What is the reason for the difference in operating profit under marginal and absorption costing? (1.4)

5   What is the best figure to use for comparison product profitability? (1.6)

Marginal and absorption costing compared

6   What are the advantages of marginal costing? (2.2)

7   What are the advantages of absorption costing? (2.3)

Exam-type questions

Question 1

A company made 17,500 units at a total cost of £16 each. Three quarters of the costs were variable and one quarter fixed. 15,000 units were sold at £25 each. There were no opening stocks.

By how much will the profit calculated using, absorption costing principles differ from the profit if marginal costing principles had been used?

A   The absorption costing profit would be £22,500 less

B   The absorption costing profit would be £10,000 greater

C   The absorption costing profit would be £135,000 greater

D   The absorption costing profit would be £10,000 less.

Question 2

When comparing the profits reported under marginal and absorption costing during a period when the level of stocks increased

A   absorption costing profits will be higher and closing stock valuations lower than those under marginal costing

B   absorption costing profits will be higher and closing stock valuations higher than those under marginal costing

C   marginal costing profits will be higher and closing stock valuations lower than those under absorption costing

D   marginal costing profits will be lower and closing stock valuations higher than those under absorption costing.

Question 3

Dundee makes cakes, for which the standard cost card is as follows:

	£ per cake
Materials and labour	5
Variable production overhead	3
Fixed production overhead	4
Variable selling cost	1
Fixed selling overhead	2
Profit	5
Sales price	20

Both types of fixed overheads were based on a budget of 10,000 cakes a year.

In the first year of production, the only difference from the budget was that Dundee produced 11,000 cakes and sold 9,000.

(a)   The profit reported under an absorption costing system is £ [   ]

(b)   The profit reported under an marginal costing system is £ [   ]

Question 4

Over-absorbed overheads occur when:

A   absorbed overheads exceed actual overheads

B   absorbed overheads exceed budgeted overheads

C   actual overheads exceed budgeted overheads

D   budgeted overheads exceed absorbed overheads

For the answers to these questions, see the 'Answers' section at the end of the book.

Practice question

Rayners plc

Rayners plc manufactures and sells electric blankets. The selling price is £12 per blanket. Each blanket has the following unit cost:

	£
Direct material	2
Direct labour	1
Variable production overhead	2
Fixed production overhead	3
	8

Administration costs are incurred at the rate of £20,000 per annum.

The company achieved the following production and sales of blankets:

Year	1	2	3
Production ('000 units)	100	110	90
Sales ('000 units)	90	110	95

The following information is also relevant:

- The overhead costs of £2 and £3 per unit have been calculated on the basis of a budgeted production volume of 90,000 units.
- There was no inflation.
- There was no opening stock at the beginning of the year 1.

You are required:

(a)   to prepare an operating statement for each year using:

   (i)   marginal costing

   (ii)   absorption costing.

(b)   to explain why the profit figures reported under the two techniques disagree.

For the answer to this question, see the 'Answers' section at the end of the book.

Feedback to activities

Activity 1

	£	£
Sales		48,000
Cost of sales:		
Production (6,000 × £8)	48,000	
Closing stock (1,200 × £8)	9,600	
		38,400
Operating margin		9,600
Over-absorbed fixed overhead ((6,000 units × £2) − £10,000)		2,000
Operating profit		11,600

Activity 2

	£	£
Sales		48,000
Variable cost of sales:		
Production costs (6,000 × £6)	36,000	
Closing stock (1,200 × £6)	7,200	
		28,800
Contribution		19,200
Fixed costs		10,000
Operating profit		9,200

Activity 3

(a) **Net profit statement (fixed overhead absorbed)**

	1st quarter	2nd quarter	3rd quarter	4th quarter
Sales units	10,000	9,000	7,000	5,500
	£	£	£	£
Sales value (£5 per unit)	50,000	45,000	35,000	27,500
Cost of sales:				
Prime costs (£3.50 per unit)	35,000	31,500	24,500	19,250
Production overhead absorbed (£0.75 per unit)	7,500	6,750	5,250	4,125
Under-absorbed production overhead (W)	–	500	1,500	2,250
	42,500	38,750	31,250	25,625
Gross profit	7,500	6,250	3,750	1,875
Less: Selling and administration overhead (10,000 × £0.30)	3,000	3,000	3,000	3,000
Net profit/(loss)	4,500	3,250	750	(1,125)

Working

Fixed production overhead absorption rate:

$$\frac{\text{Fixed production overhead}}{\text{Budgeted production}} = \frac{£5,000}{10,000 \text{ units}} = £0.50 \text{ per unit}$$

As finished stock is maintained at 1,000 units, production volume = sales volume. Therefore fixed overhead under absorbed in each quarter = £5,000 − (Sales units × £0.50).

(b)   **Net profit statement (fixed overhead charged against period sales)**

	1st quarter	2nd quarter	3rd quarter	4th quarter
Sales units	10,000	9,000	7,000	5,500
	£	£	£	£
Sales value	50,000	45,000	35,000	27,500
Less: Variable cost of sales (£3.75 per unit) (W)	37,500	33,750	26,250	20,625
Contribution	12,500	11,250	8,750	6,875
Less: Fixed production, selling and administration overhead	8,000	8,000	8,000	8,000
Net profit/(loss)	4,500	3,250	750	(1,125)

Working

Variable cost per unit:

	£
Prime cost	3.50
Variable production overhead (£0.75 = £0.50 fixed)	0.25
	3.75

Chapter 5

MATERIALS: ACCOUNTING AND CONTROL

Syllabus content

- Materials: accounting and control procedures.

In this chapter consideration will be given to the control of and accounting for the materials purchases of an organisation. This ranges from the initial order, purchase and receipt of goods through to the storekeeping function, recording of receipts and classification and coding of materials.

We shall also be looking at the ways in which materials stock may be valued when it is issued from stores to production, and how the chosen method can affect reported profits.

Contents

1   Purchasing of materials

2   Accounting for materials: cost collection

3   Costing material issues

4   Checking the level of stock

5   Materials classification and coding

1 Purchasing of materials

1.1 Types of materials

In a manufacturing business, materials purchased fall into three main categories:

(a) raw materials from which the product is made, e.g. sheet steel from which car body sections are made

(b) consumable stores used in production, e.g. grease, nuts, screws

(c) materials used in operating the business as opposed to making the product, e.g. machine parts and fuel for power generation.

Categories (b) and (c) are generally treated as indirect materials which form part of overhead costs, so the remainder of this chapter will concentrate on the costing and control procedures relating to direct materials.

1.2 Procedures and documentation for purchasing materials

Materials can form the largest single item of cost so it is essential that the material purchased is the most suitable for the intended purpose from the aspects of utility and cost. Purchasing a great variety of materials is expensive and ideally the business should seek to use standard materials wherever possible; classification and coding of all materials used will help to this end.

1.3 Purchase requisition

It is important to control the placing of orders with suppliers. That function normally is centralised in the purchasing department. Any request for material must therefore be made on a purchase requisition. The purchasing manager will verify that requisitions are authorised in accordance with established policy before placing orders.

1.4 Specimen purchase requisition

PURCHASE REQUISITION								
Date 20						Serial No:		
Purpose*: stock/special production/consumables capital equipment/ (budget reference) *Delete as appropriate.								
Quantity and units	Description	Material code	Job or dept. code	Delivery required		Purchase order		
				Date	Place	No.	Date	Supplier
Origination department: . . . . Authorisation								

1.5 Ordering procedure

On receipt of a properly authorised requisition, the purchasing manager will select a supplier and place an order. The selection will be based upon a number of factors, including price, delivery promise, quality and past performance.

1.6 Specimen purchase order

```
                        PURCHASE  ORDER

  To:.........................        Serial No:.................
     .........................        Date:......................
     .........................        Purchase Req. No:...........

  Please supply, in accordance with the attached conditions
```

Quantity	Description	Code	Delivery date	Price	Per

```
  Your quotation.........................
  To be delivered, carriage paid, to................... Terms
  Please quote our Purchase Order number on all correspondence.
                        For ABC Ltd
                        .........................
```

A copy of the purchase order is sent to the goods receiving department as confirmation of expected delivery.

If a supplier fails to meet a delivery promise, sections of the factory may be brought to a standstill and prevent the company from keeping its delivery promises to its own customers. It is essential that close contact is maintained with suppliers to obtain advance warning of delayed delivery.

1.7 Goods receiving procedure

When goods are received, the goods receiving department will:

- determine what they are, in terms of quantity, apparent quality, the supplier and purchase order number to which they relate

- check the advice or delivery note accompanying the materials to see that it agrees with the goods sent and then check the order copy to see that the goods are as ordered. Full details of the goods are entered on a goods received note (GRN).

Activity 1

Design a goods received note.

Feedback to this activity is at the end of the chapter.

1.8 Purchase invoices

A copy of the GRN will be sent to the purchasing department attached to the copy purchase order. When the supplier's invoice is received, the three documents will be passed to the appropriate individual to approve payment of the invoice.

1.9 Computers and stock control

In reality, of course, in a modern business, this would all be done by electronic means, either via a specialised messaging system (which would be part of the stock control module of an accounting package), or via internal e-mail.

2 Accounting for materials: cost collection

2.1 Stores ledger

Accounting for direct materials is carried out in the stores ledger, which contains a detailed record for each class of material handled. The ledger may be in the form of a loose-leaf binder, a card index or, more commonly these days, a computer application (at least a spreadsheet, but more probably a specialised package).

This record of materials is often referred to as a 'perpetual inventory'.

Perpetual inventory is the recording as they occur of receipts, issues, and the resulting balances of individual items of stock in either quantity or quantity and value. (CIMA *Official Terminology*)

2.2 Specimen stores ledger card

STORES LEDGER CARD									
Description . . . . Unit . . . . Location . . . . Code									
Maximum . . . . Minimum . . . . Reorder level . . . . Reorder quantity									

Receipts			Issues				On order		
Date	Ref.	Quantity	Date	Ref.	Quantity	Physical balance	Date	Ref.	Quantity

In the above illustration values have been omitted. Materials are frequently valued at standard or predetermined prices; this allows value columns to be dispensed with.

2.3 Use of bin cards

A bin card is a record of receipts, issues and balances of the quantity of an item of stock handled by a store. (CIMA *Official Terminology*).

The bin card is a duplication of the quantity information recorded in the stores ledger but storekeepers frequently find that such a ready record is a very useful aid in carrying out their duties.

2.4 Materials requisition and issues

Materials issued to production departments (and to other departments for internal use) are controlled by a materials requisition. This document performs two functions – it authorises the storekeeper to release the goods and acts as a posting medium to the stores ledger and bin card.

2.5 Specimen materials requisition

			Cost office only				
Code No.	Description	Quantity or weight	Rate	Unit	£	£	Stores ledger

MATERIAL REQUISITION   Serial No: . . . .

Charge Job/ Cost Centre No: . . . .   Date: . . . .

Authorised by: Storekeeper: Prices entered by:

Received by: Bin card entered: Calculations checked:

2.6 Other materials movements

When unused materials are returned to store, the transaction will be recorded on a document of similar format to the materials requisition but printed in a different colour. This document is called a materials returned note.

Similarly, materials which are transferred from one production order to another (or from one department to another) should be documented for control and accounting purposes, on a materials transfer note.

Use of the materials returned note and materials transfer note ensures that the correct cost centre or cost unit is charged with the use of the materials concerned.

3 Costing material issues

3.1 Allocating direct materials cost to production

If materials were purchased exactly as required for production, the cost of a particular consignment could be immediately attributed to a specific job or production order. Frequently, however, materials are purchased in large quantities at different prices and issued to production in smaller lots. In attempting to ascertain unit costs of output, therefore, the cost accountant is faced with the problem of identifying the material cost of a particular issue.

3.2 Stock valuation methods (issue pricing)

Various different methods may be used by the cost accountant in order to solve the problem of allocating direct materials cost to production. The three that are required for this syllabus are:

- FIFO (first in, first out)

- LIFO (last in, first out)

- Weighted average cost.

The following example is used to illustrate each of these methods.

Example

In November 1,000 tonnes of 'Grotti' were purchased in three lots:

3 November	400 tonnes at £60 per tonne
11 November	300 tonnes at £70 per tonne
21 November	300 tonnes at £80 per tonne

During the same period four materials requisitions were completed for 200 tonnes each, on 5, 14, 22 and 27 November.

There were no stocks of 'Grotti' at the beginning of November.

In order to calculate the actual material cost of each requisition the cost accountant would need to identify physically from which consignment(s) each issued batch of 200 was drawn. Such precision is uneconomic as well as impractical, so a conventional method of pricing materials issues is adopted.

Using the data in the above example, we shall illustrate the three methods listed above.

Solution 1 – first in first out (FIFO) price

Each issue is valued at the price paid for the material first taken into the stocks from which the issue could have been drawn.

The stores ledger account (in abbreviated form) would appear as below.

Grotti

Date	Receipts (issues) Quantity	Price £	Value £	Balance (quantity) @ £60	@ £70	@ £80
3 Nov	400	60	24,000	400		
5 Nov	(200)	60	(12,000)	(200)		
11 Nov	300	70	21,000		300	
14 Nov	(200)	60	(12,000)	(200)		
21 Nov	300	80	24,000			300
22 Nov	(200)	70	(14,000)		(200)	
27 Nov	(200)	75	(15,000)		(100)	(100)
30 Nov (bal)	200	80	16,000	–	–	200

KEY POINT

Under FIFO the closing stock is valued at the latest price.

Note that the value of the stock at 30 November is at the latest price. Note also that the balance at any time requires analysis by purchase price so that each consignment is exhausted before charging issues at the next price.

Activity 2

You are given the following information about one line of stock held by Tolley plc:

		Units	Cost £	Selling price £
Opening stock	1 January	50	7	
Purchase	1 February	60	8	
Sale	1 March	40		10
Purchase	1 April	70	9	
Sale	1 May	60		12

Assuming that there are no further transactions in the month of May, what would be the stock valuation at that date, using a FIFO valuation method?

Feedback to this activity is at the end of the chapter.

Solution 2 – last in first out (LIFO) price

Each issue is valued at the price paid for the material last taken into the stock from which the issue could have been drawn.

Grotti

Date	Quantity	Receipts (issues) Price £	Value £	Balance (quantity) @ £60	@ £70	@ £80
3 Nov	400	60	24,000	400		
5 Nov	(200)	60	(12,000)	(200)		
11 Nov	300	70	21,000		300	
14 Nov	(200)	70	(14,000)		(200)	
21 Nov	300	80	24,000			300
22 Nov	(200)	80	(16,000)			(200)
27 Nov	(200)	75	(15,000)		(100)	(100)
30 Nov (bal)	200	60	12,000	200	–	–

Under LIFO the closing stock is now valued at £60 per tonne, the earliest price. The issue on 27 November exhausts the latest receipt (at £80) so that the previous latest is used to price the remaining 100 tonnes issued.

Solution 3 – weighted average price

Each time a consignment is received a weighted average price is calculated as:

$$\frac{\text{Stock value} + \text{Receipt value}}{\text{Quantity in stock} + \text{Quantity received}}$$

The price so calculated is used to value subsequent issues until the next consignment is received.

Grotti

Date	Quantity	Receipts (issues) Price £	Value £	Weighted average price £
3 Nov	400	60	24,000	
5 Nov	(200)	60	(12,000)	
11 Nov	300	70	21,000	
Balance	500		33,000	66
14 Nov	(200)	66	(13,200)	
21 Nov	300	80	24,000	
Balance	600		43,800	73
22 Nov	(200)	73	(14,600)	
27 Nov	(200)	73	(14,600)	
30 Nov (bal)	200	73	14,600	

A fresh calculation is required after each receipt but analysis of the balance is unnecessary.

Alternatively, in a computer system, where data is stored for, say, a month and then processed all at once, an average price for the month could be calculated and used to value all issues during the month, irrespective of sequence.

This average can be based on either of the following:

- **Periodic simple average** – Average of all the prices of the period irrespective of quantity delivered (only used where prices do not fluctuate significantly).

- **Periodic weighted average** – Average of all the prices of the period weighted by quantity delivered at each price.

For both alternatives, opening stock is treated as the first delivery of the month.

- Periodic simple average $= \dfrac{£(60+70+80)}{3} = $ £70 per tonne.

- Periodic weighted average $= \dfrac{£(24{,}000+21{,}000+24{,}000)}{(400+300+300)} = $ £69 per tonne

The closing balance, 200 tonnes at £70 or at £69, would be treated as the first receipt in the following month to be included in that month's average.

Activity 3

Using the data for Tolley plc (Activity 2) recompute the stock valuation at 31 May assuming:

(a)   a LIFO valuation method

(b)   a moving weighted average valuation method.

Feedback to this activity is at the end of the chapter.

3.3   Comparison of methods – the effect on profit of the stock valuation method selected

The relative advantages and disadvantages of each system are discussed below, particularly in relation to inflationary situations that are now accepted as being normality.

FIFO

Advantage:

- Produces realistic stock values.

Disadvantages:

- Produces out of date production costs and therefore potentially overstates profits.

- Complicates stock records as stock must be analysed by delivery.

LIFO

Advantage:

- Produces realistic production costs and therefore more realistic/prudent profit figures.

KEY POINT

Whichever method of stock valuation is adopted it should be applied consistently from period to period and its limitations should be recognised when material cost information is being used.

KEY POINT

If selling prices are based on ascertained costs, the use of FIFO or weighted average price could lead to under-pricing, since costs may reflect out of date material prices

Disadvantages:

- Produces unrealistically low stock values.

- Complicates stock records as stock must be analysed by delivery.

Not acceptable under SSAP 9, although it is acceptable under IAS 2 with certain additional disclosures.

Weighted average price

Advantage:

- Simple to operate – calculations within the stock records are minimised.

Disadvantage:

- Produces both stock values and production costs that are far from current values.

Whichever method is adopted it should be applied consistently from period to period and its limitations should be recognised when material cost information is being used. For example, if FIFO is in use and a business is tendering for a special order, it may be dangerous to estimate on the basis of past costs. Such costs probably include the cost of materials purchased some time ago. Additionally, if selling prices are based on ascertained costs, the use of FIFO or weighted average price could lead to under-pricing, since costs may reflect out of date material prices.

Note that these are only methods of **costing**. In physical terms stocks should and would be used up on a FIFO basis.

Activity 4

(a) Using the data for Tolley plc (Activity 2) and your results from activities 2 and 3, calculate the gross profit for January to May using each of the stock valuation methods.

(b) Comment on the results.

Feedback to this activity is at the end of the chapter.

4   Checking the level of stock

4.1   Stocktaking

The process of stocktaking involves checking regularly the physical quantity of stock held against the balance recorded on the perpetual inventory system, i.e. the balance recorded on the bin card and/or stores ledger card. The stock check can be carried out on a periodic basis or on a continuous basis.

A periodic stock check involves checking the balance of every stock item on the same date, usually at the end of an accounting period. The chief disadvantages of periodic stocktaking are that it causes disruption to production operations and that it can be some time before discrepancies are revealed.

4.2   Continuous stocktaking

Continuous stocktaking involves counting and valuing selected items at different times on a rotating basis. In a continuous stocktaking system:

- all items are checked at least once a year

- valuable items, or those subject to specially frequent use, are checked

- checks are carried out by staff unconnected with the stores, being those responsible to the chief accountant or internal auditor.

DEFINITION

Continuous stocktaking is
the process of counting and
valuing selected items at
different times on a rotating
basis.

If stock checking regularly discloses significant differences between book and
physical stocks, the recording system and/or security arrangements should be
reviewed. If differences are within acceptable limits, however, the need for an
annual stocktaking, with its consequent disruption, is avoided, since the stock
shown by the stores ledger can be assumed to be sufficiently accurate.

- more often

4.3 Accounting for stock differences

In theory any differences between 'book' stock and physical stock arise through
faulty recording. The stores ledger, therefore, should be adjusted to the physical
balance by posting a correcting document for the discrepancy once it has been
identified. If the error cannot be traced, the value of the difference (calculated
on a FIFO or LIFO, etc. basis) will be recorded as an issue in the stores ledger
but charged to a special account pending authority for write-off.

4.4 Slow-moving and obsolete stocks

These may arise through faulty purchasing and/or storekeeping and also as a
result of changing circumstances. It is important that such stocks should not be
allowed to accumulate as they will tie up space and capital. The stock controller
must regularly bring slow-moving and obsolete stocks to the attention of
production and sales management for decisions to be taken as to their disposal if
necessary. Certain items, e.g. maintenance materials or product spares, must be
kept although they are slow-moving.

5 Materials classification and coding

5.1 Materials coding system

DEFINITION

A code is a system of
symbols designed to be
applied to a classified set of
items to give a brief,
accurate reference,
facilitating entry, collation
and analysis. (CIMA *Official
Terminology*).

Where a business uses many types of material there are often at least two ways
of describing any one material and a coding system becomes necessary.

A code is a system of symbols designed to be applied to a classified set of items
to give a brief, accurate reference, facilitating entry, collation and analysis.
(CIMA *Official Terminology*).

The advantages of using a materials code are:

- clerical effort is reduced because the writing out of precise descriptions
  becomes unnecessary

- ambiguity is avoided because everyone knows what material is being
  referred to

- it becomes easier to refer to items and to categorise them

- it is normally essential when processing materials data by computer.

5.2 Classifications of materials

DEFINITION

Classification is the
arrangement of items in
logical groups having regard
to their nature (subjective
classification) or purpose
(objective classification).
(CIMA *Official Terminology*).

Classification is the arrangement of items in logical groups having regard to
their nature (subjective classification) or purpose (objective classification).
(CIMA *Official Terminology*).

Here are some common materials classifications.

- **Raw materials** – materials that are converted by production processes
  into a saleable product.

- **Packing materials** – materials that do not form part of the product being sold but are necessary to enable the product to be distributed to the customer.

- **Maintenance materials** – materials which are not required for production or distribution but are necessary to keep machines and plant in working order.

- **Patterns, templates and tools** – materials that do not form part of the product but are necessary in its production.

- **Other indirect materials** – among these would be stationery, protective clothing, fuels, etc.

5.3 Allocation of codes

The most common coding system is to code the material according to its characteristics. For instance BOLT.S.075 might be the code for a 75mm steel bolt. This method avoids duplication, assists storekeeping and can be structured to aid the memory.

Summary

Materials are likely to be a significant cost of most manufacturing organisations and therefore it is essential that control is exercised over all aspects of materials from their purchase through to their issue to production departments. This chapter has looked at many of those aspects of control and most specifically the important area of valuation of materials and closing stock. This valuation and the comparison of the various methods of valuation tend to be a popular examination topic.

By the time you have finished this chapter you should be able to:

- explain raw material accounting and control procedures

- explain FIFO, LIFO and weighted average stock valuation methods

- calculate stock, cost of sales and gross profit under LIFO, FIFO and weighted average.

Self-test questions

Purchasing of materials

1   What are the three main categories of materials purchases in a manufacturing business? (1.1)

Accounting for materials: cost collection

2   Which document is used to record the return of excess materials to the stores? (2.6)

3   What is a perpetual inventory system? (2.1)

Costing material issues

4   Under the LIFO method of stock valuation at what price is closing stock valued? (3.2)

5   What are the advantages and disadvantages of the weighted average price method of stock valuation? (3.3)

Checking the level of stock

6 State two disadvantages of periodic stocktaking. (4.1)

7 What is continuous stocktaking? (4.2)

Exam-type questions

Question 1

During a period of rising prices, tick the boxes to indicate the correct alternatives:

(a) Closing stock values with the LIFO method, compared with the FIFO method, will be:

higher [ ]   lower [ ]

(b) Reported profits with the LIFO method, compared with the FIFO method, will be:

higher [ ]   lower [ ]

Question 2

M Ltd uses a raw material, T. Movements in T for the month of August are set out below.

	Goods received			Issues to production	
Date	kgs	Price £/kg		Date	kgs
12 August	4,000	5.00		15 August	3,900
19 August	1,200	6.00		21 August	1,100
24 August	2,800	7.50			

There were no stocks of T held at 1 August.

(a) The stock valuation at 31 August on a FIFO basis, to the nearest £, would be   £ [ ]

(b) The closing stock valuation at 31 August on a weighted average cost basis, to the nearest £, would be   £ [ ]

Question 3

Aberdeen Ltd holds stocks of ratchets that it uses in production. Over the last month receipts and issues were as follows:

	Receipts		Issues	
Opening balance	200 @ £5		7th	400
5th	300 @ £4.50		23rd	400
12th	100 @ £6		30th	200
22nd	400 @ £5.50			
29th	200 @ £7			

(a) If a FIFO stock valuation method were used, the value of stocks at the month end would be   £ [ ]

(b) If a LIFO stock valuation method were used, the cost of ratchets issued to production in the month would be   £ [ ]

Question 4

A firm has a high level of stock turnover and uses the FIFO (first in first out) issue pricing system. In a period of rising purchase prices, the closing stock valuation is:

A   close to current purchase prices

B   based on the prices of the first items received

C   much lower than current purchase prices

D   the average of all goods purchased in the period

Question 5

The purchase and movements of a particular item of material are recorded using the following documents. Indicate the order in which the documents would be raised by writing 1, 2, 3, 4 and 5 in the boxes as appropriate.

Goods received note

Purchase requisition

Materials requisition

Purchase order

Materials returned note

For the answers to this question, see the 'Answers' section at the end of the book.

Practice question

Material X

(a)   Explain the meaning of:

    (i)   continuous stocktaking

    (ii)   perpetual inventory

    in the context of a material control system.

(b)   A company uses the weighted average method of pricing raw material issues. A weighted average price (to 3 decimal places of a pound £) is calculated after each purchase of material.

Receipts and issues of Material X for a week were as follows:

Receipts into stock			Issues to production	
Day	*Kgs*	*£*	*Day*	*Kgs*
1	1,400	1,092.00	2	1,700
4	1,630	1,268.14	5	1,250

At the beginning of the week, stock of Material X was 3,040 kgs at a cost of £0.765 per kg. Of the issues of material on Day 2, 60 kgs were returned to stock on Day 3. Of the receipts of material on Day 1, 220 kgs were returned to the supplier on Day 4. Invoices for the material receipts during the week remained unpaid at the end of the week.

Required:

Prepare a tabulation of the movement of stock during the week, showing the changes in the level of stock, its valuation per kilogram and the total value of stock held.

For the answer to this question, see the 'Answers' section at the end of the book.

Feedback to activities

Activity 1

GOODS RECEIVED NOTE

Supplier: . . . .   Serial No: . . . .

. . . .   Date issued: . . . .

Carrier: . . . .   Purchase Order No: . . . .

Date of delivery: . . . .

Description	Code	Quantity	Packages	Gross weight

INSPECTION REPORT			Received by: . . . .
Quantity passed	Quantity rejected	Remarks	Required by: . . . .
Inspector . . . . Date			Accepted: . . . . Date: . . . .

The goods received note (GRN) is the basis for entering receipts in the stores record.

Certain goods will need to be critically inspected and/or possibly chemically analysed. Normally inspection will be on a sampling basis, i.e. a number of items selected at random will be investigated and checked against the detailed specification in the purchase order.

Activity 2

FIFO results in later purchases remaining in stock.

	Units
Opening stock	50
Purchases	130
Sales	(100)
Closing stock	80

			£
Comprising			
1 April	70 × £9 =		630
1 February	10 × £8 =		80
			710

Activity 3

Note: closing stock is 80 units, as computed in Activity 2.

(a) LIFO results in earlier purchases remaining in stock. However, care must be taken as some of the earliest priced stock may have been used up before the month end.

The issue of 40 units on 1 March will be valued at £8 (Feb purchase)

The issue of 60 units on 1 May will be valued at £9 (April purchase)

This leaves:

	£
50 units from opening stock @ £7	350
20 units from Feb purchase @ £8	160
10 units from April purchase @ £9	90
	600

(b) **Weighted average**

Here we have to work through the averaging process:

Date	Quantity	Receipts (issues) Price	Value	Weighted average price
		£	£	£
1 Jan	50	7.00	350	
1 Feb	60	8.00	480	
	110		830	7.55
1 Mar	(40)	7.55	(302)	
1 April	70	9.00	630	
	140		1,158	8.27
1 May	(60)	8.27	(496)	
31 May	80	8.27	662	

Activity 4

(a) Profit for January to May

	FIFO	LIFO	Weighted average
	£	£	£
Cost of purchases	1,110	1,110	1,110
Less closing stock (from activity 2 & 3)	(710)	(600)	(662)
Cost of sales	400	510	448
Sales ((40 × £10) + (60 × £12)	1,120	1,120	1,120
Gross profit	720	610	672

(b) FIFO reports the highest profit because this method charges the older, lower prices to cost of sales. Conversely, LIFO charges the later prices to cost of sales and thus a lower profit is reported in times of rising prices. The weighted average method produces a profit figure which lies between the FIFO and LIFO result.

Chapter 6

MATERIALS: STOCK CONTROL

Syllabus content

- Materials: re-order quantity, re-order level, maximum stock, minimum stock, economic order quantity.

We continue on the theme of materials, looking particularly at the ways in which stock levels are 'controlled', in other words, how you make sure that you have raw materials when you need them. The principles can also be applied to the control of finished goods stocks. This is a mixture of practical approaches and theoretical models.

Contents

1   Investment in stock

2   Practical stock control systems

3   Re-order level system – control levels

4   Theoretical stock control – the EOQ

1 Investment in stock

1.1 The benefits of holding stocks

The object of holding stocks is to increase sales and thereby increase profit. If stocks are held customer demand is more immediately satisfied because the product is available and this should prevent prospective customers from going elsewhere.

Also, stockholding of materials and components will prevent hold-ups in production.

1.2 The costs of holding stocks

Holding stock is an expensive business – it has been estimated that the cost of holding stock each year is one-third of its cost. Holding costs include interest on capital (the money tied up in stock), the cost of storage space and equipment, and administration costs.

However, running out of stock (known as a **stock-out**) also incurs a cost. If, for example, a shop is persistently out of stock on some lines, customers will start going elsewhere. Stock-out cost is difficult to estimate, but it is an essential factor in inventory control.

Finally, set-up or handling costs are incurred each time a batch is ordered. Administrative costs and, where production is internal, costs of setting up machinery will be affected in total by the frequency of orders.

1.3 Principles of stock control

Determining the best re-order levels and order quantities involves striking the optimum balance between two of the three cost categories above – holding costs, stock-out costs and order costs.

The questions asked in maintaining stock at optimum levels are:

DEFINITION

Lead time – the time expected to elapse between the start of a process or activity and its completion (CIMA), for example placing and receiving an order for stock.

Buffer stock – a stock of materials, or of work in progress, maintained in order to protect user departments from the effect of possible interruptions to supply.

- **How much to re-order?** – Large order quantities cut ordering and set-up costs each year. On the other hand, stock volumes will on average be higher, and so holding costs increase. The problem is balancing one against the other. The order quantity that minimises total annual cost is the economic order quantity.

- **When to re-order?** – A gap (known as the lead time) inevitably occurs between placing an order and its delivery. Where both that gap and the rate of demand are known with certainty, an exact decision on when to re-order can be made. In the real world both will fluctuate randomly and so the order must be placed so as to leave some buffer stock if demand and lead time follow the average pattern. The problem is again the balancing of increased holding costs if the buffer stock is high, against increased stock-out costs if the buffer stock is low. The quantity of stock at the time of placing the order is the re-order level.

2 Practical stock control systems

2.1 Inventory control systems

It is important that inventory levels are maintained at a high enough level to service the production facility while at the same time minimising the working capital tied up in inventory. The following sections look at both the physical aspects of different control systems and the mathematical techniques supporting control.

2.2 Two-bin system

Under this system the existence of two bins is assumed, say A and B. Stock is taken from A until A is empty. A is then replenished with the order quantity. During the lead time (the time taken between ordering goods and receiving them) stock is used from B. The standard stock for B is the expected demand in the lead time, plus any buffer stock. When the new order arrives, B is filled up to its standard level and the rest placed in A. Stock is then drawn as required from A, and the process repeated.

In considering the costs of stock control, the actual costs of operating the system must be recognised. The costs of a continual review as implied by the two-bin system may be excessive, and it may be more economic to operate a periodic review system.

2.3 Periodic review system

Under this system the stock levels are reviewed at fixed intervals, e.g. every four weeks. The stock in hand is then made up to a predetermined level, which takes account of likely demand before the next review and during the lead time. Thus, a four-weekly review in a system where the lead time was two weeks would demand that stock be made up to the likely maximum demand for the next six weeks.

This system is described in some textbooks as the constant order cycle system.

Advantages of two-bin system

Stock can be kept at a lower level because of the ability to order whenever stocks fall to a low level, rather than having to wait for the next re-order date.

Advantages of periodic review system

The purchasing department's workload is more evenly spread and easier to plan. For this reason the system is also more popular with suppliers.

2.4 ABC inventory analysis

This is a technique that divides stocks into sub-classifications based on an annual usage value and involves using different control systems for each classification.

It is based on a Pareto analysis that states that approximately 20% of the total quantity of stock lines may account for about 80% of the total value of stock.

The idea is to gear the quality of stock control procedures to the value of the stock and therefore to help ensure that the stock control methods adopted are cost effective.

Illustration

An example of ABC analysis is the classification of stock as follows:

	No of days' supply held in stock
Class A	2 days
Class B	5 days
Class C	10 days
Class D	20 days or more

Stock levels of high value category A items are kept low in order to save on holding costs.

The priority with category D items is to avoid stockouts, hence much higher stocks are held. The company could use the 'two bin system' for this category of items.

3 Re-order level system – control levels

DEFINITION

Re-order level – a level of stock at which a replenishment order should be placed.

Minimum stock level – a stock level, set for control purposes, below which stockholding should not fall without being highlighted.

Maximum stock level – a stock level, set for control purposes, which actual stockholding should never exceed.

3.1 Re-order level system

This is a more sophisticated version of the two-bin system, which involves the setting of three control levels, as defined in CIMA Official Terminology.

- Re-order level – a level of stock at which a replenishment order should be placed.

- Minimum stock level – a stock level, set for control purposes, below which stockholding should not fall without being highlighted. (If the stocks fall below that level the storekeeper will consider the need for an emergency order.)

- Maximum stock level – a stock level, set for control purposes, which actual stockholding should never exceed. (If the stock rises above this level, it is an indication of decline in usage/demand, and the re-order quantity may need to be reviewed.)

The following diagram illustrates the re-order level system:

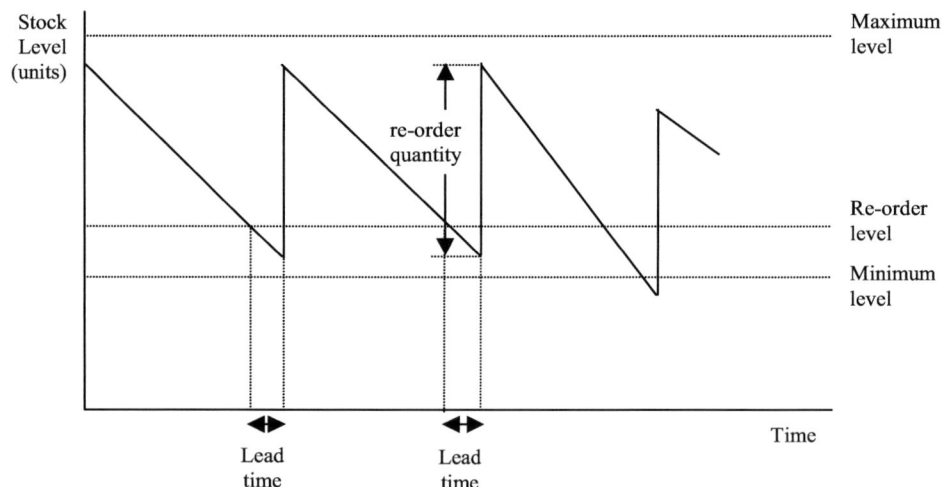

3.2 The minimum level

The minimum level can be described as the buffer stock

Buffer stock = Re-order level – (average usage per day × average lead time (days))

Example

ABC Limited uses between 75 and 90 litres of oil per day. Delivery times vary between 2–3 days. It has set its re-order level at 270 litres, and orders 500 litres each time.

Using simple averages, the minimum level is:

$$270 - (82.5 \times 2.5)$$

$$= 63.75 \text{ litres}$$

Activity 1

Calculate the minimum stock level from the following data:

Re-order level	2,400 units
Lead time	2–5 days
Maximum usage	400 units per day
Minimum usage	100 units per day

Feedback to this activity can be found at the end of the chapter.

3.3 The maximum level

The maximum level is the level above which stock should not normally rise. It is given by:

$$\frac{\text{Reorder}}{\text{level}} + \frac{\text{Reorder}}{\text{quantity}} - \left(\frac{\text{minimum usage}}{\text{per day}} \times \frac{\text{minimum lead}}{\text{time (days)}}\right)$$

Example

In the example of ABC Limited, the maximum level is:

$270 + 500 - (75 \times 2)$

$= 620$ litres

3.4 The reorder level

The reorder level is the level of stock at which a replenishment order should be placed.

Reorder level = maximum usage × maximum lead time

Example

In the example of ABC Limited the re-order level can be calculated as:

reorder level = $90 \times 3 = 270$ litres

3.5 Average stock level

Although the average stock level is not a control level as such, an examination question might require you to apply your knowledge of the control level system to determine the average stock.

If we assume that a replenishment order arrives at the point at which stock reaches the buffer or safety stock level, and that thereafter stock is used evenly until it reaches the re-order level and an order is placed, the average stock level can be calculated as:

average stock = safety stock + ½ reorder quantity

Example

In the example of ABC Limited, if we assume that the minimum stock level is the safety stock, then the average stock will be:

average stock = $63.75 + (0.5 \times 500) = 313.75$ litres

If we assume that no safety stock is held, so that a delivery is received just as stock falls to zero (an assumption that you will see is made in the economic order quantity model) then the formula for calculating the average stock level becomes:

average stock = ½ reorder quantity

3.6 Free stock

Free stock is stock on hand or on order which has not been scheduled for use.

Free stock = physical stock + stock ordered – stock scheduled (CIMA *Official Terminology*)

It will be important for the storekeeper to monitor this stock level in an efficient stock control system. For example at a single point in time there may be a high level of physical stock, but if a large proportion of this stock has already been requisitioned for use on a particular job then it may be necessary to place a replenishment order.

Monitoring the free stock balance against the predetermined control levels helps to avoid the occurrence of stock-outs.

Example

K Limited has 3,400 units of material Y in stock. Of these units, 2,600 have been requisitioned by a production cost centre for a job to commence in two days. An order has been placed with the supplier for 1,500 units. Delivery is expected in three days.

The free stock balance is 3,400 + 1,500 – 2,600 = 2,300 units.

If this stock level is at or below the re-order level then it will be necessary to place another order with the supplier.

4 Theoretical stock control – the EOQ

4.1 Introduction

At the start of this chapter, we showed that in any stock control system there are two basic questions to answer:

- how much to re-order (re-order quantity)

- when to re-order (re-order level).

Having used given figures, or simple models, for these in the systems considered so far, we now turn to the theoretical approach for the determination of their optimum values. You should, however, note the various simplifying assumptions built into the models.

4.2 Calculation of economic order quantity

Consider the following situation. Watallington Ltd is a retailer of beer barrels. The company has an annual demand of 30,000 barrels. The barrels are purchased for stock in lots of 5,000 and cost £12 each. Fresh supplies can be obtained immediately (i.e. nil lead time) ordering and transport costs amounting to £200 per order. The annual cost of holding one barrel in stock is estimated to be 10% of the price of a barrel, i.e. £12 × 0.1 = £1.20.

The stock level situation could be represented graphically as follows:

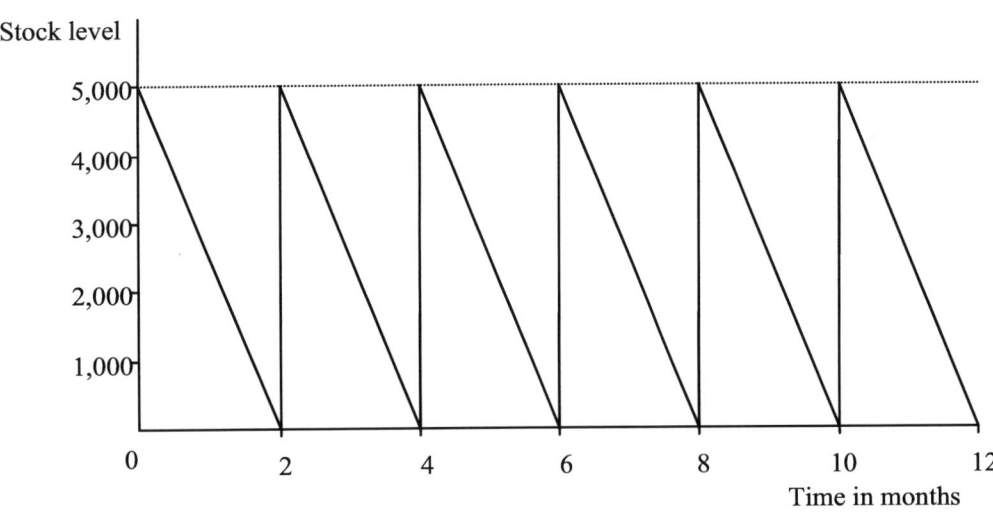

Thus, Watallington Ltd orders 5,000 barrels at a time and these are used from stock at a uniform rate.

Every two months stock is zero and a new order is made and received. The average stock level is $\dfrac{5,000}{2}$ barrels, i.e. half the replenishment level. So the fluctuating stock levels are equivalent to holding 2,500 barrels for the whole of the year.

Watallington's total annual inventory costs are made up as follows:

		£
Ordering costs	$\dfrac{30,000}{5,000} \times £200$	1,200
Cost of holding stock	$\dfrac{5,000}{2} \times £1.20$	3,000
Total inventory costs		4,200

Thirty thousand barrels are purchased annually in lots of 5,000. If each order costs £200, the total ordering costs are £1,200. The cost of holding each barrel in stock was estimated at £1.20. With the average stock being half the replenishment level, the annual stockholding costs are £3,000.

Compare these costs with those of ordering 4, 6, 8, 10 and 15 times a year.

A No of orders per year	B Annual ordering costs £(A × 200)	C Order size 30,000 ÷ A	D Average stock C ÷ 2	E Stockholding costs per annum £(D × £1.20)	F Total inventory cost (B + E)
	£	barrels	barrels	£	£
4	800	7,500	3,750	4,500	5,300
6	1,200	5,000	2,500	3,000	4,200
8	1,600	3,750	1,875	2,250	3,850
10	2,000	3,000	1,500	1,800	3,800
15	3,000	2,000	1,000	1,200	4,200

To minimise total inventory costs (column F), make between eight and fifteen orders a year, i.e. order size should be between 3,750 and 2,000 barrels a time. A more explicit solution could be achieved by calculating costs at 9, 10, 11, 12, 13 and 14 orders per year.

However, rather than continue with the trial and error process, the results from the table could be shown graphically, plotting actual cost against size of order. Three curves result:

- annual ordering costs curve (column B) – falling as the order quantity rises

- annual stockholding costs curve (column E) – rising as the order quantity rises

- total inventory costs curve (column F).

Graph of costs of ordering and storing stock

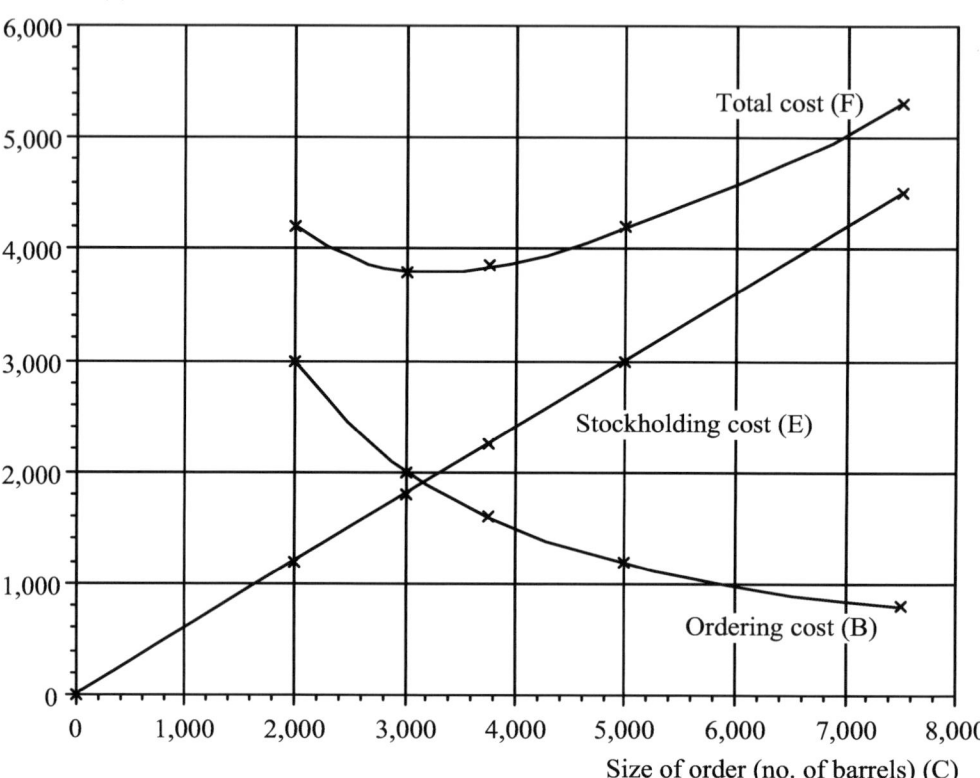

From the graph the order quantity which gives the lowest total cost is somewhere between 3,000 and 3,200 barrels. It is difficult, however, to be much more accurate than this by reading the graph.

4.3 Economic Order Quantity (EOQ) formula

The exact quantity to be ordered to minimise the total cost of ordering and storing stock is the economic order quantity (EOQ)

The EOQ can be calculated by the following formula:

$$EOQ = \sqrt{\frac{2C_0 D}{C_h}}$$

where

C_0 = cost of placing an order

D = expected annual demand

C_h = cost of holding one unit in stock for one year.

In the example of Watallington Ltd, the values to be inserted in the formula are:

$C_0 = £200$

$D = 30,000$ barrels

$C_h = £1.20$

$$EOQ = \sqrt{\frac{2C_0 D}{C_h}}$$

$$= \sqrt{\frac{2 \times 200 \times 30,000}{1.20}}$$

$$= 3,162 \text{ barrels}$$

Activity 2

Calculate the economic order quantity given the following data:

Annual demand	5,000 units
Ordering cost	£150 per order
Annual holding cost	£2 per unit

Feedback to this activity is at the end of the chapter.

Summary

To keep stock levels under control management will need a regular flow of information on stock levels to act upon. For economy the stock control system is frequently restricted to the most important items. It has been estimated that in many businesses, about 20% of the items comprise about 80% of total materials cost.

A stock control system will contain the following features:

- Prediction of likely usage and delivery period (lead time); expressed as maximum, minimum and average.
- Calculation of order quantity.
- Establishment of control levels - minimum stock, reorder level and maximum level, and monitoring of these levels against the free stock balance.
- Regular reports.

As you have seen, a number of formulae are involved in establishing a stock control system. You will be provided with the formula for the EOQ in the examination if you need it. However you must learn all of the other formulae as they will not be provided in the examination.

By the time you have finished this chapter you should be able to:

- explain and calculate re-order quantity, re-order level, maximum stock minimum stock, and economic order quantity.

Self-test questions

Investment in stock

1   State two benefits and the costs associated with holding stock. (1.1–1.2)

Practical stock control systems

2   Explain the meaning of the two-bin system of inventory control. (2.2)

Re-order level system – control levels

3   How is the maximum stock control level calculated? (3.3)

4   What is the formula for the reorder level? (3.4)

Theoretical stock control – the EOQ

5   Explain the objective of using the EOQ model. (4.2)

Exam-type questions

Question 1

There are 27,500 units of Part Number X53 on order with the suppliers and 16,250 units outstanding on existing customers' orders. The free stock balance is 13,000 units.

The physical stock of Part Number X53 is [   ] units.

The following information is to be used for questions 2 and 3.

A national chain of tyre fitters stocks a popular tyre for which the following information is available:

Average usage	140 tyres per day
Minimum usage	90 tyres per day
Maximum usage	175 tyres per day
Lead time	10 to 16 days
Re-order quantity	3,000 tyres

Question 2

Based on the data above, a replenishment order should be issued when the stock

balance reaches [   ] tyres.

Question 3

Based on the data above, the maximum stock level is [   ] tyres.

The following information is to be used for questions 4 and 5.

A large retailer with multiple outlets maintains a central warehouse from which the outlets are supplied. The following information is available for Part Number SF525.

Average usage	350 per day
Minimum usage	180 per day
Maximum usage	420 per day
Lead time for replenishment	11 – 15 days
Re-order quantity	6,500 units
Re-order level	6,300 units

Question 4

Based on the data above, the maximum level of stock is [   ] units.

Question 5

Based on the data above, the minimum stock level is [   ] units.

Question 6

The objective of the EOQ as part of a stock control policy is to ensure that

A   the company never runs out of stock, except in exceptional circumstances

B   the cost of being out of stock is minimised

C   the combined cost of ordering and holding stock is minimised

D   stock is purchased from suppliers at the cheapest price

For the answers to these questions, see the 'Answers' section at the end of the book.

Practice question

Computer bureau order quantity

It has been estimated that a computer bureau will need 1,000 boxes of line printer paper next year. The purchasing officer of the bureau plans to arrange regular deliveries from a supplier, who charges £15 per delivery.

The bureau's accountant advises the purchasing officer that the cost of storing a box of line printer paper for a year is £2.70. Over a year, the average number of boxes in storage is half the order quantity (that is the number of boxes per delivery).

The ordering cost is defined as the delivery cost plus the storage cost, where the annual costs for an order quantity of x boxes will be:

Delivery cost:

$$\text{Number of deliveries} \times \text{Cost per delivery} = £\frac{1{,}000}{x} \times 15$$

Storage cost:

$$\text{Average stock level} \times \text{Storage cost per box} = £\frac{x}{2} \times 2.70$$

You are required:

(a)   to calculate the delivery cost, storage cost and ordering cost for order quantities of 50, 100, 150, 200 and 250 boxes to estimate the order quantity that will minimise cost.

(b)   use the values calculated in (a) to estimate the order quantity that will minimise cost.

(c)   use the EOQ formula to calculate the exact order quantity that will minimise cost.

For the answers to this question, see the 'Answers' section at the end of the book.

Feedback to activities

Activity 1

$$2{,}400 - (250 \times 3.5)$$

$$= 1{,}525 \text{ units.}$$

Activity 2

$$\sqrt{\frac{2 \times £150 \times 5{,}000}{£2}}$$

= 866 units (to nearest unit).

Chapter 7

LABOUR: ACCOUNTING AND CONTROL

Syllabus content

- Labour: accounting and control procedures.

- Factory incentive schemes for individuals and groups

So far, we have looked at the principles and computations relating to overheads (indirect costs) and materials (usually, but not exclusively, a direct cost). We complete our studies of the 'Cost determination' part of the syllabus by looking at the third main category of costs – labour. Again, we concentrate on the direct cost aspects, but supervisory and management salaries would in fact form part of indirect costs.

Contents

1 Labour documentation

2 Payroll

3 Remuneration methods

4 Incentive schemes

5 Labour cost accounting

6 Labour cost control reports

1   Labour documentation

1.1   Personal history

The personnel department will maintain a history record for each employee. The record will include such details as:

(a)   full name and address

(b)   previous employment

(c)   clock number issued

(d)   date engaged

(e)   department, job title and pay rate upon engagement

(f)   amendments to (e) above, recorded as and when they occur

(g)   on the termination of employment, the date and reason for leaving.

1.2   Time recording

Time recording is required both for payment purposes and also for determining costs to be charged to specific jobs. These may be described diagrammatically:

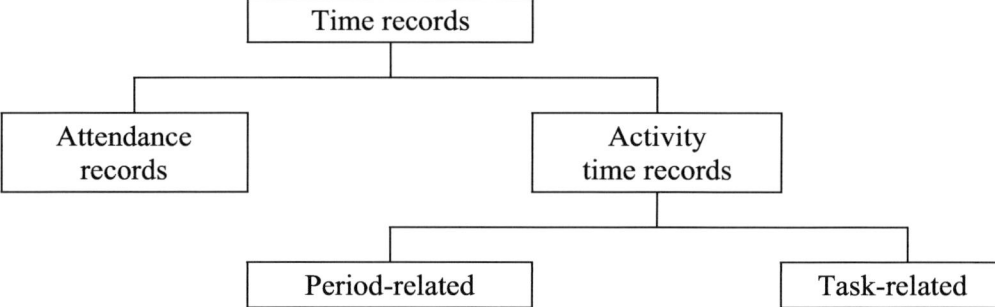

1.3   Attendance records

Wages cost represents payments for direct and indirect labour. Both types of workers will be supplied with time cards (gate or clock cards) or other records on which to record their time of arrival and departure from the factory. Such records will provide the basis for wages calculation at time rates.

A clock card is a document on which is recorded the starting and finishing time of an employee, e.g. by insertion into a time-recording device, for ascertaining total actual attendance time. (CIMA, Official Terminology)

The most sophisticated time recorders use plastic 'swipe' cards and are directly linked to a central computer.

1.4   Activity-time records

The precise arrangements for activity-time recording should be adapted to the nature and organisation of production, and so will vary from one factory to another. In some cases a card for each job may accompany that job through the factory, each worker involved noting or 'clocking' the time spent on the one card. Alternatively a separate job card or ticket may be issued to each worker for each job.

However, most such records can be categorised as being either period-related or task-related. However recorded, it will be essential to reconcile activity time and attendance time to ensure accuracy of the information.

1.5 Period-related activity time records

These may be for daily, weekly, or sometimes longer periods. An example of a weekly time sheet is given below.

Weekly Time Sheet			Dept:				
Employees No		Name	Wk Edg				
To be completed by employee					For Office Use		
Day	Start	Finish	Job		Code	Hrs	Amounts £ p
Supervisor's Signature:					Gross Wages		

1.6 Task related activity time records

Known variously as job sheets, operations charts or piece-work tickets. They are generally more accurate and reliable than time-related activity time records, and are essential for use with incentive schemes. An example is given below.

Time Sheet

Employee name: No:
Start date: Finish date:
Department: Operation:

Day	Start	Finish	Time	Production	Supervisor's Signature
1					
2					
3					
4					
5					
Total					
Time allowed					
Time saved					

	Hours	Rate £	Paid £
Time wages			
Bonus			
Total wages			

2 Payroll

2.1 Payroll preparation

Because of the sums of money involved, security control is necessary at all stages of the task of payroll preparation and payment. One major area of risk is the introduction of fictitious employees ('dummies' or 'ghosting') in the payroll.

The payroll preparation involves:

- calculating gross wages from time and activity records
- calculating net wages after PAYE and other deductions, and properly recording the deductions
- preparing a cash analysis of total cash required for payment, if necessary.

3 Remuneration methods

3.1 Introduction

There are two basic approaches to remuneration, time-related or output-related. The two basic methods are time rate and piece rates.

3.2 Time rates

The most common method of payment is time rate, whereby employees are paid a basic rate per hour, day, week or month irrespective of production achieved. Basic time rate provides no incentive to improve productivity and close supervision is necessary.

A variation is known as 'higher time rates', where rates above the basic level are offered and paid, to attract more enthusiastic and skilled employees.

3.3 Piece-work

The direct alternative to time rate is piece-work, whereby a fixed amount is paid per unit of output achieved, irrespective of time spent. Rigid inspection procedures are required to ensure work is of an adequate standard.

Straight piece-work is almost extinct today as a result of employment legislation and trade union resistance. Most employees are paid a guaranteed minimum wage within the piecework system.

Piece-workers are usually required to keep time records for disciplinary and security purposes.

A variation is 'differential piece rates'. This is almost a penal system, with a low piece rate for the first units of production, and a high piece rate for subsequent units.

KEY POINT

The two basic approaches to remuneration are time-related or output-related.

Example

A company operates a differential piece-rate system and the following weekly rates have been set:

Weekly production	*Rate of pay per unit in this band*
	£
1 to 500 units	0.20
501 to 600 units	0.25
601 units and above	0.55

Employees are paid a guaranteed minimum wage of £130 per week.

How much would be paid to the following employees for the week?

Employee A – output achieved = 800 units

Employee B – output achieved = 570 units.

Solution

Employee A = (500 units × £0.20) + (100 units × £0.25) + (200 units × £0.55) = £235

Employee B = (500 units × £0.20) + (70 units × £0.25) = £117.50. This is less than the guaranteed minimum therefore employee B would be paid £130.

3.4   Incentive schemes

These have developed from the piece rate approach, but attempt to avoid the crudities of the system described above.

The variety of approaches are described by the diagram below:

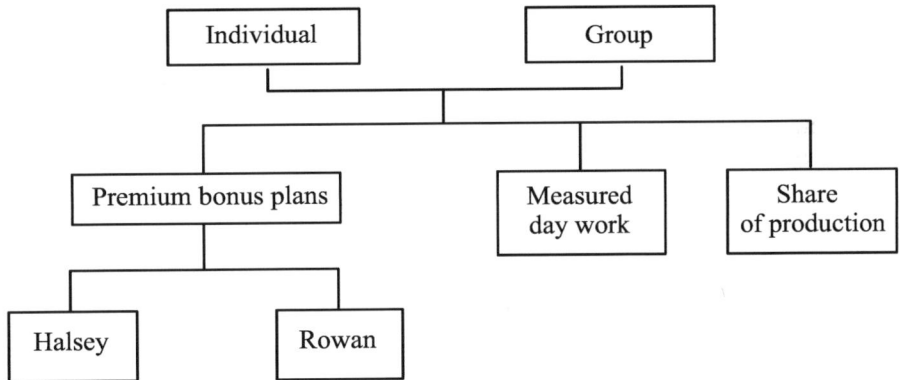

These are all explained in the sections below:

As a general rule, any incentive scheme should be:

- related closely to effort
- agreed by prior consultation between employer and employees
- understandable and simple to operate
- capable of being beneficial to the average worker.

4 Incentive schemes

4.1 Premium bonus plans

The basic idea of all premium bonus plans is to pay a basic time rate, plus a portion of the time saved as compared to some agreed allowed time. Examples of such schemes are Halsey and Rowan.

(a) **Halsey** – The employee receives 50% of the time saving, i.e.

$$\text{Bonus} = \frac{\text{Time allowed} - \text{Time taken}}{2} \times \text{Time rate}$$

Example

Employee's basic rate	=	£4.80 per hour	
Allowed time for Job A	=	1 hour	
Time taken for Job A	=	36 minutes	
			£
Bonus	=	$\dfrac{60-36}{2} \times \dfrac{£4.80}{60}$	0.96
Basic rate	=	$\dfrac{36}{60} \times £4.80$	2.88
			———
Total payment for Job A			3.84
			———

(b) **Rowan** – The proportion paid to the employee is based on the ratio of time taken to time allowed, i.e.

$$\text{Bonus} = \frac{\text{Time taken}}{\text{Time allowed}} \times \text{Time rate} \times \text{Time saved}$$

Example

Using the facts in (a) above.

			£
Bonus	=	$\dfrac{36}{60} \times \dfrac{£4.80}{60} \times 24$	1.15
Basic rate	=	$\dfrac{36}{60} \times £4.80$	2.88
			———
Total payment for Job A			4.03
			———

Activity 1

What would be the bonus under each plan if the time taken in the previous example was 18 minutes?

Feedback to this activity is at the end of the chapter.

Premium bonus schemes of the type described are really appropriate only for skilled craftsmen. In continuous production the output of the individual worker is largely governed by the speed of the flow line, although such schemes may be suitable for special jobs, e.g. fitting radios in motorcar assembly. As with straight piece-work, production under bonus for timesaving requires strict inspection to prevent poor quality work.

Many different schemes exist in practice for calculating the bonus payable. In an examination you should follow the instructions carefully to calculate the bonus from the data supplied.

4.2 Measured day work

The concept of this approach is to pay a high time rate, but this rate is based on an analysis of past performance. Initially, work measurement is used to calculate the allowed time per unit. This allowed time is compared to the time actually taken in the past by the employee, and if this is better than the allowed time an incentive is agreed.

Example

Allowed time – 1 hour.

Average time taken by employee over last three months – 50 minutes.

Normal rate – £4.80/hour.

Agreed incentive rate (say) – £5.00/hour.

Note: the incentive rate will be a matter of negotiation.

This incentive wage rate will be reviewed periodically in the light of the employee's actual performance.

4.3 Share of production plans

In order to understand this plan, it is necessary to introduce the concept of added value. This is explained below:

		£
Sales		X
Less:	Cost of bought in materials and services (i.e. all costs except payroll and depreciation)	X
Value added		X

Generally, wages tends to maintain a constant relationship to value added, usually about 40%.

Share of production plans are based on acceptance by both management and labour representatives of a constant share of value added for payroll. Thus, any gains in value added – whether by improved production performance or cost savings – are shared by employees in this ratio.

Example

	£
Sales	100,000
Less: bought in materials and services	55,000
Value added	45,000
Agreed wages share 40% value added	18,000
Wages paid	15,000
Balance paid as bonus	3,000

4.4 Group incentive schemes

All of the schemes discussed above can be operated as group incentive schemes. This more closely relates to reality, in that improved performance is the result of group rather than individual effort.

Example

Ten employees work as a group. When production of the group exceeds the standard – 200 pieces per hour – each employee in the group is paid a bonus for the excess production in addition to wages at hourly rates.

The bonus is computed thus: the percentage of production in excess of the standard quantity is found, and one half of the percentage is regarded as the employees' share. Each employee in the group is paid as a bonus this percentage of a wage rate of £5.20 per hour. There is no relationship between the individual worker's hourly rate and the bonus rate.

The following is one week's record:

	Hours worked	*Production*
Monday	90	24,500
Tuesday	88	20,600
Wednesday	90	24,200
Thursday	84	20,100
Friday	88	20,400
Saturday	40	10,200
	480	120,000

You are required:

(a) to compute the rate and amount of bonus for the week

(b) to calculate the total pay of Jones, who worked 42 hours and was paid £3.00 per hour basic, and that of Smith, who worked 44 hours and was paid £3.75 per hour basic.

Solution

(a) Standard production for the week = 480 hours × 200 = 96,000 pieces

Actual production for the week = 120,000 pieces

Bonus rate $= \dfrac{24,000}{96,000} \times 0.5 \times £5.20$

= 65p per hour

Total bonus = 480 hours × 65p

= £312

(b)

		Jones £		*Smith* £
Basic	42 × £3.00	126.00	44 × £3.75	165.00
Bonus	42 × £0.65	27.30	44 × £0.65	28.60
Total pay		153.30		193.60

4.5 Incentives to non-production workers

The main incentive schemes are only appropriate where production can be measured in saleable output. However, the principle of relating reward to achievement is capable of adaptation to many activities; for example, sales order staff could be paid a group bonus based on the number of orders correctly processed in a period.

Alternatively, managerial and skilled technical employees may be given objectives for achievement in the period ahead and, if they agree that the objectives are attainable, their rewards, in terms of bonus of increased salary, would be related to success in meeting the objectives.

5 Labour cost accounting

5.1 Direct and indirect wages

The distinction between direct and indirect costs has previously been explained. Indirect wages represent:

- the cost of time spent by direct labour on non-productive work, e.g. cleaning machines or waiting for materials

- the gross wage of factory personnel not actually engaged in production, e.g. maintenance staff, forklift truck operators, supervisors.

The gross wages total provided from the payroll represents a control figure for cost analysis and gross wages comprise basic pay, overtime, bonuses and allowances. For cost ascertainment purposes, direct wages will be charged to cost units and indirect wages will be charged to cost centres for later allotment to cost units. Therefore it is important that the system should distinguish between direct and indirect wages.

One further point may require clarification. The distinction between wages and salaries is meaningless for cost accounting purposes. What is important is whether the payment can be regarded as direct or indirect.

5.2 Accounting treatment of overtime premium

The treatment of the overtime premium depends on the reason for the overtime being worked. If the overtime is worked at the specific request of a customer the premium should be charged to the customer and therefore to work in progress control.

If the overtime arises as a result of company policy to increase production generally, then the premium should be charged to production overhead along with other indirect wage costs and charged to the product via the overhead recovery rate.

6 Labour cost control reports

6.1 Productivity

One of the major responsibilities of production management is to improve productivity. To assist in this, regular reports analysed by process, machine group or department are required, showing:

- numbers of employees (direct and indirect)

- labour costs (analysed into basic, premium and bonuses)

- production achieved

- hours worked, hours lost and hours spent on non-productive work
- ratios and trends.

Such reports are most effective when a comparison plan is incorporated. A central feature of such a comparison is the productivity index. This expresses the actual number of units produced as a percentage of the standard or budgeted production for the period, e.g. actual production in June was 1,100 units, standard production was 1,000 units. The productivity index is 110%.

Note the difference between production and productivity. Production is output in terms of units, e.g. 1,000 units per month. Productivity is this output expressed relative to a vital resource, e.g. 10 cars per man per year, or 12 tons of steel per man per month.

6.2 Idle time

Idle time is a cost that represents waste and warrants close control. To assist control, time booking procedures should permit analysis of idle time by cause, and analysis should disclose whether idle time was capable of being avoided by action within the business.

The three main causes of idle time are:

- **Production disruption** – due to machine breakdown, shortage of materials, inefficient scheduling, etc.
- **Policy decisions** – run-down of stocks, changes in product specification, retraining schemes, seasonal factors, etc.
- **Outside influences** – sudden fall in demand due to economic changes, a strike affecting vital supplies, etc.

6.3 Labour turnover

A key objective of the personnel department is to retain staff: in other words to minimise turnover of labour. It is evident that each time an employee is replaced, the business incurs direct costs of:

- advertising and selection
- administering departure and replacement
- training
- reduced efficiency until the new employee reaches the required skill.

Furthermore, a high rate of turnover tends to lower the performance of continuing employees, who may become restless and resentful of the extra burden of training new members and of additional temporary duties imposed upon them.

Labour turnover can be calculated as:

$$\frac{\text{number of employees leaving and replaced}}{\text{average number of employees in period}} \times 100$$

To assist control of labour turnover, the personnel department will maintain records of employees leaving, analysed to show:

(a)   personnel details – sex, age groups, etc.

(b)   department or section in which employed

(c)   length of service

(d)   reason for leaving.

Analysis in respect of (d) would be useful to disclose whether a particular cause is recurring, especially if the cause can be avoided by action within the business. Such statistics should, however, be regarded with caution, as employees frequently hide the true reason, or neglect to explain it clearly.

Summary

This chapter has considered the remuneration methods available together with appropriate incentive schemes to improve productivity.

The collection of costs has been explained by reference to the appropriate documentation and labour cost reporting considered.

By the time you have finished this chapter you should be able to:

- explain labour accounting and control procedures

- discuss and calculate factory incentive schemes for individuals and groups.

Self-test questions

Labour documentation

1   What is a clock card? (1.3)

2   What is a time sheet? (1.5)

3   What is a job sheet? (1.6)

Payroll

4   What does payroll preparation involve? (2.1)

Remuneration methods

5   What are the two main approaches to calculating the remuneration paid to employees? (3.1)

Incentive schemes

6   What is measured day work? (4.2)

7   What is value added? (4.3)

8   What is a group incentive scheme? (4.4)

Labour cost accounting

9   How is an overtime premium treated? (5.2)

Labour cost control reports

10   State three possible causes of idle time. (6.2)

11   How is labour turnover calculated? (6.3)

Exam-type questions

Question 1

A job requires 2,400 actual labour hours for completion and it is anticipated that there will be 20% idle time. If the wage rate is £10 per hour, the budgeted labour cost for

the job is £ ⬚

Question 2

A manufacturing firm is very busy and overtime is being worked.

The overtime premium would normally be classed as:

A   part of prime cost

B   factory overheads

C   direct labour costs

D   administrative overheads

Question 3

The following graph shows the wages earned by an employee during a single day.

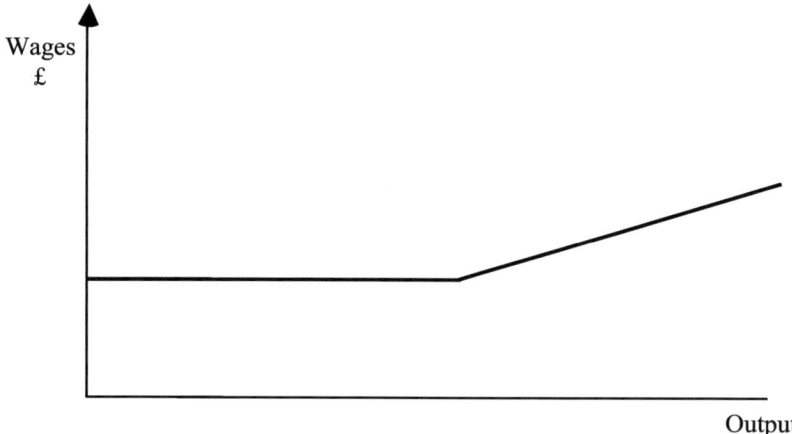

Which one of the following remuneration systems does the graph represent?

A   Differential piecework

B   A flat rate per hour with a premium for overtime working

C   Straight piecework

D   Piecework with a guaranteed minimum daily wage.

For the answers to these questions, see the 'Answers' section at the end of the book.

Practice question

Components A, B and C

A factory manufactures three components A, B and C.

During week 26, the following was recorded:

Labour grade	Number of employees	Rate per hour £	Individual hours worked
I	6	6.00	40
II	18	5.00	42
III	4	4.80	40
IV	1	4.80	44

Output and standard times during the same week were:

Component	Output	Standard minutes(each)
A	444	30
B	900	54
C	480	66

The normal working week is 38 hours, and overtime is paid at a premium of 50% of the normal hourly rate.

A group incentive scheme is in operation. The time saved is expressed as a percentage of hours worked and is shared between the members of the group as a proportion of the hours worked by each grade.

The rate paid is 75% of the normal hourly rate.

You are required:

(a) to calculate the total payroll showing the basic pay, overtime premium and bonus pay as a separate total for each grade of labour.

(b) to journalise the payroll assuming:

- income tax deducted is £884.00

- national insurance payable by employee is 6% of gross pay

- national insurance payable by employer is 5% of gross pay

- 12 employees are members of the Social Club whose weekly subscription is 25 pence.

(c) to summarise two advantages and two disadvantages of group incentive schemes.

For the answer to this question, see the 'Answers' section at the end of the book.

Feedback to activity

Activity 1

Halsey

$$\text{Bonus} = \frac{60-18}{2} \times \frac{£4.80}{60} = £1.68$$

Rowan

$$\text{Bonus} = \frac{18}{60} \times 42 \times \frac{£4.80}{60} = £1.00$$

Chapter 8

RELEVANT COST CONCEPTS

Syllabus content

- Relevant cost concepts, including sunk costs, committed costs and opportunity costs.

This is the first main chapter of the 'marginal costing and decision-making' part of your syllabus. The marginal costing concepts studied earlier are here applied in the context of decision-making rather than stock valuation, with the contribution concept being central to the next three chapters. In this chapter we look at the different way costs are viewed and used in a short-term decision-making situation in contrast to an historic financial account reporting approach.

Contents

1 The decision making process

1.1 Structure of a decision

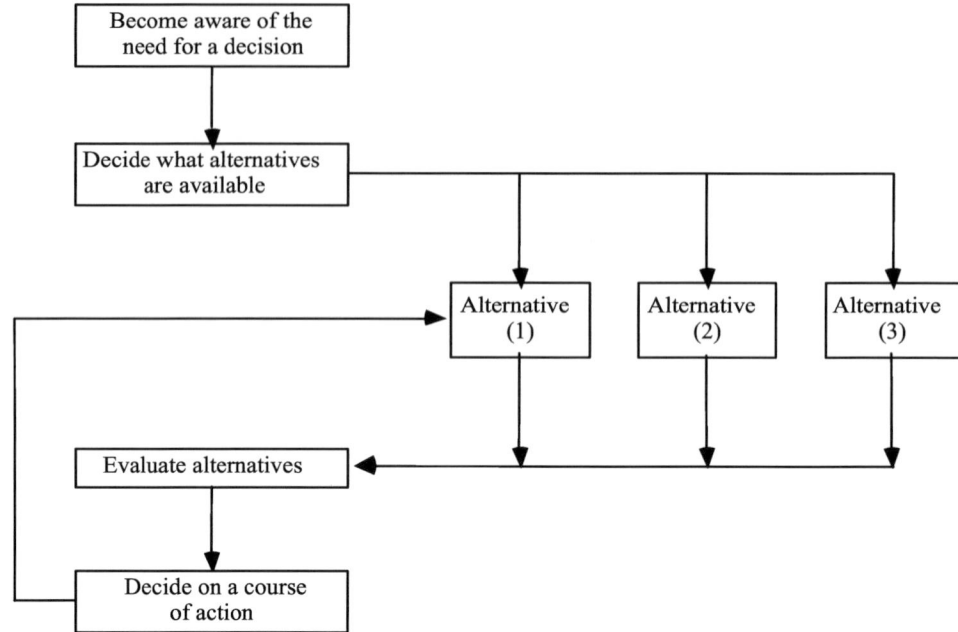

Although the cost accountant may be involved in all four stages, the main concern is with the evaluation process.

1.2 Quantitative and qualitative factors

In an evaluation of the alternatives the manager will take account of factors of two types:

- those which may be quantified in monetary terms

- those that may not as easily be quantified, e.g. effect on customer relations.

1.3 Quantitative information

Although often measured in financial terms using costs and revenues measured in monetary units, other forms of quantitative information may be used in a decision-making situation. For example the quantity of resources required (materials, labour, machines), or the effects of the decision on percentage market shares could be useful quantitative information.

1.4 Qualitative information

Qualitative information is often in the form of opinions that show the effects of decisions on people and the community within which the entity operates. Interested groups include the following.

- **Employees** will be affected by certain decisions that may threaten their continued employment, or cause them to need re-training.

- **Customers** will be interested to know about new products, but will want to be assured that service arrangements, etc. will continue for existing products.

- **Suppliers** will want to be aware of the entity's plans, especially if smart orders are used within a Just In Time (JIT) environment.

- **Competitors** will want to assess their market position following the entity's decision. They may have to make their own decisions as a consequence.

In addition the following other qualitative factors need to be considered when making a decision including:

- **The effects on the environment** – certain decisions may affect emissions and pollution of the environment. The green issue and the entity's responsibility towards the environment may seriously affect its public image.

- **Legal effects** – there may be legal implications of a course of action, or a change in law may have been the cause of the decision requirement.

- **Timing of decision** – the timing of a new product launch may be crucial to its success.

Each of these factors must be considered before making a final decision. Each of these factors is likely to be measured by opinion. Such opinions must be collected and co-ordinated into meaningful information.

1.5 Short and long term decisions

The decisions faced by management may affect the future of the business in the long term, the short term or both.

Factors that are relevant in the short term may be irrelevant in the long term or vice versa but in evaluating the factors, only the revenues and costs that are affected by the decision are relevant.

2 Relevant costs

Example

Suppose you had a car that you bought two years ago for £5,000. A friend has just offered you £2,000 for it. Would you accept? Considerations would include:

- **Historical cost** – will you automatically turn the offer down because it is less than the original cost? These are not comparable – one was spent some time ago and you cannot change that. It is a sunk cost. The decision you should be making is 'Would I rather have £2,000 or keep the car?' To answer that you need to look at alternative uses for the car, that you would give up if you sold to your friend.

- **Dealer buy price** – If you don't need the car, you need to consider the best price you could get elsewhere.

- **Benefits from retaining and using** – If you keep the car what cash benefits will this bring? Savings in bus/train fares? The possibility of earning a living as a taxi driver?

These initial thoughts ignore qualitative aspects such as being willing to give your friend a 'good deal' or the non-quantified benefit of the convenience of owning a car. Based purely on quantitative aspects alone, the decision should be based on comparing:

- **relevant revenues** – the inflow of £2,000 from your friend with

- **relevant costs** – extra costs incurred, e.g. valeting cost before sale, benefits forgone, e.g. lost revenue from dealer or lost benefits from retaining and using.

2.1 Some more formal definitions

Relevant costs and revenues are those that change as a result of a decision. Since it is not possible to change what happened in the past, then relevant costs and revenues must be future costs and revenues.

An opportunity cost may be described as the cost of a particular course of action compared to the next best alternative course of action. For example losing revenue that could be obtained from an alternative course of action (e.g. dealer buy price).

DEFINITION

Relevant costs and revenues are cash flows that are different as a consequence of the decision made or its recommended course of action being taken.

2.2 Which costs are not relevant in decision making?

Factors that are not relevant to decision making include:

DEFINITION

Opportunity cost is the value of the benefit sacrificed when one course of action is chosen, in preference to an alternative.

- **Sunk costs**. Costs that have already been incurred, e.g. costs already incurred in market research. The information gained from the research will be useful in making the decision, but the costs are irrelevant as the decision will not change them. This includes the original cost of your car (£5,000).

- **Book values and accounting depreciation**. Both of these figures are determined by accounting conventions. For decision making purposes it is the cash flow considerations that are important.

    Illustration

    A machine which cost £10,000 four years ago has a written down value of £6,000 and the depreciation to be charged this year is £1,000. It has no alternative use, but it could be sold now for £3,000. In one year's time it will be unsaleable.

    The cost of keeping it and using it for a further year will be the amount you missed out on if you don't sell it now, i.e. £3,000. All the other figures are irrelevant.

    - **Common costs.** Future costs that are common to all alternative courses of action are irrelevant when deciding which alternative to choose.

    - **Committed costs**. Future costs that cannot be avoided, whatever decision you make, are irrelevant. If, for example, you would have to tax your car before sale to either your friend, or to the dealer, or even if you kept it yourself, this cost should be ignored in the decision.

2.3 Cost behaviour and decision making

You should recall from your earlier studies that many different classifications of cost might be used depending upon the purpose of the information. For decision making purposes one of the most useful forms of classification is by behaviour, i.e. how costs change as the activity level changes. Look back at chapter 2 to revise fixed costs, variable costs, step costs and semi-variable costs.

Relevant costs have been described as those that change as a consequence of the decision. Variable costs are those costs that change in proportion to changes in the level of activity. Thus whenever the decision involves increases or decreases in activity it is almost certain that variable costs will be affected and therefore will be relevant to the decision.

Fixed costs are generally regarded as those costs that are not affected by changes in the level of activity and therefore are irrelevant to decisions. However, a stepped fixed cost may be relevant.

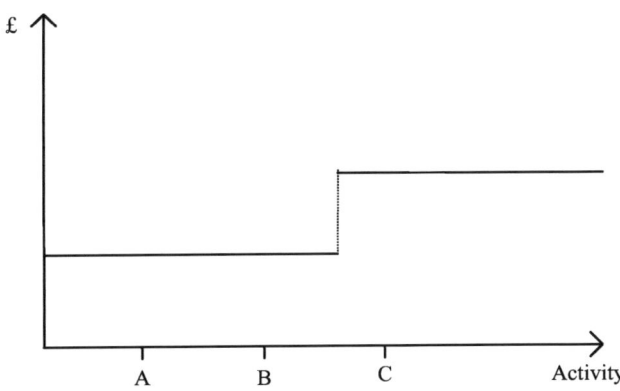

A change in activity from point A to point B does not affect the level of total fixed costs because both activity levels lie on the same fixed cost step. For such a decision the fixed cost is irrelevant because it is not changing. However a change in activity from point B to point C does affect the level of total fixed costs. Thus such a decision causes the total fixed costs to change and in such circumstances they are relevant. When fixed costs become relevant to a decision by changing in this way, the extra fixed cost is usually referred to as the incremental fixed cost or differential cost.

Semi-variable costs comprise both a fixed and variable element. The variable element is relevant to the decision, the fixed element is irrelevant (unless it is a stepped fixed cost). It is therefore necessary to separate the fixed and variable components of semi-variable costs to isolate the relevant and non-relevant parts of the cost.

3   Decision making with relevant costs

3.1   General approach to decision making problems

In the examples that follow, remember the key question:

Do the relevant revenues exceed the relevant costs? If they do, the proposals are to be recommended, at least on financial grounds.

Example

A decision has to be made whether to use production method A or B.

The cost figures are as follows:

	Method A		Method B	
	Costs last year	Expected costs next year	Costs last year	Expected costs next year
	£	£	£	£
Fixed costs	5,000	7,000	5,000	7,000
Variable costs per unit:				
Labour	2	6	4	12
Materials	12	8	15	10

Which costs are relevant to the decision?

- First, reject past costs (though in practice they may be used as a guide to future costs).

- Second, reject expected fixed costs because, although they are not past, they are the same for both alternatives and may therefore be ignored.

- Hence the only relevant costs are:

	Method A £	Method B £
Expected future variable costs per unit:		
Labour	6	12
Materials	8	10
	14	22

It is concluded that, in decision making, the analysis should eliminate all irrelevant figures, i.e. those unaffected by the decision.

This, of course, considerably simplifies the decision, because it eliminates from consideration many irrelevant costs.

Note that, as discussed earlier, fixed costs are not always irrelevant. If they vary between decision alternatives, they are relevant and must be taken into account.

3.2 Determining the relevant costs of materials

In any decision situation the cost of materials relevant to a particular decision is their opportunity cost. This can be represented by a decision tree:

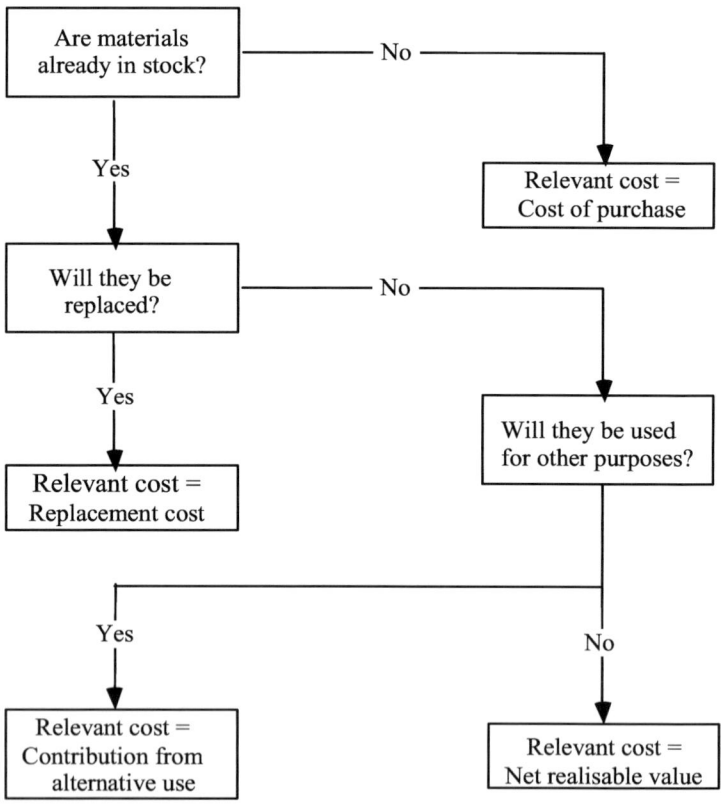

This decision tree can be used to identify the appropriate relevant cost of materials.

Activity 1

Z Ltd has 50kg of material P in stock that was bought five years ago for £70. It is no longer used but could be sold for £3/kg.

Z Ltd is currently pricing a job that could use 40kg of material P. What is the relevant cost of P that should be included in the price?

Feedback to this activity is at the end of the chapter.

3.3 Determining the relevant costs of labour

A similar problem exists in determining the relevant costs of labour. In this case the key question is whether spare capacity exists and on this basis another decision tree can be produced:

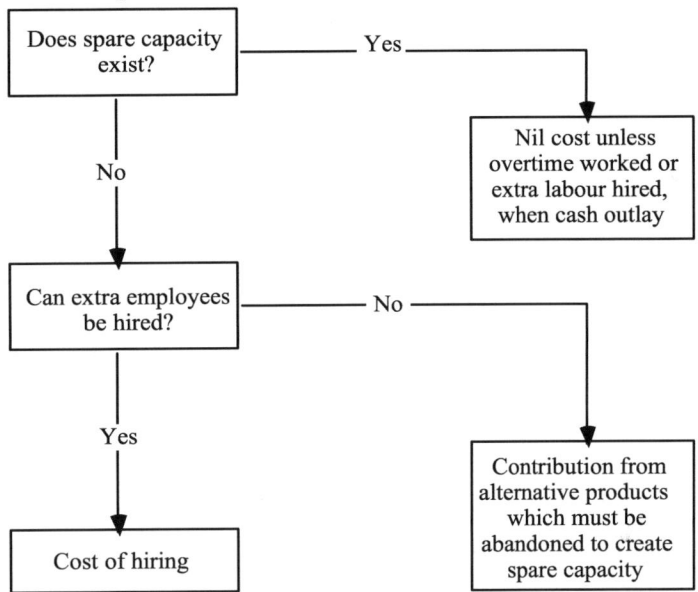

Again this can be used to identify the relevant cost.

Activity 2

The job Z Ltd is pricing involves the use of 20 hours of skilled labour and 50 hours of semi skilled labour.

The four existing skilled workers are paid £15 per hour with a minimum weekly wage of £450. They are currently working 24 hours a week.

The semi-skilled workforce is currently fully utilised. They are paid £10 per hour, with time and a half overtime. Additional workers may be hired for £12 per hour.

What labour costs should be included in the price for Z Ltd's job?

Feedback to this activity is at the end of the chapter.

4   A worked example

4.1   Introduction

The following example illustrates the approach to determining relevant costs for various items commonly included in examination questions. Each section is self-contained so you may work through the information and the solution for each in turn if you wish.

Note the overall approach used at the beginning of the solution to determine the incremental or relevant costs. Although this can be a bit long winded if applied to some of the simpler examples, it is a very useful technique to remember when the information given is not so straightforward.

4.2   The example

Teewhy plc manufactures a wide range of soft toys. The managers of the business are considering whether to add a new type of toy animal, the Bealie, to the product range. A recent market research survey, undertaken at a cost of £2,000, has indicated that demand for the Bealie would last for only one year, during which time 100,000 of these could be sold at £9.50 each.

It is assumed that production and sales of the Bealie would take place evenly throughout the year. Manufacturing cost data is available as below.

Raw materials

Each Bealie would require three types of raw material, A, B and C. Material A is used regularly in the business and stocks are replaced as necessary. Material B is currently being held as surplus stock as a result of over-ordering on an earlier contract. This material is not used regularly by Teewhy plc and would be sold if not required for the manufacture of the Bealie. Material C would have to be bought in especially for the Bealie, since stocks of this item are not normally held.

Current stock levels and costs of each raw material are shown below.

Raw Material	Amount required per Bealie (m)	Current stock level (m)	Original cost (£/m)	Replacement cost (£/m)	Realisable value (£/m)
A	0.8	200,000	1.05	1.25	0.90
B	0.4	30,000	1.65	1.20	0.55
C	0.1	0	–	2.75	2.50

Labour

In producing one Bealie, half an hour of skilled labour and a quarter of an hour of unskilled labour would be required, at wage rates of £8 per hour and £5 per hour respectively. One supervisor would be required full-time at an annual salary of £12,000.

Skilled labour for the production of Bealie would have to be recruited specially, whilst 25,000 surplus unskilled labour hours are expected to be available during the coming year if Bealies are not manufactured. However, company policy dictates that no unskilled worker will be made redundant in the foreseeable future.

The supervisor has agreed to delay immediate retirement for one year, and to waive his annual pension of £7,000 in return for his annual salary during this period.

Machinery

Two machines, X and Y, would be required to manufacture Bealies, details of which are as below.

	X	Y
Written down value	£11,000	£7,000
Estimated remaining useful life	1 year	2 years
Estimated cash resale value – now	£7,000	£4,000
– in one year	£5,000	£3,000
– at end of useful life	£5,000	£1,000
Current replacement cost	£40,000	£30,000

If machine X were not used for the manufacture of Bealies then it would be used to manufacture existing products, the sale of which would result in an estimated £50,000 net receipts.

Machine Y is the only one of its type within the firm and if not used in the manufacture of Bealies would be sold immediately.

Overheads

Variable overhead costs attributable to Bealies are estimated at £1.50 per item produced. Production fixed overheads are allocated by Teewhy plc to products on the basis of labour hours, and the rate for the coming year has been established at £2.50 per labour hour. The manufacture of Bealies will not result in any additional fixed costs being incurred.

4.3 Solution

We can now turn our attention to assessing whether, on the basis of the information given, the manufacture and sale of Bealies represents a profitable opportunity to Teewhy plc. In doing so, the relevant cost of using each resource required to produce Bealies must be identified. For each resource, a comparison is required showing the cash flows associated with manufacture and those associated with non-manufacture. The difference between the two represents the incremental cost of applying each resource to the production of Bealies.

For further explanation of the figures, see the notes following the cash flow table.

Cash flows

	Bealie Manufacture £	*Non-manufacture* £	*Incremental costs* £
Raw materials			
A	(100,000)	0	(100,000)
B	(12,000)	16,500	(28,500)
C	(27,500)	0	(27,500)
			(156,000)
Labour			
Skilled	(400,000)	0	(400,000)
Unskilled	(125,000)	(125,000)	0
Supervisor	(12,000)	(7,000)	(5,000)
			(405,000)
Machinery			
X	(40,000)	0	(40,000)
Y	3,000	4,000	(1,000)
			(41,000)
Overheads			
Variable	(150,000)	0	(150,000)
Fixed	–	–	–
			(150,000)
Total incremental cost			(752,000)
Total sales revenue			950,000
Net cash inflow (contribution)			198,000

Thus, £752,000 is the relevant cost to Teewhy plc for producing 100,000 Bealies during the forthcoming year. Taking the cash generated from sales into consideration a net cash inflow of £198,000 would result from this trading opportunity.

At this stage you are advised to review critically the build-up of incremental cost shown above before reading further, in order to establish whether or not the principle of relevance has been fully understood. The basis for establishing the relevant cost of each resource is examined below.

Raw materials

- **A:** since this material is used regularly within the business and stocks are replaced as used, the 80,000 metres required would be replaced for subsequent use on other jobs at the current replacement cost of £1.25 per metre.

- **B:** if Bealies are manufactured a further 10,000 metres would have to be purchased at £1.20 per metre. The historical cost of the 30,000 metres already in stock is a sunk cost and is therefore not relevant. If Bealies were not manufactured, the existing stock would be sold off at the realisable value of £0.55 per metre.

- **C:** the only cash flow arising here is that relating to the special purchase of 10,000 metres at £2.75 per metre if Bealies are produced.

To summarise, the relevant cost of raw materials is identified as being their current replacement cost, unless the material in question is not to be replaced, in which case the relevant cost becomes the higher of current resale value or the value if applied to another product (economic value).

Labour

- **Skilled:** in manufacturing Bealies additional wage payments of £400,000 would be made, i.e. 50,000 hours @ £8 per hour. These payments relate to specifically recruited labour.

- **Unskilled:** the cost of 25,000 hours of unskilled labour will be incurred by Teewhy plc regardless of whether Bealies are produced. Company policy has effectively turned this unskilled labour wages element into a fixed cost that cannot be adjusted in the short term and is therefore not relevant to the decision at hand.

- **Supervisor:** the relevant cost of the supervisor is the difference between the wages paid if Bealies are produced, and the pension cost that would be avoided in this situation.

In assessing the relevant cost of labour the avoidable costs of production have been identified, i.e. those that will not be incurred unless Bealies are produced. If any element of the labour resource could be used for some other profitable purpose, then the opportunity cost representing the income forgone would have to be included in the analysis.

Machinery

- **X:** As this machine can earn £50,000 net receipts from use elsewhere, it will be worth replacing it at a cost of £40,000 if it is to be diverted to manufacture of Bealies (or indeed, buying a new one for manufacturing Bealies). Either way the cost of obtaining a machine X for the project will be £40,000.

- **Y:** the manufacture of Bealies would delay the sale of machine Y by one year, during which time the resale value of the machine would have been reduced by £1,000 (from £4,000 to £3,000) as shown in the table of machine details.

In determining the relevant costs associated with the use of plant and machinery, similar considerations apply as to those identified in respect of raw materials. If plant and equipment is to be replaced at the end of its useful life, or would be immediately replaced should the business be deprived of the use of an asset, then current replacement cost is the relevant cost. If the asset is not to be replaced, then the relevant cost becomes the higher of resale value or associated net receipts arising from use of the asset (economic value).

Overheads

KEY POINT

For decision purposes, only those costs that will vary as a result of the decision taken are relevant.

Variable costs of £1.50 per Bealie are avoidable, being incurred only if Bealies are produced. In contrast, fixed overhead may be assumed to be fixed regardless of the product being produced and the level of activity over a given range. Since fixed overhead is unaffected by the opportunity being considered, any apportionment of fixed cost is meaningless and would serve only to distort the profitability of the project.

For decision purposes, only those costs that will vary as a result of the decision taken are relevant.

4.4 Further points

From a purely financial viewpoint the production and sale of Bealies appears to be worthwhile. However, as was noted earlier, there may be other factors of interest to the decision-maker. Non-quantifiable qualitative factors such as the effect on longer term marketing strategy, customer reaction, competitor reaction, etc. should be identified and incorporated into the analysis so that a balanced judgement may be made.

In the above analysis the principle of relevance was applied in the evaluation of the financial factors surrounding the manufacture of Bealies. At no time was historical cost suggested as being an appropriate measure of the relevant cost of a resource.

This presents a practical problem since conventional cost accounting records deal with costs already incurred, i.e. historical cost. It may therefore be difficult to extract replacement costs or opportunity costs from the organisation's information system. Moreover, if the relevant cost approach is to be adopted, the accountant is faced with the task of educating managers, if the correct interpretation is to be placed on the figures presented.

However, despite these obstacles to adopting the correct approach to decision making, the alternative route of applying conventional cost accounting principles is likely to lead to sub-optimal decisions.

Summary

This chapter has looked at the concept of relevant costs, which is fundamental to decision-making. You should apply the principles illustrated here whenever possible in answering examination questions unless you are specifically asked to apply historic cost accounting approach.

Two key points to remember:

- Relevant costs/revenues = incremental future cash flows arising as a result of the proposed action being taken.

- These may be identified by comparing:

Future cash flows if action taken, with future cash flows if no action taken.

By the time you have finished this chapter you should be able to:

- identify relevant costs and revenues.

Self-test questions

The decision making process

1   Give three examples of qualitative information that may be taken into account in decision making. (1.4)

Relevant costs

2   What are relevant costs? (2.1)

3   What is an opportunity cost? Give an example. (2.1)

4   Explain sunk costs and why they are not relevant in decision making. (2.2)

5   What is a committed cost? (2.2)

6   What is a differential cost? (2.3)

Exam-type questions

Question 1

The most relevant costs to be used in decision-making are:

A   costs already incurred which are known with certainty

B   current costs

C   estimated future costs

D   notional costs

Question 2

A sunk cost is:

A   a cost committed to be spent in the current period

B   a cost that is irrelevant for decision-making

C   the lower of two step costs

D   a cost unaffected by fluctuations in the level of activity

Question 3

A firm has some material that originally cost £45,000. It has a scrap value of £12,500 but if reworked at a cost of £7,500, it could be sold for £17,500.

What would be the incremental effect of reworking and selling the material?

A   A loss of £27,500.

B   A loss of £2,500.

C   A profit of £5,000.

D   A profit of £10,000.

Question 4

In order to utilise some spare capacity, Z Ltd is preparing a quotation for a special order that requires 1,000 kg of material R.

Z Ltd has 600 kg of material R in stock (original cost £5.00 per kg). Material R is used in the company's main product Q.

The resale value of material R is £4.00 per kg. The present replacement price of material R is £6.00 per kg. Material R is readily available in the market.

The relevant cost of the 1,000 kg of material R to be included in the quotation is

£ _____ .

Question 5

A company is considering accepting a one-year contract that will require four skilled employees. The four skilled employees could be recruited on a one-year contract at a cost of £40,000 per employee. The employees would be supervised by an existing manager who earns £60,000 per annum. It is expected that supervision of the contract would take 10% of the manager's time.

Instead of recruiting new employees, the company could retrain some existing employees who currently earn £30,000 per year. The training would cost £15,000 in total. If these employees were used they would need to be replaced at a total cost of £100,000.

The relevant labour cost of the contract is £ _____ .

For the answers to these questions, see the 'Answers' section at the end of the book.

Practice question

Civil engineering

A company in the civil engineering industry with headquarters located 22 miles from London undertakes contracts anywhere in the United Kingdom.

The company has had its tender for a job in north-east England accepted at £288,000 and work is due to begin in March 20X3. However, the company has also been asked to undertake a contract on the south coast of England. The price offered for this contract is £352,000. Both of the contracts cannot be taken simultaneously because of constraints on staff site management personnel and on plant available. An escape clause enables the company to withdraw from the contract in the northeast, provided notice is given before the end of November and an agreed penalty of £28,000 is paid.

The following estimates have been submitted by the company's quality surveyor:

Cost estimates

	North-east £	South coast £
Materials:		
In stock at original cost, Material X	21,600	
In stock at original cost, Material Y		24,800
Firm orders placed at original cost, Material X	30,400	
Not yet ordered – current cost, Material X	60,000	
Material Z		71,200
Labour – hired locally	86,000	110,000
Site management	34,000	34,000
Staff accommodation and travel site management	6,800	5,600
Plant on site – depreciation	9,600	12,800
Interest on capital, 8%	5,120	6,400
Total local contract costs	253,520	264,800
Headquarters costs allocated at rate of 5% on total contract costs	12,676	13,240
	266,196	278,040
Contract price	288,000	352,000
Estimated profit	21,804	73,960

Notes:

1   X, Y and Z are three building materials. Material X is not in common use and would not realise much money if re-sold; however, it could be used on other contracts but only as a substitute for another material currently quoted at 10% less than the original cost of X. The price of Y, a material in common use, has doubled since it was purchased. Its net realisable value if re-sold would be its new price less 15% to cover disposal costs. Alternatively it could be kept for use on other contracts in the following financial year. Material Z would only be required if the South coast contract is undertaken.

2   With the construction industry not yet recovered from the recent recession, the company is confident that manual labour, both skilled and unskilled, could be hired locally on a sub-contracting basis to meet the needs of each of the contracts.

3   The plant that would be needed for the south coast contract has been owned for some years and £12,800 is the year's depreciation on a straight-line basis. If the northeast contract is undertaken, less plant will be required but the surplus plant will be hired out for the period of the contract at a rental of £6,000.

4   It is the company's policy to charge all contracts with notional interest at 8% on estimated working capital involved in contracts. Progress payments would be receivable from the contractee.

5   Salaries and general costs of operating the small headquarters amount to about £108,000 each year. There are usually ten contracts being supervised at the same time.

6 Each of the two contracts is expected to last from March 20X3 to February 20X4 which, coincidentally, is the company's financial year.

7 Site management is treated as a fixed cost.

You are required, as the management accountant to the company:

(a) to present comparative statements to show the net benefit to the company of undertaking the more advantageous of the two contracts

(b) to explain the reasoning behind the inclusion in (or omission from) your comparative financial statements, of each item given in the cost estimates and the notes relating thereto.

For the answer to this question, see the 'Answers' section at the end of the book.

Feedback to activities

Activity 1

- Materials in stock? – Yes
- Will they be replaced? – No (no longer used)
- Used for other purposes? – No
- Net realisable value – 40kg @ £3/kg = £120

Activity 2

Skilled workers: Minimum weekly wage covers £450/£15 = 30 hours work. Each worker therefore has 6 hours per week spare capacity which is already paid for: $6 \times 4 = 24$ hours which is sufficient for the job.

Relevant cost = £0.

Semi-skilled workers: Overtime cost = $£10 \times 1\frac{1}{2} = £15$ per hour. It is therefore cheaper to hire additional workers.

Relevant cost = 50 hours $\times$ £12 = £600.

Chapter 9

CVP ANALYSIS

Syllabus content

- Contribution concept.

- Break-even charts, profit volume graphs, break-even point, profit target, margin of safety, contribution/sales ratio.

We continue our studies of decision-making by looking at 'cost-volume-profit analysis (CVP)'. This uses the marginal costing/contribution based approach in assessing the volume of activity required to reach a target profit (commonly zero, i.e. a break-even point).

In contrast to the previous chapter, it is a technique most often applied to the longer- term decisions relating to a business's main product(s), which are generally assumed to have constant unit selling price, and variable cost.

We shall start with the crucial concept of contribution: Contribution is the sales value less variable cost of sales.

Contents

1   The contribution concept

2   Cost-volume-profit (CVP) analysis

3   Break even charts

4   Assumptions and limitations of CVP analysis

1 The contribution concept

1.1 Introduction

DEFINITION

Contribution is the sales value less variable cost of sales.

In earlier chapters we have considered two approaches to product costing:

- absorption costing – where all production overheads, fixed and variable, are attributed to cost units

- marginal costing – where only variable costs are attributed to cost units, with fixed costs being treated as a total period cost.

Whilst absorption costing is required for financial reporting purposes, we have stated that marginal costing is essential for decision making. We shall now look at this in greater detail.

Example

You are given the following information about MC Ltd's main product:

	£/unit	£/unit
Selling price		100
Production costs:		
Labour	20	
Material	15	
Variable overheads	5	
Fixed overheads	20 *	
		(60)
Gross profit		40

* This represents budgeted costs of £200,000 spread over budgeted production (= sales) of 10,000 units.

Suppose you wish to answer the following questions.

(a) What is budgeted gross profit?

(b) What would be the effect on gross profit of a 20% fall in sales volume?

(c) How many units need to be sold to make a gross profit of £500,000?

Have a go yourself at these questions before reading on.

Solution

(a) Budgeted gross profit = 10,000 × £40 = £400,000.

(b) The following approach is incorrect:

20% fall in sales volume ⇒ 20% fall in gross profit = 20% of £400,000 = £80,000 decrease in gross profits.

Why?

Because within the £400,000 there are some elements that vary proportionately with volume (sales revenue, variable costs and therefore contribution) and some that stay constant (fixed overheads):

	£/unit	£000	£000
Sales revenue	100		1,000
Variable production costs:			
Labour	20	200	
Materials	15	150	
Variable overheads	5	50	
	40		400
Contribution	60		600
Fixed overheads			(200)
Gross profit			400

If the activity level decreases by 20% the contribution will decrease by 20% but the fixed overheads will stay the same:

	£000
New contribution (600 × 80%)	480
Fixed overheads	(200)
New gross profit	280

This represents a fall of £120,000, i.e. 2,000 units at a unit contribution of £60. This is a 30% fall.

Gross profit does not change proportionately with activity level; contribution does.

(c) The following approach is incorrect:

Gross profit per unit = £40

Required profit = £500,000

$$\Rightarrow \text{Required sales volume} = \frac{£500,000}{£40} = 12,500 \text{ units.}$$

Why?

First we can prove it is incorrect by computing the gross profit at 12,500 units.

	£/unit	£000	£000
Sales revenue	100		1,250
Variable production costs			
Labour	20	250.0	
Materials	15	187.5	
Variable overheads	5	62.5	
	40		(500)
Contribution	60		750
Fixed overheads			(200)
Gross profit			550

The problem is that the gross profit per unit includes a £20 fixed overhead cost per unit that is only correct at the budgeted level of activity.

We can, however, compute the required volume via the contribution that stays constant for all levels of activity, by working backwards from (1) to (2).

	£000
Contribution required (2)	700
Less: Fixed overheads	(200)
Gross profit required (1)	500

Total contribution required = £700,000

Contribution per unit = £60

$$\Rightarrow \text{Required sales volume} = \frac{£700,000}{£60} = 11,667 \text{ units}$$

1.2 And the moral of the story is . . .

Remember that profits are made up of two very differently behaving elements.

	£	
Sales	X	
Less: Variable costs	(X)	
Contribution	X	⇐ varies with activity level
Less: Fixed costs	(X)	⇐ remains constant
Profit	X	

Contribution per unit provides a fixed link between activity level and total contribution (and thus profit); there is no such relationship between a pre-determined gross profit per unit and total profits.

So since most decision making problems involve changes in activity levels – use CONTRIBUTION!

2 Cost-volume-profit (CVP) analysis

2.1 Introduction

Cost-volume-profit (CVP) analysis is a technique that uses cost behaviour theory to identify the activity level at which there is neither a profit nor a loss (the breakeven activity level).

It may also be used to predict profit levels at different volumes of activity based upon the assumptions of cost and revenue linearity.

2.2 Cost and revenue assumptions

CVP analysis assumes that selling prices and variable costs are constant per unit and that fixed costs are constant in total.

2.3 Break even point

Break even is where there is no profit or loss, i.e. total revenue = total costs. Or, to put it another way:

	£
Contribution	X
Less: Fixed costs	(X)
Equals	Nil

Thus, at break even

Total contribution = Total fixed costs

... and since

Total contribution = Unit contribution × volume

... then break even volume must be where

Unit contribution × volume = total fixed costs

...so

$$\text{Break even volume} = \frac{\text{Total fixed costs}}{\text{Unit contribution}}$$

Example

Company	:	Widgets Ltd
Product	:	Widgets
Selling price	:	£3 per unit
Variable costs	:	Raw materials, £1 per unit
Fixed costs	:	Factory rent, £500 pa.

How many widgets must be sold per annum to break even?

$$\text{Break even volume target} = \frac{\text{Fixed costs}}{\text{Selling price - variable costs per unit}}$$

$$= \frac{£500}{£3 - £1} = 250 \text{ widgets.}$$

At sales volume of 250 units per annum, Widgets Ltd will make nil profit or loss:

		£
Sales	250 × £3	750
Variable costs	250 × £1	250
		500
Fixed costs		500
Profit/(loss)		Nil

2.4 Profit targets

Break even analysis is a special case of 'profit target' analysis where the profit target is zero.

We can apply the same principles to determine the required activity level to generate any other profit target (as we did in our earlier example):

	£
Contribution target	X
Less: Fixed overheads	(X)
= Profit target	X

Working back via contribution (the golden rule):

Contribution target = profit target + fixed overheads

[Volume target × unit contribution] = profit target + fixed overheads

So,

$$\text{Volume target} = \frac{\text{Contribution target}}{\text{Unit contribution}} = \frac{\text{Profit target + fixed overheads}}{\text{Unit contribution}}$$

As you can see, if profit target is zero, we revert back to the break even formula.

Example

Using the same data for Widgets Ltd as in the previous example (2.3)

(a) If rent goes up by 10% and Widgets Ltd aims to make £200 pa profit, what annual output is needed?

$$\text{Volume target} = \frac{\text{Contribution target}}{\text{Unit contribution}} = \frac{£500 + £50 + £200}{£3 - £1} = 375 \text{ widgets}$$

(b) Assuming the maximum possible output of Widgets Ltd is 250 widgets pa, what selling price would achieve the required profit target of £200 (assuming the increased rent)?

Contribution target   =   Fixed costs + Profit target

                              =   £550 + £200 = £750

and

Total contribution   =   Volume × (Selling price per unit − Variable costs per unit)

∴   750   =   250 × (SP − 1)

        750   =   250 SP − 250

    1,000   =   250 SP

The required selling price (SP) is therefore, £4 per unit, giving:

		£
Sales	250 widgets × £4 =	1,000
Variable costs	250 × £1	250
Contribution		750
Fixed costs		550
Profit target		200

The simple examples above illustrate that, given the cost/selling price structure, a range of alternative predictions can be easily calculated. Any change in selling price or variable costs will alter unit contribution; changes in fixed costs or profit required will affect the contribution target.

DEFINITION

The difference between budgeted sales volume and break even sales volume is known as the margin of safety.

2.5 Margin of safety

The difference between budgeted sales volume and break even sales volume is known as the margin of safety.

It indicates the vulnerability of a business to a fall in demand. It is usually expressed as a percentage of budgeted sales.

Example

Budgeted sales	:	80,000 units
Selling price	:	£8 per unit
Variable costs	:	£4 per unit
Fixed costs	:	£200,000 pa

$$\text{Break even volume} = \frac{£200,000}{£(8-4)}$$

$$= \quad 50,000 \text{ units}$$

$$\therefore \text{ Margin of safety} = \quad 80,000 - 50,000$$

$$= \quad 30,000 \text{ units or } 37\tfrac{1}{2}\% \text{ of budget.}$$

The margin of safety may also be expressed as a percentage of actual sales or of maximum capacity.

Activity 1

Assuming Widgets Ltd, in the previous example (2.3) has a budgeted sales volume of 320 units (ignore rent increase and capacity constraint). What is its margin of safety?

Feedback to this activity is at the end of the chapter.

2.6 Contribution to sales ratio (C/S ratio)

This is an alternative measure of contribution generation to unit contribution, evaluating it in relation to sales revenue rather than volume.

$$\text{C/S ratio} = \frac{\text{Contribution}}{\text{Sales revenue}}$$

It may be expressed as a ratio or a percentage.

This may be used in CVP analysis where physical unit information is unavailable, or where the answer is required in revenue rather than volume terms.

Example

	£
Sales revenue	200,000
Variable costs	(100,000)
Contribution	100,000
Fixed costs	(20,000)
Profit	80,000

$$\text{C/S ratio} = \frac{100,000}{200,000} = 1:2, \ 0.5 \text{ or } 50\%.$$

This means that for every £1 of sales revenue generated, 50% (50p) is available to contribute to fixed costs and profit (the rest having gone to cover variable costs).

Suppose we wish to know the amount of sales revenue needed to yield a profit of £120,000.

This is a 'profit target' problem, and we will tackle it the same way as before, substituting the C/S ratio for unit contribution:

$$\text{Revenue target} = \frac{\text{Contribution target}}{\text{C/S ratio}}$$

$$= \frac{£120,000 + £20,000}{0.5}$$

$$= £280,000$$

Check this is correct (note variable costs change proportionately with sales).

	£
Sales revenue	280,000
Variable costs	(140,000)
Contribution	140,000
Fixed costs	(20,000)
Profit	120,000

Note: You may come across the C/S ratio described as a 'P/V ratio' (profit volume ratio).

Activity 2

A product has the following budgeted operating statement for the sale of 1,000 units.

	£
Sales	10,000
Variable costs	6,000
Contribution	4,000
Fixed costs	2,500
Profit	1,500

You are required to compute:

(a)   the C/S ratio

(b)   break even sales and units

(c)   margin of safety

(d)   the sales volume required to increase profits to £2,000.

Feedback to this activity is at the end of the chapter.

3   Break even charts

3.1   The conventional break even chart

The conventional break-even chart plots total costs and total revenues at different output levels.

Conventional break even chart

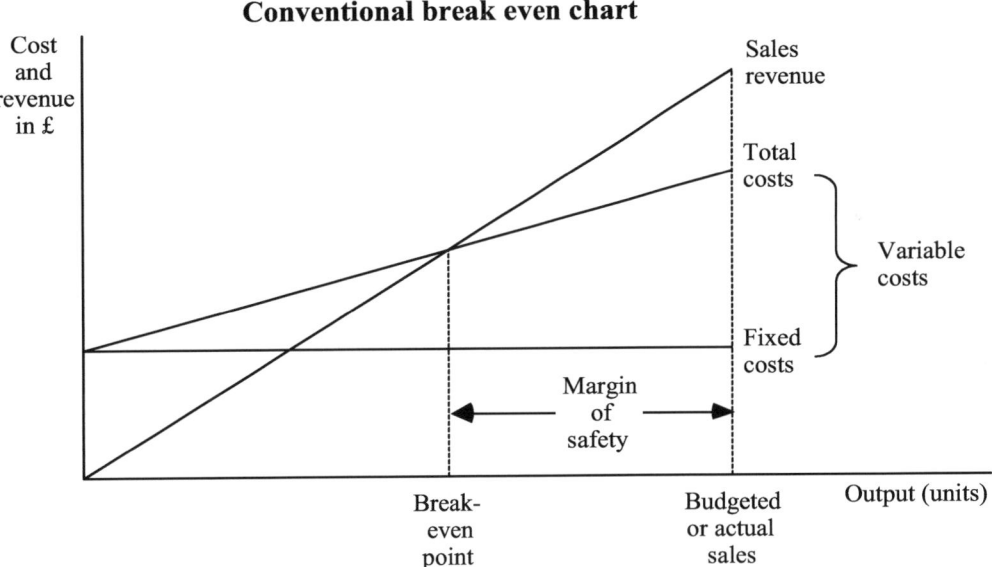

The chart or graph is constructed by:

- plotting fixed costs as a straight line parallel to the horizontal axis

- plotting sales revenue from the origin

- total costs represent fixed plus variable costs.

The point at which the sales revenue and total cost lines intersect indicates the break-even level of output. The amount of profit or loss at any given output can be read off the chart.

The chart is normally drawn up to the budgeted sales volume.

The difference between the budgeted sales volume and break even sales volume may be shown as the margin of safety.

Activity 3

Sketch the break even chart using the data from the example in 2.5.

Feedback to this activity is at the end of the chapter.

3.2 Contribution break even chart

A break even chart variant that you should be aware of is the contribution break even chart.

In the contribution break even chart, the variable cost line is substituted for the fixed cost line. This means that the contribution can be read directly from the chart.

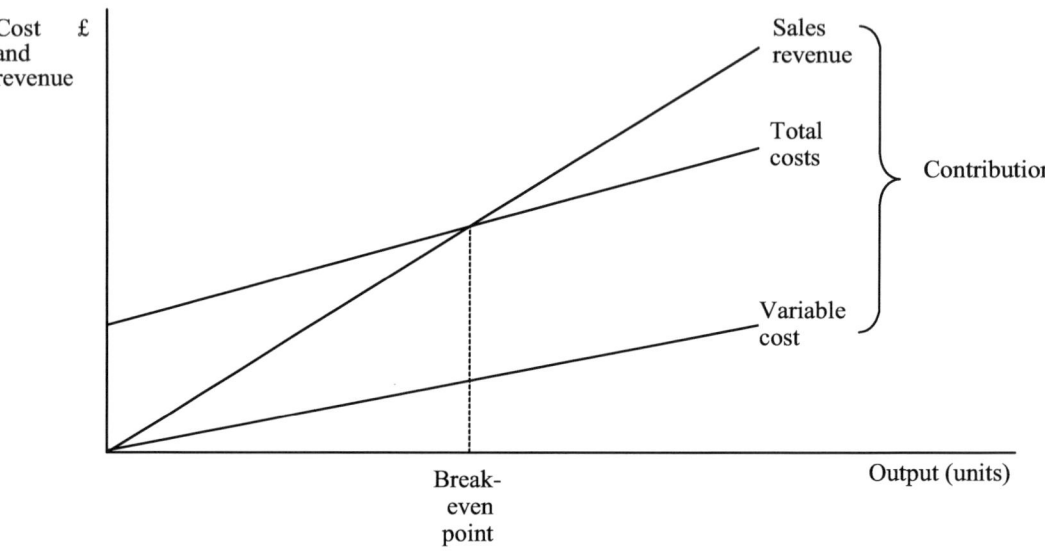

If you look back at the conventional break even chart you will see that it was more difficult to read contribution directly from that chart.

3.3 Profit volume chart

Break even charts usually show both costs and revenues over a given range of activity and they do not highlight directly the amounts of profits or losses at the various levels. A chart that does simply depict the net profit and loss at any given level of activity is called a profit-volume chart (or graph).

Profit-volume chart (1)

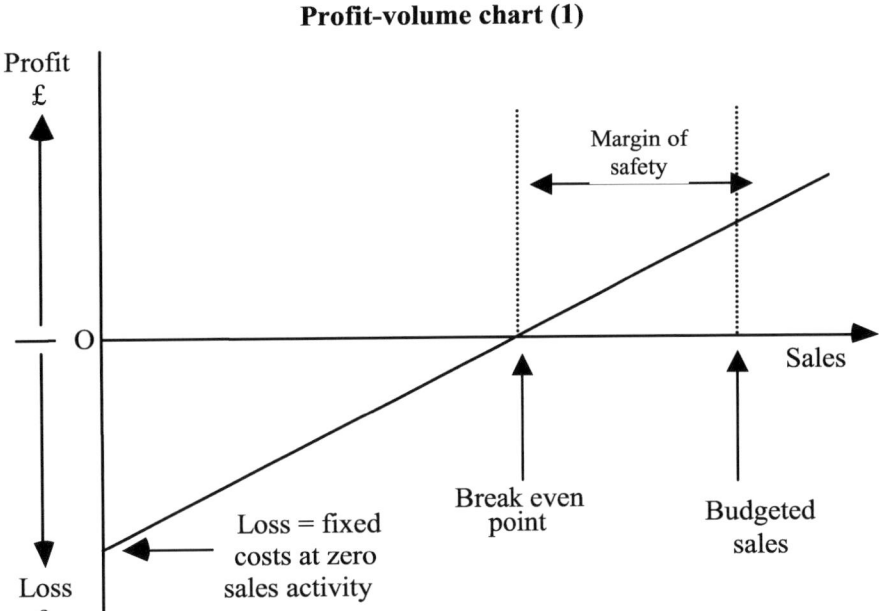

From the above chart the amount of net profit or loss can be read off for any given level of sales activity.

The points to note in the construction of a profit-volume chart are the following.

(a)   The horizontal axis represents sales (in units or sales value, as appropriate). This is the same as for a break even chart.

(b)   The vertical axis shows net profit above the horizontal sales axis and net loss below.

(c)   When sales are zero, the net loss equals the fixed costs and one extreme of the 'profit volume' line is determined – therefore this is one point on the graph or chart.

(d)   If variable cost per unit and fixed costs in total are both constant throughout the relevant range of activity under consideration, the profit-volume chart is depicted by a straight line (as illustrated above). Therefore, to draw that line it is only necessary to know the profit (or loss) at one level of sales. The 'profit-volume' line is then drawn between this point and that determined in (c) and extended as necessary.

(e)   If there are changes in the variable cost per unit or total fixed costs at various activities, it would be necessary to calculate the profit (or loss) at each point where the cost structure changes and to plot these on the chart. The 'profit-volume' line will then be a series of straight lines joining these points together, as simply illustrated as follows:

Profit-volume chart (2)

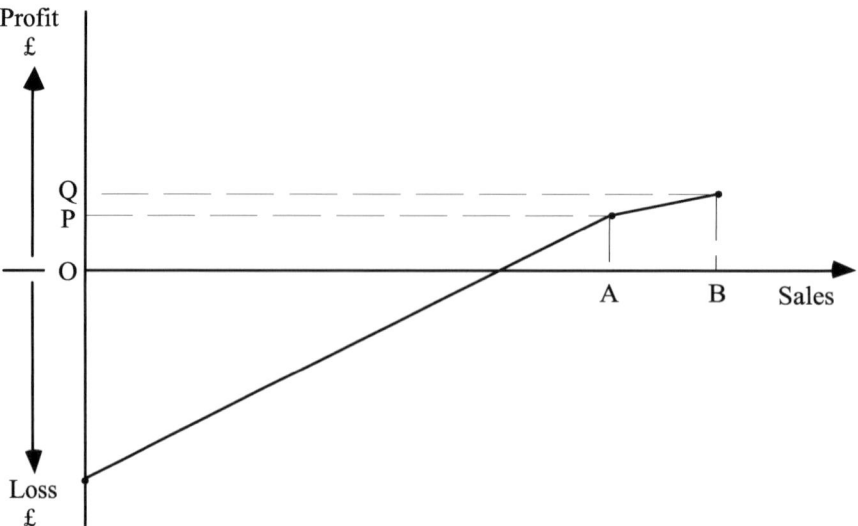

This illustration depicts the situation where the variable cost per unit increases after a certain level of activity (OA), e.g. because of overtime premiums that are incurred when production (and sales) exceed a particular level.

Points to note:

- The profit (OP) at sales level OA would be determined and plotted.

- Similarly the profit (OQ) at sales level of OB would be determined and plotted.

- The loss at zero sales activity (= fixed costs) can be plotted.

- The 'profit-volume' line is then drawn by joining these points, as illustrated.

Activity 4

Sketch the profit volume chart for the same data as in Activity 3 using sales value on the horizontal axis.

Feedback to this activity is at the end of the chapter.

3.4 Changes to variables

Break even charts can also be used to illustrate the effects of changes to variables:

Break even chart showing increasing selling price

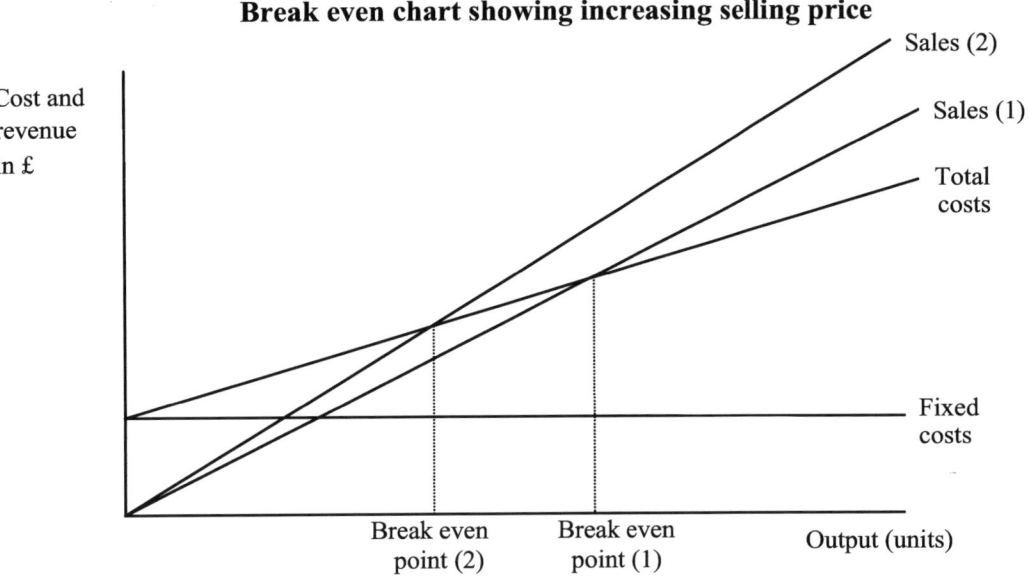

The diagram above shows the effect on the break even point of an increase in the selling price.

Contribution break even chart showing increasing variable costs/unit

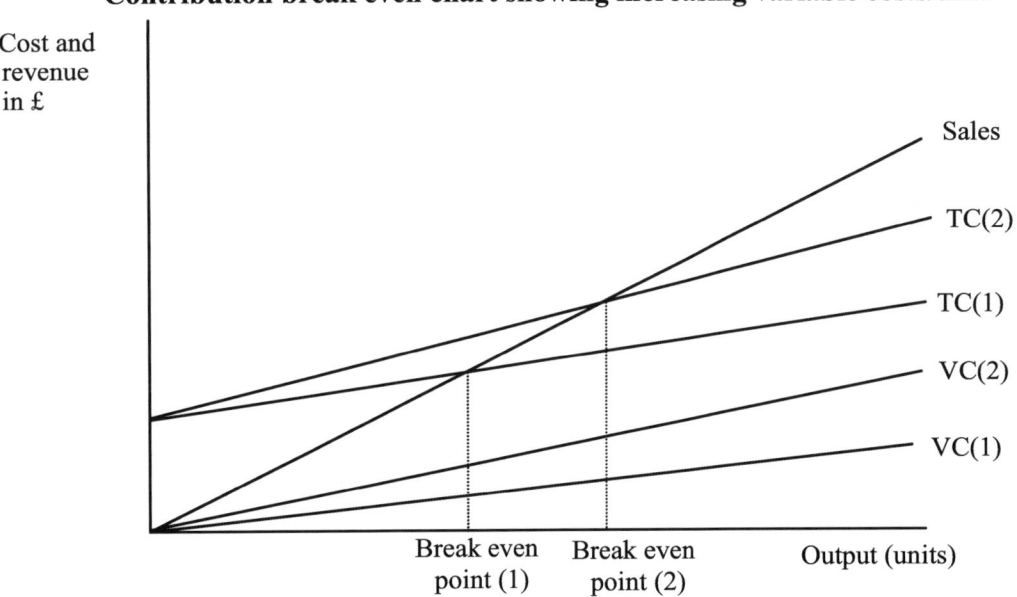

Note how a change in a variable cost automatically changes the total cost.

4   Assumptions and limitations of CVP analysis

4.1   The conventional (accountant's) break even chart

CVP analysis, including the accountant's break even chart that we have studied, makes certain assumptions concerning the linearity of costs and revenues:

- that selling price is constant per unit irrespective of the number of units to be sold

- that fixed costs are constant in total

- that variable costs are constant per unit irrespective of the number of units produced.

There is also an assumption that if there is any difference between sales and production volumes such stocks are valued at their variable cost.

The accountant's break even chart is thus depicted with costs and revenues as straight lines as shown below.

Accountant's break even chart

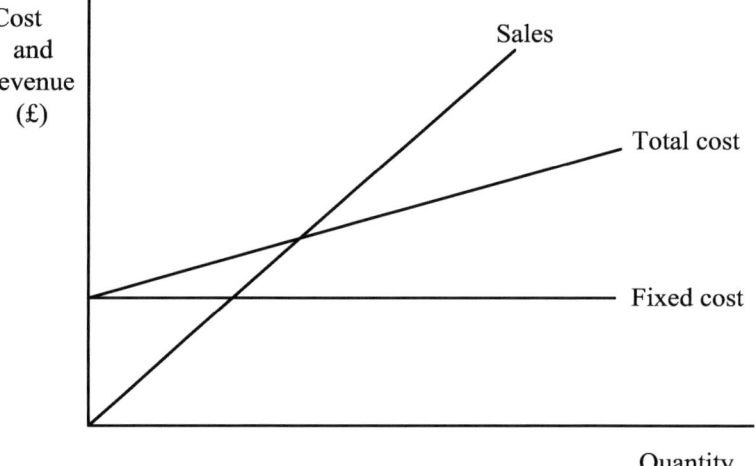

4.2   The economist's break even chart

However, most firms would ultimately encounter the conditions generally postulated by the economist:

- It is unlikely the last unit could be sold for the same price as the first.

- Material costs and labour costs rise as output tends upward. The effect of quantity discounts is offset by less efficient production and overtime rates or less skilled labour force.

The economist's break even chart has two break even points thus:

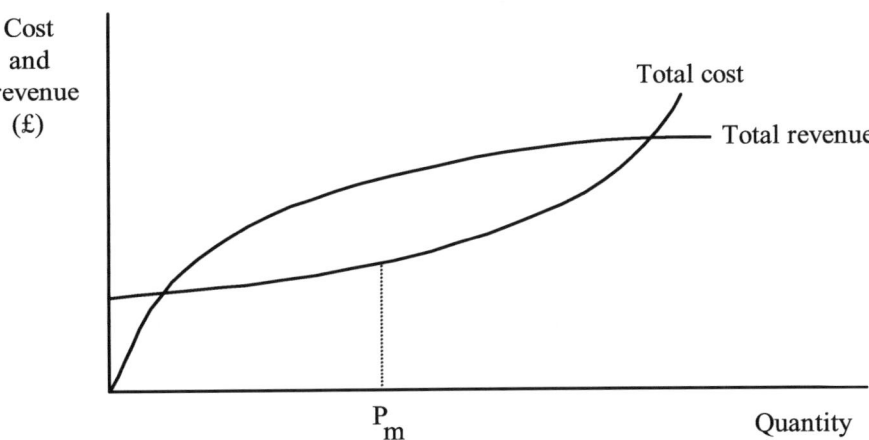

Economist's break even chart

Profit is maximised at the level of output P_m where there is the greatest vertical difference between the total cost and total revenue curves.

However, if we limit the range of activity considered we could show that these two views can be reconciled.

4.3 Revenue curves

To sell more units demand must be increased, and to do this the price must be reduced. Thus sales revenue may be depicted:

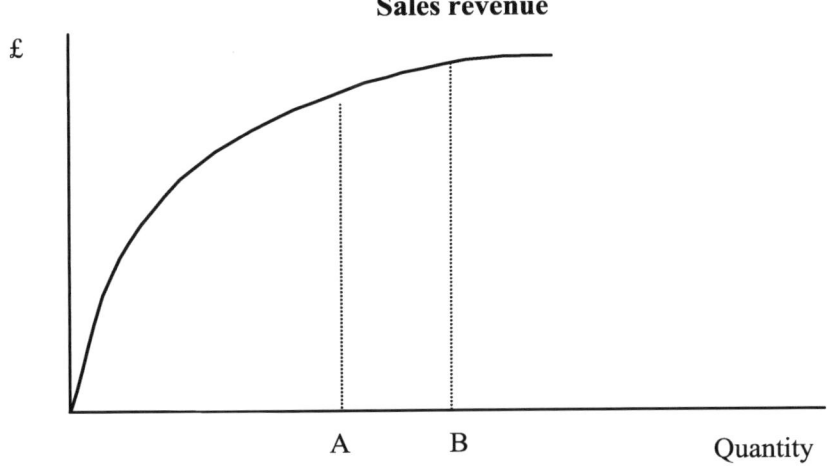

Sales revenue

However, in such a chart the range of activity levels depicted is from zero to maximum and this is unlikely to occur in reality. It is more likely that the range of activity will lie between points A and B. It can be seen that between these points the revenue curve is virtually a straight line.

4.4 Curvi-linear variable costs

A similar principle applies to variable costs where it could be argued that the effects of quantity discounts on materials, and overtime/inefficiencies on labour costs cause these to be depicted as curves:

Materials

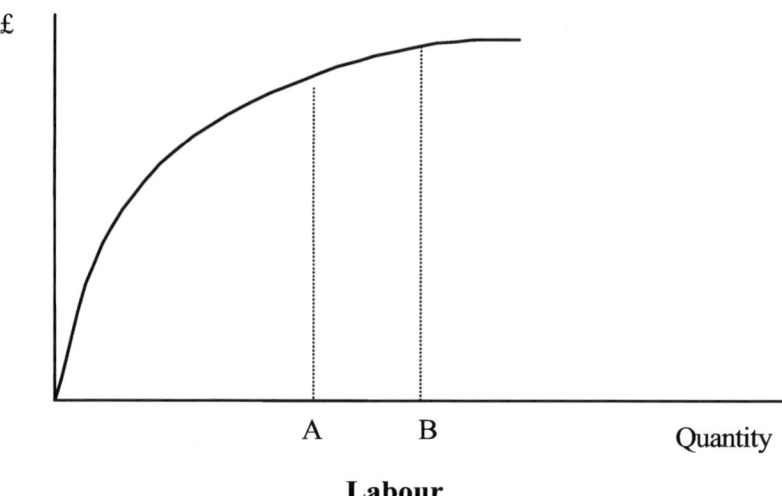

Labour

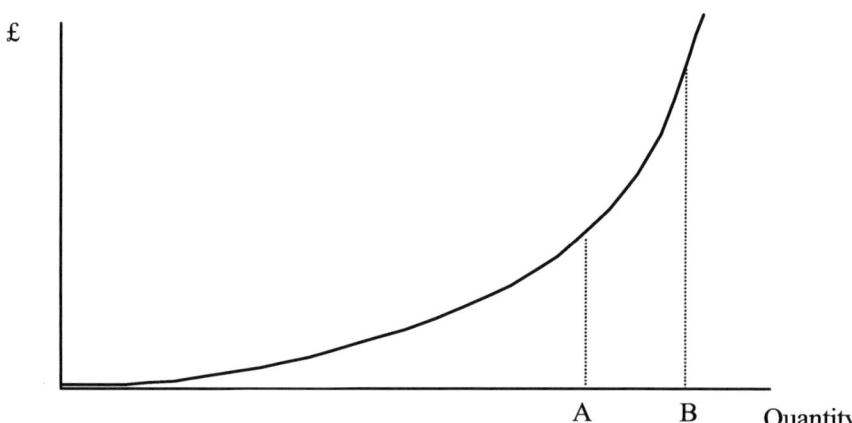

However, the following two arguments exist to support the accountant's linear model in respect of these costs.

- If each of these types of cost is added together, their total will approximate to a straight line.

- Within a likely range of activity the curves themselves are virtually linear.

4.5 Other limitations of CVP analysis

- **Multi-product situations** – When an organisation sells more than one product there is always difficulty in identifying the fixed costs relating to a specific product, and inevitably there will be some fixed costs that are not product specific. Consequently a particular sales mix has to be assumed in order to use the model, and then the break even point can only be quantified in terms of sales values.

- **Uncertainty** – The model is over-simplistic by assuming that variable costs are constant per unit and fixed costs are constant in total. In reality there will be economies and diseconomies of scale that occur, although it is uncertain as to the level of activity which causes them, and the extent to which the costs will be affected. The CVP model cannot be manipulated to deal with these and other forms of uncertainty.

Summary

We started this chapter by explaining the contribution concept, an idea fundamental to decision making.

We then saw how this is applied in CVP analysis which looks at the relationship between activity level and profits, and in particular the level at which profits are zero, i.e. the break even point.

These relationships can be illustrated graphically by the way of break even charts and profit volume graphs.

By the time you have finished this chapter you should be able to:

- explain the contribution concept

- calculate and interpret the break even point, profit target, margin of safety and profit/volume ratio for a single product

- prepare break even charts and profit/volume graphs for a single product

- discuss CVP analysis.

Self-test questions

The contribution concept

1 How are fixed production overheads treated under the marginal costing approach? (1.1)

2 Why doesn't total gross profit vary proportionately with sales volume? (1.1)

Cost-volume-profit (CVP) analysis

3 How is break even volume computed? (2.3)

4 How can you compute the volume required to achieve a given profit target? (2.4)

5 What is the margin of safety? (2.5)

6 What is the C/S ratio? (2.6)

Break even charts

7 What is the difference between a break even chart and a profit-volume chart? (3.1, 3.3)

8 Sketch a contribution break even chart (3.2)

Exam-type questions

Question 1

The standard cost of the only type of quartz watch made in the Wells factory of a jewellery firm based on an expected monthly level of production and sales of 1,000 units is as follows:

	£ per unit
Variable production costs	5.60
Fixed production costs	5.80
Variable selling costs	3.40
Fixed selling costs	4.60
Profit	5.50
Selling price	24.90

The break even point is [   ] units.

Question 2

If both the selling price per unit and variable cost per unit of a company rise by 10%, the break even point will:

A   remain constant

B   increase

C   fall

D   be impossible to determine

Question 3

Tindall Ltd sells a single product for £40 per unit. Fixed costs are £48,000 and variable costs 80% of revenue. If fixed costs increase by £8,000 the break even number of units will increase by: [   ] units.

Question 4

H Ltd manufactures and sells two products – J and K. Annual sales are expected to be in the ratio of J:1 K:3. Total annual sales are planned to be £420,000. Product J has a contribution to sales ratio of 40% whereas that of product K is 50%. Annual fixed costs are estimated to be £120,000.

The budgeted break even sales value (to the nearest £1,000) is £ [   ] .

Question 5

A Ltd makes a single product that it sells for £10 per unit. Fixed costs are £48,000 per month and the product has a contribution to sales ratio of 40%.

In a period when actual sales were £140,000, A Ltd's margin of safety, in units, was: [   ] units.

Question 6

E plc operates a marginal costing system. For the forthcoming year, variable costs are budgeted to be 60% of sales value and fixed costs are budgeted to be 10% of sales value.

If E plc increases its selling prices by 10%, but if fixed costs, variable costs per unit and sales volume remain unchanged, the effect on E plc's contribution would be:

A   a decrease of 2%

B   an increase of 10%

C   an increase of 25%

D   an increase of 66⅔%

For the answers to these questions, see the 'Answers' section at the end of the book.

Practice question

Shoe shop

The following details relate to a shop that currently sells 25,000 pairs of shoes annually:

Selling price per pair of shoes	£40
Purchase cost per pair of shoes	£25

Total annual fixed costs:

	£
Salaries	100,000
Advertising	40,000
Other fixed expenses	100,000

Requirements:

Answer each part independently of data contained in other parts of the requirement.

(a) Calculate the break even point and margin of safety in number of pairs of shoes sold.

(b) Assume that 20,000 pairs of shoes were sold in a year.

Estimate the shop's net income (or loss).

(c) If a selling commission of £2 per pair of shoes sold was to be introduced, how many pairs of shoes would need to be sold in a year in order to earn a net income of £10,000?

(d) Assume that for next year an additional advertising campaign costing £20,000 is proposed, whilst at the same time selling prices are to be increased by 12%.

What would be the break even point in number of pairs of shoes?

For the answer to this question, see the 'Answers' section at the end of the book.

Feedback to activities

Activity 1

$320 - 250 = 70$ units, or $^{70}/_{320} \times 100 = 21.9\%$ of budget.

Activity 2

(a) C/S ratio $= \dfrac{£4,000}{£10,000}$

$= 40\%$

(b) Break even sales $= \dfrac{£2,500}{0.4}$

$= £6,250$

Sales price per unit = £10, thus break even volume = 625 units

(c)   Margin of safety   =   £10,000 - £6,250

$$= £3,750$$

$$\text{Margin of safety} \quad = \quad \frac{£3,750}{£10,000}$$

$$= \quad 37.5\% \text{ of budgeted sales}$$

(or this can be computed in terms of units)

(d) $\text{Volume target} = \dfrac{\text{Profit target + fixed costs}}{\text{Unit contribution}} = \dfrac{£2,000 + £2,500}{£4,000/1,000} = 1,125 \text{ units}$

Activity 3

Fixed costs = £200,000

Sales revenue at budget level = 80,000 × £8 = £640,000

Variable costs at budget level = 80,000 × £4 = £320,000

Total costs at budget level = £320,000 + £200,000 = £520,000

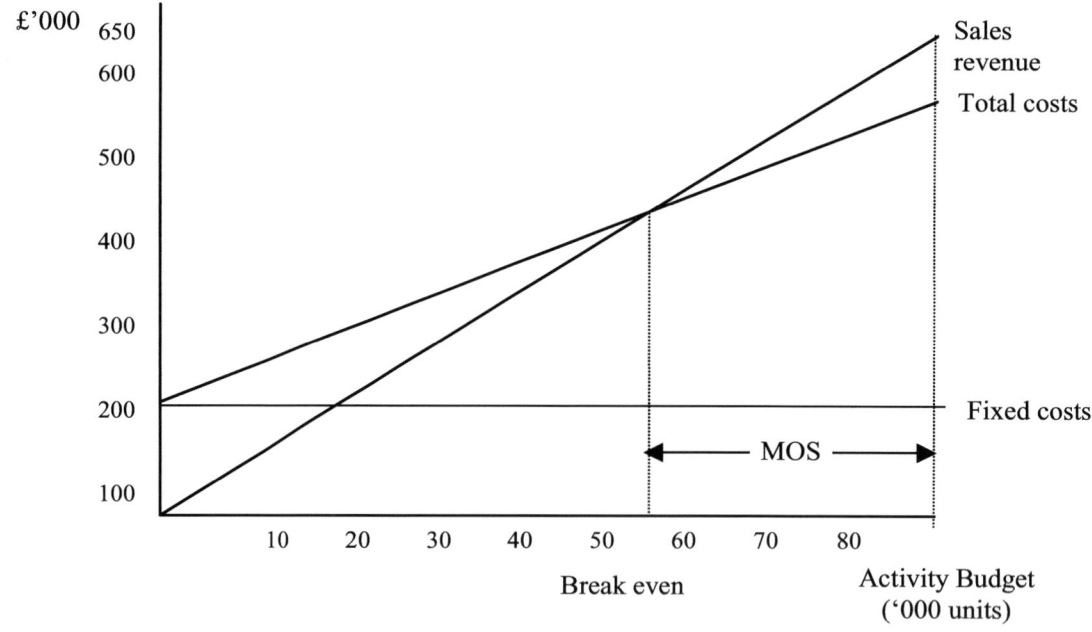

Activity 4

3 points on the line (2 to plot, 1 to check)

At sales = £0   Loss = fixed costs = (£200,000)

At sales = £400,000   Break even ⇒ zero profit/loss

At sales = £640,000   Budget ⇒ profit = 80,000 × £[8 − 4] − £200,000 = £120,000

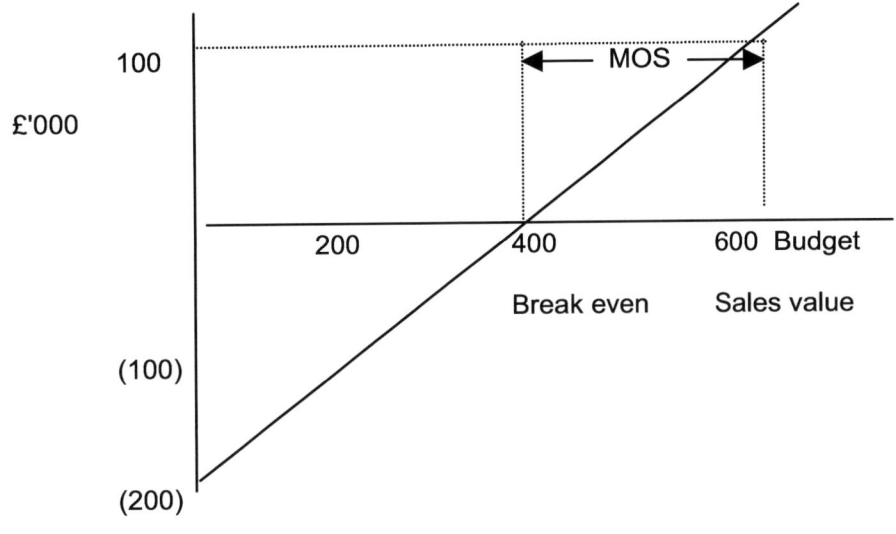

Chapter 10

LIMITING FACTOR ANALYSIS

Syllabus content

- Limiting factor analysis.

This chapter uses the contribution concept to address the problem of scarce resources – where one or more of the manufacturing inputs (materials, labour, production capacity, etc.) is in short supply. The key question is how the available supply may be allocated between products to gain maximum benefit – measured in terms of contribution.

Contents

1   Decision making objectives

2   Single scarce resource problems

3   Demand constraints

4   Applying limiting factor analysis to make or buy decisions

1 Decision making objectives

Organisational objectives are many and varied, but to evaluate a decision mathematically one single objective is assumed, that of profit maximisation – which is achieved by contribution maximisation.

Other factors may then be considered before a final decision is taken, but this is part of the management process after the profit maximising solution has been found.

2 Single scarce resource problems

DEFINITION

Economics defines a scarce resource as a good or service that is in short supply. This definition is modified in the context of decision making to a resource which is in short supply and which, because of this shortage, limits the ability of an organisation to provide greater numbers of products or service facilities.

2.1 Identifying the scarce resource

Economics defines a scarce resource as a good or service that is in short supply. This definition is modified in the context of decision making to a resource which is in short supply and which, because of this shortage, limits the ability of an organisation to provide greater numbers of products or service facilities.

In any situation it can be argued that all of the resources required are scarce. What is important is to identify the **key resource** or resources that limit the ability of the organisation to produce an infinite quantity of goods or services.

Example

X Ltd makes a single product that requires £5 of materials and 2 hours labour. There are only 80 hours labour available each week and the maximum amount of material available each week is £500.

Solution

It can be said that the supply of both labour hours and materials are limited and that therefore they are both scarce resources. However, there is more to this problem than meets the eye. The maximum production within these constraints can be shown to be:

Materials:	£500/£5	=	100 units
Labour hours:	80 hours/2 hours	=	40 units

Thus the shortage of labour hours is the significant factor – the scarcity of the materials does not limit production.

In the context of the decision in this example the materials are not a scarce resource.

2.2 Multiple product situations

When more than one product or service is provided from the same pool of resources, profit is maximised by making the best use of the resources available.

Example

Z Ltd makes two products which both use the same type of materials and grades of labour, but in different quantities as shown by the table below:

	Product A	Product B
Labour hours/unit	3	4
Material/unit	£20	£15

During each week the maximum number of labour hours available is limited to 600; and the value of material available is limited to £6,000.

Each unit of product A made and sold earns Z Ltd £5 contribution and product B earns £6 contribution per unit. The demand for these products is unlimited.

Advise Z Ltd which product they should make.

Solution

Step 1

Determine the scarce resource.

Step 2

Calculate each product's benefit per unit of the scarce resource consumed by its manufacture – in this case measured by $\dfrac{\text{Contribution per unit}}{\text{Resource units per unit}}$

Each resource restricts production as follows:

Labour hours	600/3	=	200 units of A, or
	600/4	=	150 units of B
Materials	£6,000/£20	=	300 units of A, or
	£6,000/£15	=	400 units of B

It can be seen that whichever product is chosen the production is limited by the shortage of labour hours, thus this is the limiting factor or scarce resource.

Contribution per hour

Product A contribution per labour hour

= £5/3 hours = £1.67 per hour

Product B contribution per labour hour

= £6/4 hours = £1.50 per hour

Thus Z Ltd maximises its contribution by making and selling product A.

To choose between products competing for the same scarce resource, rank them according to contribution per unit of scarce resource.

Activity 1

A Ltd makes two products, X and Y. Both products use the same machine and the same raw material that are limited to 200 hours and £500 per week respectively. Individual product details are as follows:

	Product X per unit	Product Y per unit
Machine hours	5.0	2.5
Materials	£10	£5
Contribution	£20	£15

Identify the limiting factor.

Feedback to this activity is at the end of the chapter.

Activity 2

Using the data of the activity above recommend which product A Ltd should make and sell (assuming that demand is unlimited).

Feedback to this activity is at the end of the chapter.

KEY POINT

To choose between products competing for the same scarce resource, rank them according to contribution per unit of scarce resource.

3 Demand constraints

3.1 Maximum demand

In the above examples and activities the demand for the products was unlimited and thus once the contribution per unit of the limiting factor had been determined, the product having the highest contribution was made until the scarce resource was fully utilised.

In some situations there is a maximum level of demand for each product. To solve such problems a ranking approach is used.

Example

R Ltd makes three products that use the same type of materials but in different quantities as shown by the table below:

Product	P	Q	R
Material/unit	3 kg	4 kg	5 kg
Contribution/unit	£10	£12	£20
Maximum demand per month (units)	100	150	300

The available material is limited to 1,680 kg per month.

Advise R Ltd as to the quantities of each product that they should make.

Solution

Step 1

Calculate each product's contribution per unit of the scarce resource consumed by its manufacture.

Step 2

Determine the order of production based on the products' contributions, ranking the highest first.

Step 3

Calculate the quantity of each product to be produced.

Product	P	Q	R
Contribution per kg of material	$\frac{£10}{3kg} = £3.33$	$\frac{£12}{4kg} = £3.00$	$\frac{£20}{5kg} = £4.00$
Rank order	2nd	3rd	1st

The resources are then allocated according to these rankings subject to the maximum demand constant.

Product R has the highest contribution from the use of the materials; its demand is limited to 300 units per month.

300 units of product R require 5 kg of material per unit or 1,500 kg in total (300 × 5 kg). There is no benefit from making more units of product R because they cannot be sold.

Since there is a total of 1,680 kg of material available and only 1,500 kg are used to produce product R there are 180 kg of material still available.

The next best product is product P, which has a maximum demand of 100 units, each of which requires 3 kg of material. The maximum quantity of product P would require 300 kg (100 × 3 kg) but we only have 180 kg available so we can only produce

$$\frac{180\text{kg}}{3\text{kg/unit}} = 60 \text{ units of product P.}$$

All of the available materials have now been allocated. The production plan that maximises profit is:

300 units of R	using	1,500 kgs of material
60 units of P	using	180 kgs of material
		1,680 kgs

There is insufficient material to make product Q.

Activity 3

C Ltd makes three products: A, B and C. All three products use the same type of labour that is limited to 1,500 hours per month. Individual product details are as follows:

Product	A	B	C
Contribution/unit	£25	£40	£35
Labour hours/unit	5	6	8
Maximum demand	100	200	400

Advise C Ltd as to the quantities of each product they should make.

Feedback to this activity is at the end of the chapter.

4 Applying limiting factor analysis to make or buy decisions

4.1 The situation

A manufacturer may need component parts or assemblies for use in its main product. If it has the capacity it will often be cheaper for these to be made in-house, i.e. by the manufacturer, rather than buying them in from an external supplier.

If, however, the business cannot fulfil orders because it has used up all available capacity, it may be forced to purchase the component parts or assemblies from outside in the short term (unless it is cheaper to refuse sales). In the longer term management may look to other alternatives, such as capital expenditure.

It may be, however, that a variety of components is produced in-house from common resources and management would try to arrange manufacture or purchase to use its available capacity most profitably. In such a situation the limiting factor concept makes it easier to formulate the optimum plans; priority for purchase would be indicated by ranking components in relation to the excess purchasing cost per unit of limiting factor. Here then, the benefit is in terms of cost savings rather than contribution.

Example

Fidgets Ltd manufactures three components used in its finished product. The component workshop is currently unable to meet the demand for components and the possibility of sub-contracting part of the requirement is being investigated on the basis of the following data:

	Component A £	Component B £	Component C £
Variable costs of production	3.00	4.00	7.00
Outside purchase price	2.50	6.00	13.00
Excess purchase cost (saving) per unit	(0.50)	2.00	6.00
Machine hours per unit	1	0.5	2
Labour hours per unit	2	2	4

You are required:

(a) to decide which component should be bought out if the company is operating at full capacity

(b) to decide which component should be bought out if production is limited to 4,000 machine hours per week

(c) to decide which component should be bought out if production is limited to 4,000 labour hours per week.

Solution

(a) Component A should always be bought out regardless of any limiting factors, as its variable cost of production is higher than the outside purchase price.

(b) If machine hours are limited to 4,000 hours:

	Component B	Component C
Excess cost	£2	£6
Machine hours per unit	0.5	2.0
Excess cost per machine hour	£4	£3

Component C has the lowest excess cost per limiting factor and should, therefore, be bought out.

Proof:

	Component B	Component C
Units produced in 4,000 hours	8,000	2,000
	£	£
Production costs	32,000	14,000
Purchase costs	48,000	26,000
Excess cost of purchase	16,000	12,000

(c) If labour hours are limited to 4,000 hours:

	Component B	Component C
Excess cost	£2	£6
Labour hours	2	4
Excess cost per labour hour	£1	£1.50

Therefore, component B has the lowest excess cost per limiting factor and should be bought out.

Proof:

	Component B	Component C
Units produced in 4,000 hours	2,000	1,000
	£	£
Production costs	8,000	7,000
Purchase costs	12,000	13,000
Excess cost of purchase	4,000	6,000

Summary

This chapter has looked at the technique of limiting factor analysis (sometimes referred to as key factor analysis) that facilitates the optimum allocation of scarce resources between products to maximise contribution.

Whilst the most common application is in the determination of the profit maximising sales mix, the technique can be applied in other contexts, such as the make or buy decision illustrated at the end of the chapter.

By the time you have finished this chapter you should be able to:

- calculate the profit maximising sales mix for a company with a single resource constraint that has total freedom of action.

Self-test questions

Single scarce resource problems

1   What is a scarce resource? (2.1)

2   What is the key factor or resource? (2.1)

3   How do we choose between products competing for a scarce resource? (2.2)

Applying limiting factor analysis to make or buy

4   How is priority for buying-in of components over making in-house determined? (4.1)

Exam-type questions

Question 1

A company manufactures three products (X, Y, Z) all of which pass through the same finishing process. For the coming month the number of hours available in the finishing process is 6,000.

Data relating to each product are as follows:

Product	X	Y	Z
Selling price per unit (£)	30	36	41
Variable cost per unit (£)	20	27	35
Minutes in the finishing process per unit	45	36	25
Maximum monthly demand (units)	4,500	4,500	4,500

The production plan that will maximise profits for the coming month is:

Product X [   ] units

Product Y [   ] units

Product Z [   ] units

Question 2

BB Ltd makes three components – S, T and W. The following costs have been recorded:

	Component S Unit cost £	Component T Unit cost £	Component W Unit cost £
Variable cost	2.50	8.00	5.00
Fixed cost	2.00	8.30	3.75
Total cost	4.50	16.30	8.75

Another company has offered to supply the components to BB Ltd at the following prices:

	Component S	Component T	Component W
Price each	£4.00	£7.00	£5.50

Which component(s), if any, should BB Ltd consider buying in?

A   Buy in all three components.

B   Do not buy any.

C   Buy in S and W.

D   Buy in T only.

Question 3

A company's existing production plan is as follows:

	A	B
Units	1,000	750
	£	£
Unit selling price	13.00	21.00
Unit variable costs		
Direct material	1.00	1.00
Direct labour at £2 per hour	5.00	12.00
Overhead	0.50	1.20
	6.50	14.20

This represents the maximum demand for each product. The company is limited to 7,000 labour hours availability. A contract to produce 200 units of product C is under review. These are required by a customer who will provide his own materials. Net proceeds from the contract after deducting labour and overhead costs amount to £3,000 and will utilise 1,500 labour hours.

Assuming that the company wishes to maximise profit, the optimum production plan is:

Product A [   ] units

Product B [   ] units

Product C [   ] units

Question 4

A company makes three products as follows:

	Kilts £	*Skirts* £	*Dresses* £
Material @ £5/square metre	5	2.50	10
Labour @ £2/hour	6	2.00	2
Fixed costs absorbed	6	2.00	2
Profit	6	3.50	5
Selling price	23	10.00	19

Maximum demand is 1,000 units of each product, but supplies of material are limited to 4,000 square metres while the labour force will only work 1,000 hours.

To maximise its profits the company should produce:

A   1,000 kilts

B   1,000 skirts

C   1,000 dresses

D   333 kilts

For the answers to these questions, see the 'Answers' section at the end of the book.

Practice question

Barford bakery

The Barford bakery is well known locally for its speciality breads. It bakes three different varieties: the Barford, Wilden and Roxton. The cost structure for a batch of five of each is as follows:

	Barford £	*Wilden* £	*Roxton* £
Labour (at £2.50 per hour)	0.50	1.25	0.625
Flour (at 50p per kg)	0.40	0.75	0.400
Other ingredients	0.10	0.25	0.150
Fixed overheads	0.10	0.25	0.125
	1.10	2.50	1.300
Selling price (each)	0.28	0.61	0.29

Currently, each day the bakery makes and sells the maximum market demand of 400 Barford, 300 Wilden and 600 Roxton loaves. The fixed overhead costs are apportioned to products on the basis of labour hours.

Requirements:

(a)   Produce a statement showing the costs, revenue and contribution of each product in total, and the total profit currently earned each day by the bakery.

(b)   What is the contribution/sales ratio of each product?

(c)   If labour costs increase by 10% and all other variable costs by 5% what percentage increase in selling price is necessary to give the same amount of contribution from each product? (Assume that volumes remain unchanged.)

(d)   What is the optimum daily production plan and the profit that this gives if the labour hours available are limited to 60 per day?

For the answer to this question, see the 'Answers' section at the end of the book.

Feedback to activities

Activity 1

Production is restricted as follows:

Machine hours	200/5	=	40 units of X, or
	200/2.5	=	80 units of Y
Materials	£500/£10	=	50 units of X, or
	£500/£5	=	100 units of Y

Therefore machine hours is the limiting factor since X's and Y's production are most severely limited by machine hours.

Activity 2

Contribution per machine hour:

Product X	£20/5 hours	=	£4/hour
Product Y	£15/2.5 hours	=	£6/hour

Product Y should be made.

Activity 3

Product	A	B	C
Contribution per labour hour	$\frac{£25}{5} = £5.00$	$\frac{£40}{6} = £6.66$	$\frac{£35}{8} = £4.375$
Rank order	2nd	1st	3rd

Firstly make 200 units of product B (maximum demand) and then with the remaining 300 hours make 60 units of product A.

Chapter 11

BUDGET THEORY AND FUNCTIONAL BUDGET PREPARATION

Syllabus content

- Budget theory.
- Budget preparation.

We now move on to a very important tool used by management accountants in the planning and control of a business – the budget. It is essential in communicating the short-term plans developed by management as a means of achieving the long-term objectives of the organisation. Actual results can be compared with the budget and differences investigated. In this chapter we look at the principles behind budgeting and start to look at the mechanics of budgeting itself. The next chapter completes the budget preparation aspects, and in chapter 13 we consider the use of budgets in controlling operations.

Contents

1   Why plan for the future?

2   Why prepare budgets?

3   How are budgets prepared?

4   Budget preparation

5   Preparation of the functional budgets

6   Prepartion of the budgeted profit and loss account

1 Why plan for the future?

1.1 Introduction

Given the increasing complexity of business and the ever-changing environment faced by firms (social, economic, technological and political) it is doubtful whether any firm can survive by simply continuing to do what it has always done in the past. If the firm wishes to earn satisfactory levels of profit in the future, it must plan its course of action.

DEFINITION

Corporate planning is essentially a long run activity that seeks to determine the direction in which the firm should be moving in the future.

1.2 Corporate planning

Corporate planning is essentially a long run activity that seeks to determine the direction in which the firm should be moving in the future.

A frequently asked question in formulating the corporate plan is 'Where do we see ourselves in 10 years time?'. To answer this successfully the firm must consider:

- what it wants to achieve (its objectives)

- how it intends to get there (its strategy)

- what resources will be required (its operating plans)

- how well it is doing in comparison to the plan (control).

These areas are discussed below.

DEFINITION

Objectives are simply statements of what the firm wishes to achieve.

1.3 Objectives

Objectives are simply statements of what the firm wishes to achieve.

Traditionally it was assumed that all firms were only interested in the maximisation of profit (or the wealth of their shareholders). Nowadays it is recognised that for many firms profit is but one of the many objectives pursued. Examples include:

- maximisation of sales (whilst earning a 'reasonable' level of profit)

- growth (in sales, asset value, number of employees, etc.)

- survival

- research and development leadership

- quality of service

- contented workforce

- respect for the environment.

KEY POINT

Some objectives of firms may be difficult to quantify (e.g. contented workforce) but if no attempt is made there will be no yardstick against which to compare actual performance.

A variety of objectives can therefore be suggested for the firm and it is up to the individual company to make its own decisions. For corporate planning purposes it is essential that the objectives chosen are quantified and have a timescale attached to them. A statement such as maximise profits and increase sales would be of little use in corporate planning terms. The following would be far more helpful:

- achieve a growth in profits of 5% per annum over the coming ten year period

- obtain a turnover of £x million within six years

- launch at least two new products per year, etc.

Strategy is the course of
action, including the
specification of resources
required, that the company
will adopt to achieve its
specific objective.

Some objectives of firms may be difficult to quantify (e.g. contented workforce) but if no attempt is made there will be no yardstick against which to compare actual performance.

1.4 Strategy

Strategy is the course of action, including the specification of resources required, that the company will adopt to achieve its specific objective.

Formulation of strategy is largely a creative process, whereby the firm will consider the products it makes and the markets it serves. Policies are usually developed to represent the firm's strategy and cover basic areas such as:

- product development policy (e.g. new products, discontinuation of old products)
- market development (continue in existing markets, develop new ones)
- technology
- growth (i.e. internally generated growth, or growth by acquisition).

These policies are sometimes known as 'missions'.

1.5 Operating plans

DEFINITION

Strategic plans are essentially long term. Operating plans are the short-term tactics of the organisation.

Strategic plans are essentially long term. Operating plans are the short-term tactics of the organisation.

A strategic plan might call for expansion in a particular market; whereas the operating plan will detail how the extra products are to be made and how much is to be spent on advertising. A military analogy is useful here – strategy is how to organise to win the war, operating plans (or tactics) are how to fight individual battles.

It is at this stage that budgets will start to be drawn up. We shall look at the nature and procedures of budgets later in the text. For now we shall concentrate on their role within the overall planning process.

1.6 Control

DEFINITION

Control is the comparison of the actual results with the plans and the stated objectives to assess the firm's performance, and the taking of action to remedy any differences in performance.

It is not enough merely to make plans and implement them.

Control is the comparison of the actual results with the plans and the stated objectives to assess the firm's performance, and the taking of action to remedy any differences in performance.

This is an essential activity as it highlights any weakness in the firm's corporate plan or its execution. Plans must be continually reviewed because as the environment changes so plans and objectives will need revision. Corporate planning is not a once-in-every-10-years activity, but an on-going process that must react quickly to the changing circumstances of the firm.

1.7 Importance of long-range planning for successful budgeting

No doubt some managers would argue that because long-range forecasting can never be completely accurate, it is pointless. However, a system of budgetary control introduced in isolation without any form of corporate or long-range planning is unlikely to yield its full potential benefit, and it is important to understand the reasons for this.

Firstly, a budget is not (or should not be) the same as a forecast. A forecast is a statement of what is expected to happen; a budget is a statement of what it is reasonable to believe can be made to happen. An organisation without a long-range plan probably starts with the sales forecast and perhaps tries to improve the expected results slightly by increasing the advertising budget. This modified sales forecast then becomes the budget on which the other budgets are based. However, this approach has several limitations, some of which are listed below.

- In the absence of specified long-term objectives, there are no criteria against which to evaluate possible courses of action. Managers do not know what they should be trying to achieve.

- Performance evwithaluation can only be on a superficial 'better/worse than last year' basis: no one has assessed the potential of the business.

- Many decisions, e.g. capital expenditure decisions or the decision to introduce a new product, can only be taken on a long-term basis. Long-term forecasts may be inaccurate, but they are better than no forecast at all. A company with no long-range forecasting would be in dire straits when, sooner or later, sales of its existing products decline.

- There is a limit to the influence a company can exert over events in the short term (e.g. by increased advertising). If it wishes to improve its position markedly, it must think long term.

- Eventually some factor other than sales may become the limiting factor, e.g. shortage of materials or labour. If the company has not anticipated the situation, it may simply have to live with the problem. With adequate long-range planning it might be able to avoid or overcome it.

1.8 Overview of the planning process

The overall planning process is described in the following diagram:

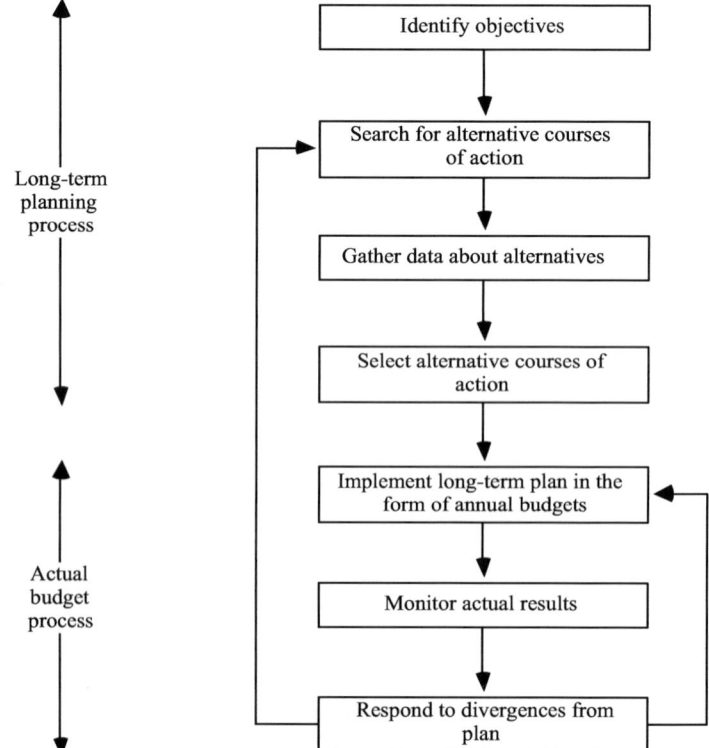

The seven stages are expanded below:

(a) **Identify objectives**

This first stage requires the company to specify objectives towards which it is working. These objectives may be in terms of:

- economic targets
- type of business
- goods/services to be sold
- markets to be served
- market share
- profit objectives
- required growth rates of sales, profits, and assets.

(b) **Search for possible courses of action**

A series of specific strategies should be developed dealing particularly with:

- developing new markets for existing products
- developing new products for existing markets
- developing new products for new markets.

(c) **Gathering data about alternatives and measuring pay-offs**

This is an information-gathering stage.

(d) **Select course of action**

Having made decisions, long-term plans based on those decisions are created.

(e) **Implementation of long-term plans**

This stage signals the move from long-term planning to annual budgeting. The budget provides the link between the strategic plans and their implementation in management decisions. The budget should be seen as an integral part of the long-term planning process.

(f) **Monitor actual outcomes**

This is the particular role of the cost accountant, keeping detailed financial and other records of actual performance compared with budget targets (variance accounting).

(g) **Respond to divergences from plan**

This is the control process in budgeting, responding to divergences from plan either through budget modifications or through identifying new courses of action.

2 Why prepare budgets?

2.1 Aims of budgeting

The principal aims relate to:

- planning and co-ordination
- authorising and delegating
- evaluating performance

- discerning trends

- communicating and motivating

- control.

2.2 Planning and co-ordination

Success in business is closely related to success in planning for the future. In this context the budget serves three functions:

(a)   It provides a formal planning framework that ensures planning does take place.

(b)   It co-ordinates the various separate aspects of the business by providing a master plan (the master budget) for the business as a whole (this is particularly important in a large organisation engaged in making several different products, where otherwise it is too easy for individual managers to concentrate on their own aspects of the business).

(c)   Though not all decisions can be anticipated, the budget provides a framework of reference within which later operating decisions can be taken.

2.3 Authorising and delegating

Adoption of a budget by management explicitly authorises the decisions made within it. This serves the following two functions.

- The need to ask for top management decisions is reduced.

- The responsibility for carrying out the decisions is delegated to individual managers.

2.4 Evaluating performance

One of the functions of accounting information is that it provides a basis for the measurement of managerial performance. By setting targets for each manager to achieve, the budget provides a benchmark, against which the manager's actual performance can be assessed objectively.

Note, however, that before a budget can successfully be used for this purpose, it must be accepted as reasonable by the individual manager whose area of responsibility it covers and whose performance is to be evaluated.

2.5 Discerning trends

It is important that management should be made aware as soon as possible of any new trends, whether in relation to production or marketing. The budget, by providing specific expectations with which actual performance is continuously compared, supplies a mechanism for the early detection of any unexpected trend.

2.6 Communication and motivating

The application of budgeting within an organisation should lead to a good communications structure. Managers involved in the setting of budgets for their own responsibility need to have agreed strategies and policies communicated down to them. A good system of downward communication should itself encourage good upward and sideways communication in the organisation. Budgets that have been agreed by managers should provide some motivation towards their achievement.

KEY POINT

When the goals have been set for the organisation, the management uses the budgetary system to control the running of the business to evaluate the extent to which those goals are achieved. By a continuous comparison of actual performance with planned results, deviations or variances are quickly identified and appropriate action initiated. This is a fundamental aspect of the whole process: if targets were set but little or no attempt were made to measure the extent to which they were achieved, then the advantages of budgeting would be severely curtailed.

2.7 Control

Once the budgets have been set and agreed for the future period under review, the formal control element of budgetary control is ready to start. This control involves the comparison of the plan in the form of the budget with the actual results achieved for the appropriate period. Any significant divergences between the budgeted and the actual results should be reported to the appropriate management so that the necessary action can be taken.

When the goals have been set for the organisation, the management uses the budgetary system to control the running of the business to evaluate the extent to which those goals are achieved. By a continuous comparison of actual performance with planned results, deviations or variances are quickly identified and appropriate action initiated. This is a fundamental aspect of the whole process: if targets were set but little or no attempt were made to measure the extent to which they were achieved, then the advantages of budgeting would be severely curtailed.

There is, however, a danger in adhering to the budget too inflexibly. Circumstances may change, and the budget should change accordingly or the control system should identify separately the variances arising due to the changed conditions. Organisations operate within a dynamic environment, and the control systems need to be appropriately flexible.

3 How are budgets prepared?

3.1 The nature of budgets

A budget is defined as a quantitative statement, for a defined period of time, which may include planned revenues, expenses, assets, liabilities and cash flows. A budget provides a focus for the organisation, aids the co-ordination of activities, and facilitates control. (CIMA, *Official Terminology*).

In general, budgets are set for specific periods of time in the future, for example the budget for next year. Sometimes budgets are constructed for specific projects that are to be undertaken but again these can be analysed into the periods of time that the projects are expected to last. Thus, if a project is planned to last two years, the total budget for it can be split into that relating to the first year and that relating to the second year.

3.2 Budget centres

A budget centre is a clearly defined part of an organisation for the purposes of operating a budgetary control system. Each function within an organisation will be sub-divided into appropriate budget centres. In determining budget centres it is important to be able to define them in terms of management responsibility. The manager responsible for a budget centre (e.g. the machining department within the production function) will be involved in the planning stage of setting the budget for this area of responsibility and the manager will be the recipient of control information in due course.

3.3 Budget period

The budget period is the period for which a budget is prepared and used, which may then be subdivided into control periods.

the length of such a period will depend on:

- **The nature of the business** – in the ship-building or power supply industries budget periods of 10 to 20 years may be appropriate; periods of less than 1 year may be appropriate for firms in the clothing and fashion industries.

- **The part of the business being budgeted** – capital expenditure will usually be budgeted for longer periods ahead than the production output.

- **The basis of control** – many businesses use a twelve-month period as their basic budget period, but at the same time it is very common to find the annual budget broken down into quarterly or monthly sub-units. Such a breakdown is usually for control purposes because actual and budgeted results need to be monitored continuously. It is not practicable to wait until the end of a twelve-month budget period before making control comparisons.

3.4 Budget committee

A typical budget committee comprises the chief executive, the management accountant (acting as budget officer) and functional heads. The functions of the committee are to:

- agree policy with regard to budgets

- co-ordinate the preparation of budgets

- suggest amendments to budgets (e.g. because there is inadequate profit)

- approve budgets after amendment, as necessary

- examine comparisons of budgeted and actual results and recommend corrective action if this has not already been taken.

The budget officer is secretary to the committee and is responsible for seeing that the timetables are adhered to and for providing the necessary specialist assistance to the functional managers in drawing up their budgets and analysing results.

3.5 Budget manual

A budget manual is a document that sets out standing instructions governing the responsibilities of persons, and the procedures, forms and records relating to the preparation and use of budgets. It sets out the procedures to be observed in budgeting, the responsibilities of each person concerned, and the timetable to be observed.

3.6 Introduction of a budgetary control system

Before a budgetary control system can be introduced, it is essential that:

- key executives are committed to the proposed system

- the long-term objectives of the organisation have been defined (as previously discussed)

- there is an adequate foundation of data on which to base forecasts and costs

- an organisation chart should be drawn up, clearly defining areas of authority and responsibility. The organisation can then be logically divided into budget centres, such that each manager has a budget for, and is given control information about, the area that the manager can control. This is the essence of responsibility accounting

- a budget committee should be set up and a budget manual produced

- the limiting factor is identified (see below).

3.7 Stages in the budgetary process

These may be identified as follows:

(a) **Communicating policy guidelines to preparers of budgets** – The long-term plan forms the framework within which the budget is prepared. It is therefore necessary to communicate the implications of that plan to the persons who actually prepare the budget.

(b) **Determining the factor which restricts output** – Generally there will be one factor which restricts performance for a given period. Usually this will be sales, but it could be production capacity, or some special labour skills. This is the principal budget factor.

(c) **Preparation of the sales budget** – On the assumption that sales is the principal budget factor, the next stage is to prepare the sales budget. This budget is very much dependent on forecast sales revenue. Various forecasting techniques may be used in this process, e.g. market research, sales personnel estimates, statistical forecasting, and so on.

(d) **Initial preparation of budgets** – Ideally budgets should be prepared by managers responsible for achieving the targets contained therein – participative budgeting. The role of the finance specialists should be to assist in turning physical budget forecasts into financial budgets. There is also a need to safeguard against budget slack, which is intentional over estimation of budget expenditure in order to provide the budget manager with a buffer against overspending.

(e) **Co-ordination and review of budgets** – At this stage the various budgets are integrated into the complete budget system. Any anomalies between the budgets must be resolved and the complete budget package subject to review. At this stage the budget profit and loss account and cash flow must be prepared to ensure that the package produces an acceptable result.

(f) **Final acceptance of budgets** – All of the budgets are summarised into a master budget, which is presented to top management for final acceptance.

(g) **Budget review** – The budget process involves regular comparison of budget with actual, and identifying causes for variances. This may involve modifying the budget as the period progresses – planning changes.

The mechanics of stages (d) to (g) are explained below and in the two next chapters.

3.8 Continuous v periodic budgeting

The effect of inflation and other environmental changes on budgets can be very serious. In the past rapid changes have led to widespread use of continuous rolling budgets. A budget is prepared for a year ahead (or whatever budget period has been chosen) and at the end of the first control period the budget for the remainder of the year is revised in the light of changes that have occurred to date or expected changes to circumstances in the future, in the light of which a budget is prepared for the first control period of the following year.

This procedure is repeated after each control period, so that a budget for a year ahead is always available and budgets are as up-to-date as possible. This continual revision of budget figures leads to more up-to-date forecasts of future performance.

While continuous budgets have a fixed planning horizon, periodic budgets have planning horizons that shorten as the period progresses. Periodic budgets are established for an accounting period, usually one year but perhaps as short as three months, and while the forecast for that year may change as the period progresses, the original periodic budget remains unchanged.

This means that management will tend only to look to the end of the period for financial planning, while with continuous budgets they must always plan a full twelve months ahead. However, periodic budgets are used extensively in practice, mainly because they are less of an administrative burden. Continuous budgets may seem like a good idea, but periodic budgets are more practical.

3.9 Budget v actual compared

One of the purposes of preparing budgets is to provide feedback to managers concerning operational performance. This is achieved by comparing actual results against the budget as shown in the following example:

	Budget £	Actual £	Difference £
Sales	100,000	104,000	+4,000
Production costs	48,000	51,500	−3,500
Selling costs	13,500	14,000	−500
Administration costs	10,000	9,500	+500
PROFIT	28,500	29,000	+500

Note: the +/− in the difference column indicates the effect of that difference on profit.

The analysis of these differences (variances) will be examined in detail in later chapters.

4 Budget preparation

4.1 How to budget – the seven steps

Preparation of the budget involves seven steps. These are illustrated diagrammatically below:

Seven steps of budgeting

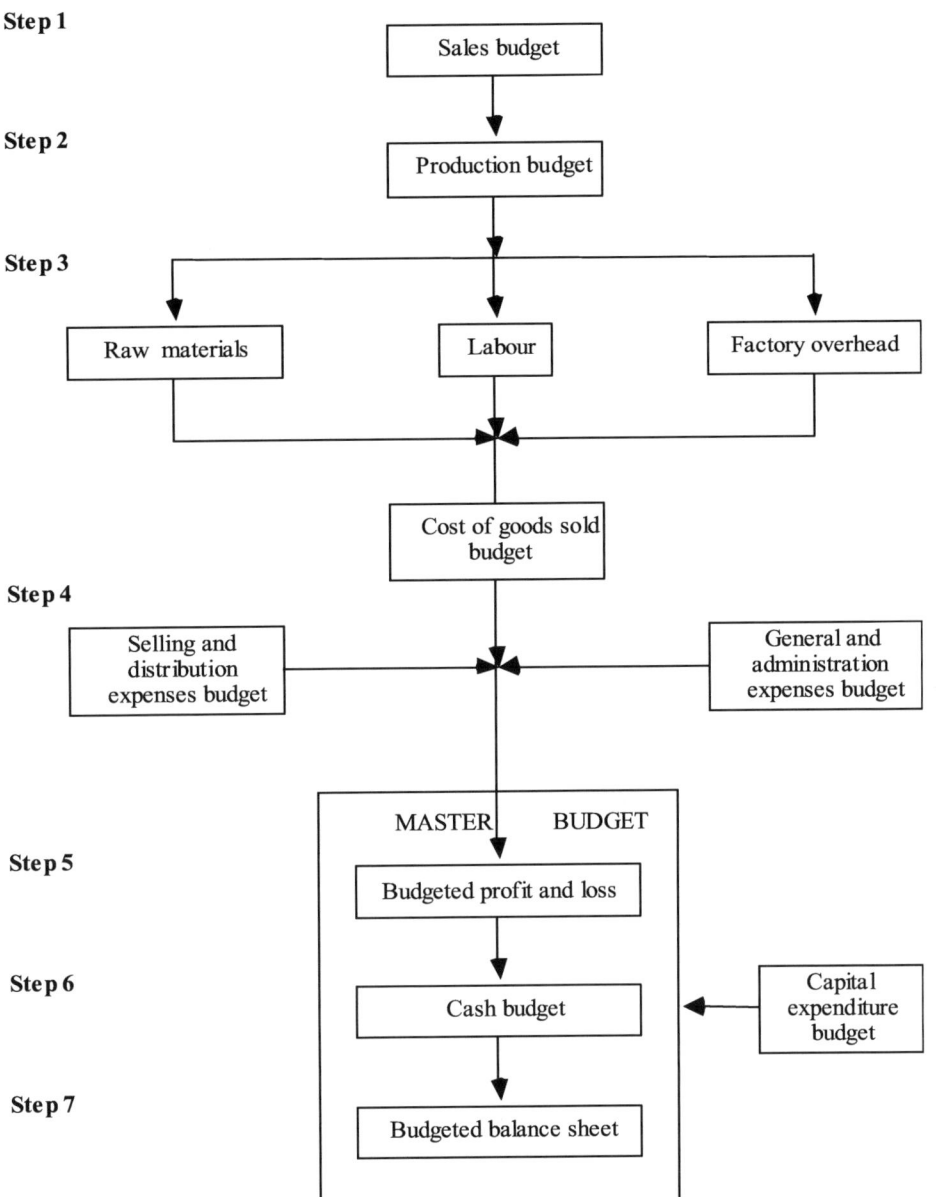

4.2 Principal budget factor

The sales budget is shown in the diagram because this is the pattern in most businesses, where it is the volume of the demand for the product or service that limits the scale of operation. It is possible, however, for there to be some other limiting factor, e.g. labour, material, cash or machinery. The limiting factor must be identified at the first stage of the budgeting process, since it will determine all the other budgets. In this context the limiting factor is referred to as the principal budget factor.

The determination and valuation of the principal budget factor is achieved using forecasting techniques.

The budgeting process is, therefore, more fully described as follows:

(a) Prepare:

- sales forecast

- raw material availability forecast

- cash availability forecast, etc.

(b) Determine the principal budget factor.

(c) Decide whether the limitations can be removed, and at what cost, e.g. by additional advertising expenditure, by intensive recruitment and training, etc. This is a matter for the budget committee.

(d) Draw up budgets on the agreed basis.

5 Preparation of the functional budgets

5.1 Introduction

A functional budget is a budget of income and/or expenditure applicable to a particular function. The main functional budgets you will be expected to prepare are those included in Steps 1 to 3 on the diagram in 4.1.

Illustration

The following data will be used to explain the technique of functional budget preparation

Hash Ltd makes two products – PS and TG. Sales for next year are budgeted at 5,000 units of PS and 1,000 units of TG. Planned selling prices are £95 and £130 per unit respectively.

Hash Ltd has the following opening stock and required closing stock.

	PS units	TG units
Opening stock	100	50
Required closing stock	1,100	50

You are also given the following data about the materials required to produce PS and TG and the whittling and fettling processes involved in production.

Finished products:

	PS per unit	TG per unit
Kg of raw material X	12	12
Kg of raw material Y	6	8
Direct labour hours	8	12
Machine hours – whittling	5	8
Machine hours – fettling	3	4

Direct materials:

	Raw material X kg	Y kg
Desired closing stock	6,000	1,000
Opening stock	5,000	5,000

Standard rates and prices:

Direct labour	£5.20 per hour
Raw material X	£0.72 per kg
Raw material Y	£1.56 per kg

Production overheads:

Variable	£1.54 per machine hour
Fixed	£0.54 per machine hour
	£2.08 per machine hour

5.2 The sales budget

The sales budget would be:

	Total	PS	TG
Sales units	6,000	5,000	1,000
Sales value	£605,000	£475,000	£130,000

In practice a business would market many more than two products. Moreover, the sales budget would probably be supported by subsidiary budgets to show analysis according to:

- responsibility, e.g. Northern area, Western area, etc.

- type of customer, e.g. wholesale, retail, government, etc.

5.3 The production budget

The production budget is usually expressed in quantity and represents the sales budget adjusted for opening/closing finished stocks and work in progress.

Production budget

	PS units	TG units
Sales budget	5,000	1,000
Budgeted stock increase (1,100 − 100)/(50 − 50)	1,000	–
Production in units	6,000	1,000

The production budget needs to be translated into requirements for:

- raw materials
- direct labour
- machine utilisation
- production overheads.

5.4 The raw materials budget

(Remember that Hash Ltd is going to produce 6,000 units of PS and 1,000 units of TG.)

		X kg		Y kg
For production of PS	6,000 × 12 kg	72,000	6,000 × 6 kg	36,000
For production of TG	1,000 × 12 kg	12,000	1,000 × 8 kg	8,000
		84,000		44,000

	X kg		Y kg
Budgeted raw material stock increase/(decrease) (6,000 – 5,000)	1,000	(1,000 – 5,000)	(4,000)
Raw materials purchases required	85,000		40,000
	£		£
Budgeted value:			
X £0.72 per kg × 85,000	61,200		
Y £1.56 per kg × 40,000			62,400

5.5 The direct labour budget

		Hours		£
For PS	6,000 × 8 hrs	48,000		
For TG	1,000 × 12 hrs	12,000		
		60,000	@ £5.20	312,000

5.6 The machine utilisation budget

		whittling hours		fettling hours
For PS	6,000 × 5 hrs	30,000	6,000 × 3 hrs	18,000
For TG	1,000 × 8 hrs	8,000	1,000 × 4 hrs	4,000
		38,000		22,000
Total hours	=			60,000

5.7 Production overheads

		£
Variable costs	60,000 hours × £1.54	92,400
Fixed costs	60,000 hours × £0.54	32,400
		124,800

6 Preparation of the budgeted profit and loss account

6.1 From functional budgets to profit and loss

We now need to bring together the individual functional budgets into a budgeted profit and loss account. To do this we need to:

- compute values for opening and closing stocks

- use these and the functional cost budgets to compute budgeted cost of sales

- compute any other non-production cost budgets

- combine sales, cost of sales, and any other non-production cost budgets into a budgeted profit and loss account.

6.2 Opening and closing stocks

Remember that we are calculating the cost of sales. So far we have calculated the amounts of material, labour and overheads used in production. To arrive at the figures for cost of sales you have to remember that production is used not just for sales but also to increase/decrease stock levels – hence the need to adjust for the opening and closing stock position of both raw material and finished goods.

Closing stock of raw materials

		£
X	6,000 kg × £0.72	4,320
Y	1,000 kg × £1.56	1,560
		5,880

Closing stock of finished goods

Standard cost of finished goods:

		PS £		TG £
Materials:				
X	12 kg × £0.72	8.64	12 kg × £0.72	8.64
Y	6 kg × £1.56	9.36	8 kg × £1.56	12.48
		18.00		21.12
Wages	8 hours × £5.20	41.60	12 hours × £5.20	62.40
Overhead	8 hours × £2.08	16.64	12 hours × £2.08	24.96
		76.24		108.48
Stock in units		1,100		50
Stock value		£83,864		£5,424

Activity 1

Calculate the values of the opening stocks of raw material and finished goods.

Feedback to this activity is at the end of the chapter.

6.3 Budgeted cost of sales

We can now bring all the above elements together.

	£	£
Opening stocks:		
Raw materials (3,600 + 7,800)	11,400	
Finished goods (7,624 + 5,424)	13,048	
		24,448
Raw materials (61,200 + 62,400)		123,600
Direct labour		312,000
Production overhead		124,800
		584,848

Less: Closing stocks:		
Raw materials	5,880	
Finished goods (83,864 + 5,424)	89,288	
		95,168
Cost of sales		489,680

6.4 Marketing and administration budget

Marketing and administration budgets will be a summary of the budget centres within those functions.

For the purposes of this example, the marketing/administration budget is assumed to be £45,000.

6.5 Budgeted profit and loss account

The budgeted profit and loss account is prepared by summarising the operating budgets.

Master budget– profit and loss account

	£	£
Sales		605,000
Cost of sales:		
Opening stocks	24,448	
Raw materials	123,600	
Direct labour	312,000	
Production overhead	124,800	
	584,848	
Closing stocks	95,168	
		489,680
Operating margin		115,320
Marketing/administration		45,000
Operating profit		70,320

Note: the above budgets are presented to highlight planned requirements rather than for costing purposes. Most businesses will obviously be more complex than that illustrated and supporting analyses would be prepared as required, e.g.

- production units by month or weeks
- raw materials by supplier
- direct labour by grade.

Summary

This chapter has considered the need for long-term planning and the conversion of these plans into short-term quantitative statements known as budgets. The procedures necessary for the set up and implementation of a budgetary system have been outlined; and the mechanics of the preparation of functional budgets, leading to a budgeted profit and loss, were studied.

By the time you have finished this chapter you should be able to:

- explain why organisations prepare budgets
- explain how organisations prepare budgets
- prepare functional budgets, profit and loss account

Self-test questions

Why plan for the future?

1   List five organisational objectives. (1.3)

2   What is the difference between a budget and a forecast? (1.7)

3   List the seven stages of the planning process. (1.8)

Why prepare budgets?

4   What are the aims of budgeting? (2.1)

How are budgets prepared?

5   What is a budget? (3.1)

6   What is a budget centre? (3.2)

7   What are the functions of budget committee? (3.4)

Budget preparation

8   Why is it important to identify the principal budget factor? (4.2)

Preparation of the budgeted profit and loss account

9   How do you adjust a production cost budget to a budgeted cost of sales? (6.2, 6.3)

Exam-type questions

Question 1

A contract-cleaning firm estimates that it will take 2,520 actual cleaning hours to clean an office block. Unavoidable interruptions and lost time are estimated to take 10% of the operatives' time. If the wage rate is £4 per hour, the budgeted labour cost

is £ [   ]   .

Question 2

A principal budget factor is:

A   the highest value item of cost.

B   a factor that limits the activities of an undertaking

C   a factor common to all budget centres

D   a factor controllable by the manager of the budget centre

Question 3

When preparing a production budget, the quantity to be produced equals:

A   sales quantity + opening stock + closing stock

B   sales quantity – opening stock + closing stock

C   sales quantity – opening stock – closing stock

D   sales quantity + opening stock – closing stock

Question 4

Budgeted sales for the first four months of the forthcoming year are as follows.

Month 1	6,000 units
Month 2	7,000 units
Month 3	5,500 units
Month 4	6,000 units

40% of each month's sales are to be produced in the month of sale and the balance is to be produced in the previous month.

The production budget for month 1 will be [   ] units.

For the answers to these questions, see the 'Answers' section at the end of the book.

Practice question

S Ltd

S Ltd manufactures three products – A, C and E – in two production departments – F and G – each of which employs two grades of labour. The cost accountant is preparing the annual budgets for Year 2 and he has asked you as his assistant to prepare, using the data given below the production budget in units for Products A, C and E.

			Product	
Data	*Total*	*A*	*C*	*E*
		£'000	£'000	£'000
Finished stocks:				
Budgeted stocks are:				
1 January, year 2		720	540	1,800
31 December, year 2		600	570	1,000
		—	—	—
All stocks are valued at				
expected cost per unit		£24	£15	£20
Expected profit:				
Calculated as percentage of selling price		20%	25%	$16\frac{2}{3}$%
	£'000	£'000	£'000	£'000
Budgeted sales:				
South	6,600	1,200	1,800	3,600

Midlands	5,100	1,500	1,200	2,400
North	6,380	1,500	800	4,080
	18,080	4,200	3,800	10,080
Normal loss in production		10%	20%	5%

For the answer to this question, see the 'Answers' section at the end of the book.

Feedback to activity

Activity 1

Raw material	X:	5,000 kg × £ 0.72	=	£3,600
Raw material	Y:	5,000 kg × £ 1.56	=	£7,800
Finished good	PS:	100 units × £ 76.24	=	£7,624
Finished good	TG:	50 units × £108.48	=	£5,424

Chapter 12

CASH BUDGETS AND IT

Syllabus content

- Budget preparation.

- IT and budgeting.

In this chapter we continue the topic of budget preparation, looking at the cash budget and the overall master budget. We also consider how IT can be of use in budgeting.

Contents

1   Cash budgets

2   The master budget

3   IT and budgeting

1 Cash budgets

DEFINITION

A cash budget is a detailed budget of cash inflows and outflows incorporating both revenue and capital items.

1.1 Objectives

A cash budget is a detailed budget of cash inflows and outflows incorporating both revenue and capital items.

The objectives of a cash budget is to anticipate cash shortages/surpluses and to provide information to assist management in short and medium-term cash planning and longer-term financing for the organisation.

1.2 Method of preparation

Remember that only cash items will appear in a cash budget. Thus, items such as depreciation and bad debts are excluded. The steps to take in preparing a cash budget are:

- forecast sales

- forecast time-lag on converting debtors to cash, and hence forecast cash receipts from credit sales

- determine stock levels, and hence purchase requirements

- forecast time-lag on paying suppliers, and thus cash payments for purchases

- incorporate other cash payments and receipts, including such items as capital expenditure and tax payments

- collate all this cash flow information, so as to determine the net cash flows.

1.3 Layout

A tabular layout should be used, with:

- columns for weeks, months or quarters (as appropriate)

- rows for cash inflows and outflows.

Example

A wholesale company ends its financial year on 30 June. You have been requested, in early July 20X5, to assist in the preparation of a cash forecast. The following information is available regarding the company's operations:

(a) Management believes that the 20X4/20X5 sales level and pattern are a reasonable estimate of 20X5/20X6 sales. Sales in 20X4/20X5 were as follows:

		£
20X4	July	360,000
	August	420,000
	September	600,000
	October	540,000
	November	480,000
	December	400,000

20X5	January	350,000
	February	550,000
	March	500,000
	April	400,000
	May	600,000
	June	800,000
Total		6,000,000

(b) The accounts receivable at 30 June 20X5 total £380,000. Sales collections are generally made as follows:

During month of sale	60%
In first subsequent month	30%
In second subsequent month	9%
Uncollectable	1%

(c) The purchase cost of goods averages 60% of selling price. The cost of the stock on hand at 30 June 20X5 is £810,000. The company wishes to maintain the stock, as of the first of each month, at a level of three months' sales as determined by the sales forecast for the next three months. All purchases are paid for on the tenth of the following month. Accounts payable for purchases at 30 June 20X5 total £370,000.

(d) Payments in respect of fixed and variable expenses are forecast for the first three months of 20X5/20X6 as follows:

	£
July	160,620
August	118,800
September	158,400

(e) It is anticipated that cash dividends of £40,000 will be paid each half year, on the fifteenth day of September and March.

(f) During the year unusual advertising costs will be incurred that will require cash payments of £10,000 in August and £15,000 in September. The advertising costs are in addition to the expenses in item (d) above.

(g) Equipment replacements are made at a rate that requires a cash outlay of £3,000 per month. The equipment has an average estimated life of six years.

(h) A £60,000 payment for corporation tax is to be made on 15 September 20X5.

(i) At 30 June 20X5 the company had a bank loan with an unpaid balance of £280,000. The entire balance is due on 30 September 20X5, together with accumulated interest from 1 July 20X5 at the rate of 12% pa.

(j) The cash balance at 30 June 20X5 is £100,000.

You are required to prepare a cash forecast statement, by months, for the first three months of the 20X5/20X6 financial year. The statement should show the amount of cash on hand (or deficiency of cash) at the end of each month. All computations and supporting schedules should be presented in clear and concise form.

Solution

The solution can be best approached as in the following activities and paragraphs. You will need to tackle Activity 1 before proceeding any further.

Activity 1

Work out the cash received from sales in each month.

Feedback to this activity is at the end of the chapter.

1.4 Payment to trade creditors

			£	£	£
(i)	10 July – Balance b/d				370,000

(ii)	10 August – purchases in July			
	Cost of goods sold (60% of July's sales 360,000)		216,000	
	Less: Opening stock	(810,000)		
	Add: Closing stock			
	60% (420,000 + 600,000 + 540,000)	936,000		
			126,000	
	Purchases			342,000

(iii)	10 September – purchases in August			
	Cost of goods sold (60% × £420,000)		252,000	
	Less: Opening stock	(936,000)		
	Add: Closing stock 60%			
	(600,000 + 540,000 + 480,000)	972,000		
			36,000	
	Purchases			288,000

Note: a quicker way to compute this would have been 60% × 480,000 (November sales) = £288,000. Opening stock covers August – September's sales; August's is sold this month, and stock is 'topped up' with November's sales, at cost.

1.5 Cash budget

	July	August	September
Receipts:			
Receipts from debtors (Activity 1)	510,000	432,000	518,400
	£	£	£
Payments:			
Payments to creditors (1.4)	370,000	342,000	288,000
Expenses (given)	160,620	118,800	158,400
Dividends (given)	–	–	40,000
Advertising (given)	–	10,000	15,000
Capital expenditure (given)	3,000	3,000	3,000
Corporation tax (given)	–	–	60,000
Bank loan (280,000 + $^3/_{12}$ × 12% × 280,000)	–	–	288,400
	533,620	473,800	852,800
Net cash inflow/(outflow)	(23,620)	(41,800)	(334,400)
Balance at beginning of month	100,000	76,380	34,580
Balance/ (deficiency) at month end	76,380	34,580	(299,820)

Activity 2

The budgeted sales for an organisation are as follows:

	Jan £000	Feb £000	March £000	April £000
Sales	600	800	400	500

These are all sales on credit and debtors tend to pay in the following pattern.

	%
In month of sale	10
In month after sale	40
Two months after sale	45

The organisation expects a bad debt rate of 5%

What are the budgeted cash receipts from debtors in April?

Feedback to this activity is at the end of the chapter.

Activity 3

You are given the following budgeted information about an organisation.

	Jan	Feb	March
Opening stock in units	100	150	120
Closing stock in units	150	120	180
Sales in units	400	450	420

The cost of materials is £2 per unit and 40% of purchases are for cash while 60% are on credit and are paid two months after the purchase. There are no budgeted changes in material stocks. What are the payments for purchases in March?

Feedback to this activity is at the end of the chapter.

2 The master budget

2.1 Components of the master budget

If you look back at the 'seven steps of budgeting' diagram in the last chapter, paragraph 4.1, you will see three budgets boxed together at the bottom, headed 'Master budget':

- Budgeted profit and loss.

- Cash budget.

- Budgeted balance sheet.

We have already looked at the preparation of the first two of these in detail.

2.2 The budgeted balance sheet

The total company plan will include a statement to show the financial situation at the end of the budget period. Subsidiary budgets will be prepared to analyse movements in fixed and working capital during the budget period based on the operating budgets and reflecting financial policy formulated by the budget committee.

You are unlikely to be asked to prepare a full balance sheet, but you may be required to calculate specific figures that would appear in a budgeted balance sheet.

Activity 4

Referring back to the cash flow example in 1.3, compute the following balances that would appear in the budgeted balance sheet as at 30 September 20X5:

(a)   Debtors

(b)   Trade creditors

(c)   Closing stock.

Feedback to this activity is at the end of the chapter.

3   IT and budgeting

3.1   The budgeting exercise

The nature of the budgeting exercise, as shown by the example earlier in this chapter, is that many of the resulting final values are dependent on the estimate made of sales units together with a few policy decisions (for example stockholding policies, payment period policies).

It is also true to say that budgets are a planning device designed to assist in the achievement of an organisation's longer-term plans.

These two factors have the following consequences.

*   There are likely to be a number of alterations made to the first draft of the budget to see the effects of such changes.

*   The alteration of one value will cause many other values to alter.

3.2   Spreadsheets and budgeting

It is these factors that have led to the preparation of budgets being computerised using spreadsheet packages. The use of a spreadsheet allows these alterations to be made accurately and very quickly by the use of formulae. This is often referred to as 'What If' analysis.

A simple example of the use of a spreadsheet to prepare a production budget is shown below.

Example

X Ltd has estimated its sales for 20X5 to be 5,000 units, and sales for 20X6 are expected to be 6,000 units.

X Ltd's stockholding policy is to hold 10% of next year's sales in stock at the end of the current year.

The spreadsheet would look something like this in Microsoft Excel.

Spreadsheet   **Underlying formulae**

	A	B	C		A	B	C
1	Sales units	5000	6000	1	Sales units	5000	6000
2	Closing stock	600		2	Closing stock	=C1*0.1	
3	Opening Stock	-500		3	Opening Stock	=-B1*0.1	
4	Production	5100		4	Production	+SUM(B1:B3)	

An alteration to the input sales unit values in row 1 would automatically alter the results of the formulae in the other cells.

This example could be extended to include costs and revenues and to finally produce a master budget that is linked by the use of formulae to the basic data.

3.3 Accounting packages and budgeting

Even entry level accounting packages such as Sage Instant or QuickBooks have facilities for entering budget figures and generating budget v actual reports, although it is likely that the budget figures would be prepared with a spreadsheet first and then entered or imported into the accounting package later.

Larger enterprises would use highly sophisticated Enterprise Resource Planning (ERP) software for budgeting, probably incorporating specialised forecasting software and statistical analysis packages. You will learn more about ERP and so on in your later studies.

Summary

This chapter has looked at the preparation of the remaining two elements of the master budget – the cash budget and the balance sheet. The key to tackling these sorts of questions is well laid out workings. Although you will not earn marks for workings, if they are clear and well laid out they will help you to arrive at the correct answer. You should, for example, be able to use one working to deduce:

- sales – for the budgeted profit and loss
- receipts from debtors – for the cash budget
- debtors – for the balance sheet.

Remember, only cash items appear in the cash budget – thus depreciation is excluded, but capital expenditure is included.

We have also considered the ways in which IT may be used to facilitate the budgeting process.

By the time you have finished this chapter you should be able to:

- prepare functional budgets, a profit and loss account, a balance sheet and a simple cash budget
- explain the use of IT in the budget process.

Self-test questions

Cash budgets

1   What are the objectives of a cash budget? (1.1)

The master budget

2   What are the components of the master budget? (2.1)

IT and budgeting

3   What is 'What if' analysis? (3.2)

4   Why is a spreadsheet particularly useful for budgeting? (3.2)

Exam-type questions

Question 1

Of the four costs shown below, which would NOT be included in the cash budget of an insurance firm?

A   Depreciation of fixed assets

B   Commission paid to agents

C   Office salaries

D   Capital cost of a new computer

Question 2

The following details have been extracted from the debtor collection records of C Ltd:

Invoices paid in the month after sale	60%
Invoices paid in the second month after sale	25%
Invoices paid in the third month after sale	12%
Bad debts	3%

Invoices are issued on the last day of each month.

Customers paying in the month after sale are entitled to deduct a 2% settlement discount.

Credit sales values for June to September 20X5 are budgeted as follows:

June	July	August	September
£35,000	£40,000	£60,000	£45,000

The amount budgeted to be received from credit sales in September 20X5 is:

A   £47,280

B   £47,680

C   £48,850

D   £49,480

Question 3

Which of the following would be included in the cash budget but would not be included in the budgeted profit and loss account (tick all that apply):

Repayment of a bank loan ☐

Proceeds from the sale of a fixed asset ☐

Bad debts write off ☐

For the answers to these questions, see the 'Answers' section at the end of the book.

Practice question

Cash budget

On January 1 the summary balance sheet of CH Ltd was as follows:

	£	£	£
Fixed asset at cost			80,000
Depreciation			(19,200)
			60,800
Current assets:			
Stock		24,200	
Debtors		25,000	
		49,200	
Current liabilities:			
Proposed dividends	1,000		
Overdraft	9,000		
		(10,000)	
Net current assets			39,200
			100,000
Long term liabilities			
Loan 15%			(40,000)
Net assets			60,000
Share capital			40,000
Accumulated profit			20,000
			60,000

The following are expected during the next three months:

	Sales £	Purchases £	Expenses £
January	150,000	100,000	20,000
February	200,000	150,000	25,000
March	300,000	280,000	30,000

All sales are on credit and the collections have the following pattern:

During the month of sale   80% (a 4% discount is given for payment in this period)

In the subsequent month   20%

Payment for purchase is made in the month of purchase in order to take advantage of a 10% prompt settlement discount, calculated on the gross purchase figures shown above. Stock levels are expected to remain constant throughout the period. Depreciation of machinery is calculated at a rate of 12% pa on cost. The appropriate portion of each month January to March is included in the expenses figures above. Expenses are paid for in the month in which they are incurred. The proposed dividend will be paid in January. Loan interest for the three months will be paid in March.

Required:

(a) Prepare a cash budget for each of the three months January to March.

(b) Prepare a forecast profit and loss account for the period.

For the answer to this question, see the 'Answers' section at the end of the book.

Feedback to activities

Activity 1

	Sales £	Cash received July £	August £	September £
May	600,000	54,000 (9%)	–	–
June	800,000	240,000 (30%)	72,000 (9%)	–
July	360,000	216,000 (60%)	108,000 (30%)	32,400 (9%)
August	420,000	–	252,000 (60%)	126,000 (30%)
September	600,000	–	–	360,000 (60%)
		510,000	432,000	518,400

Activity 2

	£000
April sales 10% × 500	50
March sales 40% × 400	160
February sales 45% × 800	360
	570

Activity 3

Purchases in units	Jan	Feb	March
Sales	400	450	420
Less: Opening stock	(100)	(150)	(120)
Add: Closing stock	150	120	180
Production in units	450	420	480
	£	£	£
Purchases of materials	900	840	960

Payment in March

	£
March purchases (960 × 40%)	384
January purchases (900 × 60%)	540
	924

Activity 4

(a) **Debtors**

Looking back at the working in Activity 1, closing debtors will be made up as follows:

		£
From August sales	10% × £420,000	42,000
From September sales	40% × £600,000	240,000
		282,000

This assumes the 1% uncollected amounts from previous months have been written off.

(b)   **Trade creditors**

The goods purchased in September will be paid for in October, and will therefore represent our creditors. In September, we purchase goods for sale in December at a cost of 60% × £400,000 = **£240,000.**

(c)   **Stock**

The closing stock at 30 September will represent October, November and December's sales, at cost:

60% (540,000 + 480,000 + 400,000) = £852,000

Chapter 13

FLEXIBLE BUDGETS

Syllabus content

- Reporting of actual against budget.

- Fixed and flexible budgeting.

In previous chapters we emphasised the role of budgets in the control of a business, by acting as comparators for actual results. It is important, however, to make meaningful comparisons, and the concept of flexible budgets is essential here.

This leads us to an introduction to variances, greater analysis of which is covered in later chapters.

Contents

1   Reporting of actual against budget

2   Flexible budgeting

3   Budget variances

1   Reporting of actual against budget

DEFINITION

Budgetary control is defined as the establishment of budgets relating the responsibilities of executives to the requirements of a policy, and the continuous comparison of actual with budgeted results, either to secure by individual action the objectives of that policy or to provide a basis for its revision. (CIMA Official Terminology)

1.1   Budgetary control

Budgetary control is defined as the establishment of budgets relating the responsibilities of executives to the requirements of a policy, and the continuous comparison of actual with budgeted results, either to secure by individual action the objectives of that policy or to provide a basis for its revision. (CIMA, *Official Terminology*)

The budgetary control cycle can be illustrated as follows:

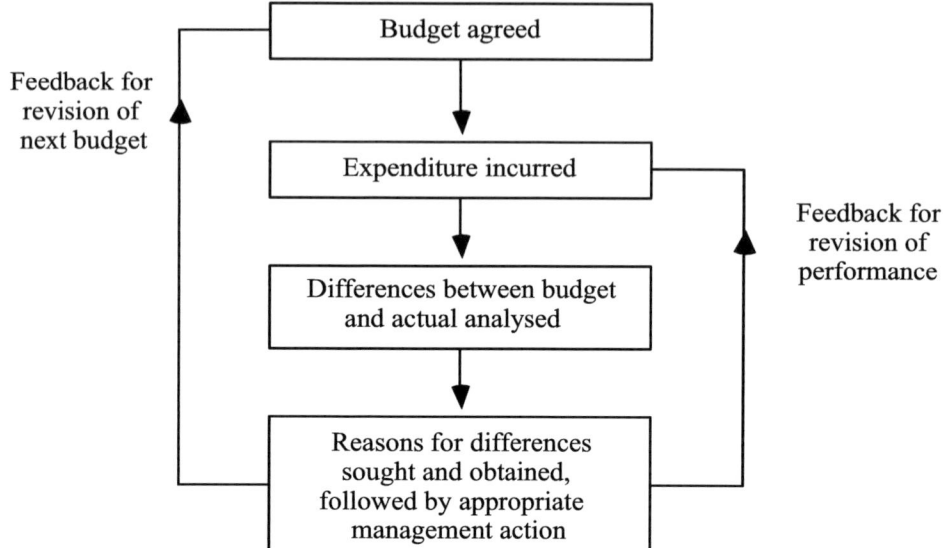

1.2   Budget reporting

The feedback loop in the control system requires a formal reporting procedure. This link is vital in that the budget system may identify variances, and hence problems, but unless these are effectively communicated to management, that knowledge is ineffective. In the context of budget systems, feedback reports consist of comparisons of budget targets and actual financial achievements, with differences highlighted as variances.

General criteria may be laid down for such reports.

- **Reports should be relevant to the information needs of their recipients**. This means that the report should contain all relevant information to the decisions to be made, and responsibilities exercised by the manager who receives the report. Generally, other information should be excluded although there is an argument for including background information on divisional/company performance.

- **Reporting should be linked to responsibility**. This is discussed in more detail below.

- **Reports should be timely**. One of the most frequent reporting problems is that reports are received after the decision for which they are required. In such cases managers must often rely on informal information sources outside the budget system. This may be less efficient, and also reduces the credibility of the budgetary control system in the eyes of that manager.

- **Reports should be reliable**. The reports should be regarded as containing reliable information (though not necessarily exact to the penny). There may be a conflict between reliability and timeliness, and often an assessment must be made of what is an acceptable error rate and/or degree of approximation.

- **Reports should be designed to communicate effectively**. Reports should be specifically designed to communicate effectively, often with managers who are not professional accountants. Reports should avoid jargon, be concise, but contain sufficient detail (often in supporting schedules). Maximum use should be made of graphical presentation.

- **Reports should be cost-effective**. A report is only worthwhile if the benefits from its existence exceed the cost of producing it.

1.3 Frequency of reports

The frequency of reports should be linked to the purposes for which they are required. This may well mean a variety of reports being produced to different time-scales for different purposes, e.g. some control information will be required weekly, or even daily. However, comprehensive budget reports are only likely to be required monthly.

1.4 Content of reports

The simplest form of budget report compares the original budget against actual results along the following lines:

	Budget	*Actual*	
Sales units	1,000	1,200	
Production units	1,300	1,250	
	£	£	£
Sales revenue	10,000	11,500	1,500 Fav
– labour costs	2,600	2,125	475 Fav
– materials costs	1,300	1,040	260 Fav
– overheads	1,950	2,200	250 Adv
	5,850	5,365	485 Fav
Cost of sales			
Profit	4,150	6,135	1985 Fav

Note:

Fav = favourable variance, i.e. is beneficial to profit

Adv = adverse variance, i.e. is detrimental to profit.

However, looking a little closer at such an analysis the following questions arise.

- Sales revenue shows a favourable variance – but how much of this is due to the higher sales volume, and how much (if any) to achieving a better price?

- Production costs have overall favourable variances, i.e. actual costs are less than budget – but this would be expected to some extent as fewer units were made.

- How much of the overhead is expected to remain fixed?

- Overall actual profits are better than budget – but can we really say why from this report?

To overcome these problems, it is more usual to compare actual results with a **flexed budget**, in other word with a budget that reflects the **actual activity level**.

2 Flexible budgeting

DEFINITION

A flexible budget is a budget, which, by recognising different cost behaviour patterns, is designed to change as volume of activity changes. (CIMA Official Terminology).

2.1 Contrast with fixed budgets

A fixed budget is one which is prepared for a single activity level. However, as we have just seen, a fixed budget might not provide particularly useful control information.

A flexible budget is a budget, which, by recognising different cost behaviour patterns, is designed to change as volume of activity changes. (CIMA, *Official Terminology*).

Activity 1

Distinguish between a fixed cost and a variable cost.

Feedback to this activity is at the end of the chapter.

2.2 The need for flexible budgets

Managers need to know when actual results for items under their control deviate from planned results.

Many of the costs for which a manager is responsible are variable costs. Since total variable cost is by definition dependent on the level of activity, a means must be found of eliminating that part of a cost variance which is due to activity level changes, so as to isolate the aspects of total variable cost for which the individual manager is accountable. The key points to note are:

- an original (fixed) budget is set at the beginning of the period based on estimated production

- this is then flexed to correspond with the actual level of activity

- the result is compared with actual monetary costs and revenues, and differences (variances) are reported to the managers responsible.

2.3 Calculation of budget variances

The following example illustrates the comparison of actual and budget results firstly using a fixed budget and then using a flexible budget.

As we have seen, the differences between the budget and actual values are known as **variances**. Where they relate to costs, if the actual cost is less than the budget cost the variance is described as **favourable**, if the actual cost is greater the variance is said to be **adverse**.

Bug Ltd manufactures one uniform product only and activity levels in the assembly department vary widely from month to month. The following statement shows the departmental overhead budget based on an average level of activity of 20,000 units production per four-week period, and the actual results for four weeks in October:

	Budget average for four week period £	Actual for 1 to 28 October £
Indirect labour – variable	20,000	19,540
Consumables – variable	800	1,000
Other variable overhead	4,200	3,660
Depreciation – fixed	10,000	10,000

Other fixed overhead	5,000	5,400
	40,000	39,600
Production (units)	20,000	17,600

You are required to:

(a) prepare a columnar flexible four-week budget at 16,000, 20,000 and 24,000 unit levels of production

(b) prepare two performance reports, based on production of 17,600 units by the department in October comparing actual with:

    (i) average four-week budget

    (ii) flexed four-week budget for 17,600 units of production.

Solution

(a)

Production level (units)	16,000 (80%)	20,000 (100%)	24,000 (120%)
	£	£	£
Variable costs:			
Indirect labour	16,000 (80%)	20,000 (100%)	24,000 (120%)
Consumables	640 (80%)	800 (100%)	960 (120%)
Other	3,360 (80%)	4,200 (100%)	5,040 (120%)
	20,000 (80%)	25,000 (100%)	30,000 (120%)
Fixed costs:			
Depreciation	10,000	10,000	10,000
Other	5,000	5,000	5,000
Total costs	35,000	40,000	45,000

(b) (i)

	Average four week budget £	Actual results £	Variances favourable/ (adverse) £
Indirect labour	20,000	19,540	460
Consumables	800	1,000	(200)
Other variable	4,200	3,660	540
Depreciation	10,000	10,000	–
Other fixed	5,000	5,400	(400)
	40,000	39,600	400

(ii)

	Flexed four week budget	Actual results	Variances favourable/ (adverse)
Production (units)	17,600	17,600	–
	£	£	£
Indirect labour	17,600	19,540	(1,940)
Consumables	704	1,000	(296)
Other variable	3,696	3,660	36

Depreciation	10,000	10,000	–
Other fixed	5,000	5,400	(400)
	37,000	39,600	(2,600)

Activity 2

Decide which comparison, (b)(i) or (b)(ii) is more useful in assessing the supervisor's effectiveness and why?

Feedback to this activity is at the end of the chapter.

2.4 The choice between fixed and flexible budgets

Despite the advantages of flexible budgets, many companies use fixed budgets for control purposes for the following reasons:

- flexible budgets involve more work, and hence are more expensive to operate

- in many businesses costs are largely fixed over the budget period – this tends to be particularly true in service industries.

It should not therefore be automatically assumed that flexible budgets should be employed for control purposes. The value of the additional information should be balanced against the incremental costs as compared to fixed budgeting.

2.5 Flexed budget computations

In some cases you may have to use cost estimation techniques studied in chapter 2 to split out semi-variable costs.

Example

Suppose you were given the following extracts from a budget report:

Flexible budgets

Production – units	1,200	1,000
Other production costs	£9,800	£8,700

What figure would you include for other production costs in a budget flexed to the actual production level of 800 units?

Solution

First note that the cost is clearly not fixed and cannot be purely variable (at 1,000 units, cost per unit is £8.70; at 1,200 it is £8.17).

Thus we need to use the high low method to analyse the cost behaviour

	Units	£
High	1,200	9,800
Low	1,000	8,700
	200	1,100

Variable cost = $\dfrac{£1,100}{200}$ = £5.50 per unit.

Fixed cost = £8,700 – (1,000 × 5.50) = £3,200

Budgeted cost allowance at 800 units = £3,200 + (800 × £5.50) = £7,600

3 Budget variances

3.1 Introduction

We have discussed why comparison of actual results against a budget flexed to actual level of activity is usually more meaningful than a comparison against an original, fixed budget, for individual revenues/costs.

However we cannot just ignore the original budget altogether – it will form part of the operational plan and management will want to see how results from actual operations have fared against budgeted profits.

Thus we can prepare a report that shows:

- Original (flexed) budget – budget activity level } differences = volume variances
- Flexed budget – actual activity level }
- Actual – actual activity level } differences = expenditure variances

The overall differences between original budget and actual results are known as total budget variances.

Example

Look back at the example. The answer to (b) (i), shows the total budget variances. The answer to (b) (ii) shows the expenditure variances.

These two statements may be combined as follows:

	Average four week budget	Flexed four week budget	Actual results	Expenditure Variances favourable/ (adverse)
Production (units)	20,000	17,600	17,600	
	£	£	£	£
Indirect labour	20,000	17,600	19,540	(1,940)
Consumables	800	704	1,000	(296)
Other variable	4,200	3,696	3,660	36
	25,000	22,000	24,200	(2,200)
Depreciation	10,000	10,000	10,000	–
Other fixed	5,000	5,000	5,400	(400)
	40,000	37,000	39,600	(2,600)

Volume variance = £3,000 Fav

We can now reconcile the variances:

	£
Volume variance	3,000 Fav
Expenditure variances	(2,600) Adv
Total budget variance	400 Fav

3.2 Volume variance

The volume variance reflects the change in cost expected from the change in volume. Budgeted variable costs at 20,000 units total £25,000. If production is reduced to 17,600 units (a drop of 12%) the expected drop in cost is 12% × £25,000 = £3,000.

3.3 Expenditure variances

The expenditure variances total £2,600 adverse. This shows that the production of 17,600 units (actual level) cost £2,600 more than expected.

In this case it is helpful to analyse this further between separate cost headings in order to isolate the main problem areas.

We can further analyse these variances to answer questions such as:

- Was indirect labour more expensive than expected because of higher rates of pay, or more hours worked per unit?

The analysis of a total labour variance is covered in the chapters on standard costing, along with other variance analysis.

Summary

This chapter has shown how budgets may be used as a control tool, by comparison with actual results. We have discussed the usefulness of flexible budgets in this respect, and how total budget variances can be analysed between volume and expenditure variances.

By the time you have finished this chapter you should be able to:

- prepare simple reports showing actual and budgeted results

- explain the differences between fixed and flexible budgets

- prepare a fixed and flexible budget

- calculate expenditure, volume and total budget variances.

Self-test questions

Reporting of actual against budget

1 What is the budgetary control cycle? (1.1)

Flexible budgeting

2 What is a fixed budget? (2.1)

3 What is a flexible budget? (2.1)

Budget variances

4 What is a volume variance? (3.2)

5 What are expenditure variances? (3.3)

Exam-type questions

Question 1

Variable costs are conventionally deemed to:

A be constant per unit of output

B vary per unit of output as production volume changes

C be constant in total when production volume changes

D vary, in total, from period to period when production is constant

Question 2

The budgeted variable cost per unit was £2.75. When output was 18,000 units, total expenditure was £98,000 and it was found that fixed overheads were £11,000 over budget whilst variable costs were in line with budget.

The amount budgeted for fixed costs was £ ⬚ .

Question 3

The flexed budgets relating to two levels of activity are as follows:

	Level 1	Level 2
Production (units)	5,000	8,000
Budgeted total cost	£76,500	£106,400

The budgeted total cost of the product includes the raw material element, which has a constant cost per unit of £4 for all units produced up to a level of 6,000 units. Above this level there is a quantity discount of 5% that applies to all units of raw material purchased. All the other unit variable cost elements and the total fixed cost element are constant throughout the relevant production range given.

The budgeted total cost of production for 7,000 units is £ ⬚ .

Question 4

The following information is taken from the production cost budget of J Limited.

	Level 1	Level 2
Production units	4,000	7,000
Production cost	£8,700	£12,600

The flexible budget cost allowance for an activity level of 5,200 units is

£ ⬚ .

Question 5

A flexible budget is:

A   a budget of variable production costs only

B   a budget that is updated with actual costs and revenues as they occur during the budget period

C   a budget that shows the costs and revenues at different levels of activity

D   a budget that is prepared for a period of six months and reviewed monthly Following such review a further one month's budget is prepared.

For the answers to these questions, see the 'Answers' section at the end of the book.

Practice question

C Ltd

C Ltd employs 300 people and has sales of £9 million. It has five producing departments, two service departments and manufactures one product.

No effective planning or financial control system has been established but after one of the directors had attended a CIMA course on 'Finance for Non-Financial Managers' he decided to introduce a budget system and performance reports related to responsibilities. Other directors and management had some reservations about the introduction of this system but they were persuaded to allow its introduction.

After the end of April, which was the first month of the current financial year, departmental performance reports were issued to all departmental supervisors. These took the form of that illustrated below for Production Department 'D' which was produced by the office manager – the senior person on the administrative staff. (A separate report was issued relating to direct material and direct labour.)

Monthly report: department 'D' – April 20X0

	Actual	*Planning budget*	*Variance*
Units produced	1,100	1,000	100
	£	£	£
Salaries and wages	10,000	10,500	500
Indirect labour	8,000	7,000	(1,000)*
Maintenance	3,500	2,750	(750)*
Overhead allocated	3,000	2,750	(250)*
Consumable stores	1,600	1,500	(100)*
Depreciation	2,500	2,500	0
Insurance	1,100	1,000	(100)*
Sundries	1,000	500	(500)*
	30,700	28,500	(2,200)

Note: considerable inefficiency; action should be taken to improve cost control in this department.

J, the supervisor for department D, was not pleased on receiving her report and declared she did not have time to bother with such paperwork and, in any case, the report was inaccurate and unfair. Her comment was typical of others who had received similar reports.

You are required to state what changes ought to be made to the report and why.

For the answer to this question, see the 'Answers' section at the end of the book.

Feedback to activities

Activity 1

(a)   **Fixed** – no variation as volume varies (within the relevant range).

(b)   **Variable** – varies directly with volume.

This distinction is important in setting up flexible budgets. You need to know which behaviour pattern individual costs fall into.

Activity 2

Clearly the flexed budget provides more useful data for comparison because:

- the fixed budget makes no distinction between fixed and variable costs

- hence no data is available about the appropriate level of costs at the actual production level

- this would lead to the conclusion that the supervisor had done well when in fact costs had not fallen as much as anticipated for the actual production

- responsibility for the production shortfall is not known.

Chapter 14

STANDARD COSTS: PRINCIPLES AND PREPARATION

Syllabus content

- Principles of standard costing.

- Preparation of standard costs under absorption and marginal costing.

Whilst this chapter marks the start of a new section of the syllabus, Standard Costing, it is closely linked with previous chapters, particularly on budgeting and cost estimation.

In order to develop a budget, we need to know what our product or service is expected to cost per unit. This is the standard cost. As well as being used as a basis for budgeting, it is also essential for variance analysis. However, you should note that standard costing and budgetary control systems are not synonymous.

In this chapter we look at how standard costs are derived. In the following chapters we look at their use in variance analysis.

Contents

1   Standard costing

2   Types of standards

3   Preparation of standard costs

1 Standard costing

1.1 Relationship of standard costing to budgetary control

DEFINITION

Standard costing is a control technique which compares standard costs and revenues with actual results to obtain variances that are used to stimulate improved performance.

Standard costing is a control technique which compares standard costs and revenues with actual results to obtain variances that are used to stimulate improved performance.

Historically, standard costing evolved as a parallel system to budgetary control, representing a different approach to the problem. Today, standard costing has become a subset of budgetary control, and is commonly used within an organisation as part of a budgetary control system.

Nevertheless, it is important to identify three factors that differentiate standard costing from other approaches to budgetary control.

- Under standard costing, for costing purposes all stocks are valued at their standard costs.

- Standard costs are incorporated in the ledger accounts; budgets are a memorandum record outside the ledger accounts.

- Standard costs are set as unit costs; budgets tend to be set as total costs.

Thus although standard costing is a subset of budgeting, it has certain distinct features of its own.

KEY POINT

Although standard costing is a subset of budgeting, it has certain distinct features of its own.

1.2 Circumstances under which each technique may be applied

The circumstances under which each of the techniques may be used are, in general terms, as below:

- **Standard costing** – This may be most effectively utilised where output or production is routine and regular and can, therefore, be easily and accurately measured. The principal advantage of standard costing is to enable a detailed comparison of individual inputs of materials, labour and other production costs to be made with the standard inputs that should be used for a given level of output. A superior variance analysis is, therefore, possible.

- **Budgetary control** – This can be used for all activities within an organisation where costs and revenues can be predicted and actual results compared. Budgetary control is, therefore, of use in the control of overhead costs and service department costs, and also perhaps in the control of sales activity. The technique is broader in its application than standard costing, and budgets may be considered to be a more basic control tool generally.

  The use of flexible budgets is suitable for cost centres where output or volume of activity has an effect on costs and in this situation there is a closer correlation with standard costing, although a broader measure of the level of output or activity will be used.

1.3 Standard cost card

This shows the standard cost for a single unit of a product.

Standard cost card – cost per unit of product X

		£
Raw materials:	5 kgs P @ £2/kg	10.00
	3 kgs Q @ £1.5/kg	4.50

Labour	4 hrs grade A @ £4/hr	16.00
	1 hr grade B @ £5.50/hr	5.50
Variable overheads	5 hrs @ £1.50/hr	7.50
		43.50 (MC)
Fixed overheads	5 hrs @ £1.30/hr	6.50
		50.00 (TAC)

This standard cost is used as a basis of comparison with actual results.

1.4 Marginal or total absorption?

We shall soon be looking at the computations of standard costs in more detail; however, note that a standard cost may be computed on either a marginal cost basis, including only variable costs, or on an absorption cost basis.

In the latter case, fixed production overheads will be absorbed into cost units, possibly using the allocation, apportionment and absorption techniques studied earlier. In this example, the absorption basis is labour hours, the same as variable costs, which is very common in examination questions.

1.5 Standard – definition

A standard cost is calculated in relation to a prescribed set of working conditions, i.e. it reflects technical specifications and scientific measurement of the resources used to manufacture a product.

- A standard is a benchmark measurement of resource usage, set in defined conditions. (CIMA *Official Terminology*).

- A **standard cost** is the planned unit cost of the products, components or services produced in a period. The standard cost may be determined on a number of bases. The main uses of standard costs are in performance measurement, control, stock valuation and in the establishment of selling prices. (CIMA *Official Terminology*).

Standard costs represent target costs. As such they represent costs that are most likely to be useful for:

- planning

- control

- motivation.

2 Types of standards

2.1 What sort of standards?

There is a whole range of bases upon which standards may be set within a standard costing system. The choice will be affected by the main purposes for which management see such a system operating. In the modern age quality control and continuous improvement are likely to be the main concerns.

The types of standard that you are most likely to meet are:

- basic standards

- ideal standards

- attainable standards

- current standards.

DEFINITION

A standard is a benchmark measurement of resource usage, set in defined conditions. (CIMA *Terminology*).

DEFINITION

A **standard cost** is the planned unit cost of the products, components or services produced in a period. The standard cost may be determined on a number of bases. The main uses of standard costs are in performance measurement, control, stock valuation and in the establishment of selling prices.

2.2 Basic standards

A basic standard is: 'a standard established for use over a long period from which a current standard can be developed'. (CIMA, 1984)

Such standards do not change from year to year. Historical trends would be highlighted by a system incorporating basic standards, but for other management control purposes the information from the analysis between actual and standard would be limited. Most businesses operate in a dynamic world of continuously changing products and production methods. This would necessitate changes to standards and, therefore, to the base period.

2.3 Ideal standards

Standards may be set 'at ideal levels which make no allowances for [normal losses, waste and machine downtime], and are only attainable under the most favourable conditions.' (CIMA, Official Terminology, 2000).

Ideal standards are set on the assumption of maximum efficiency. So, for example, no allowance for breakdowns, no wastage, working at full capacity would all be features of such ideal or theoretical standards. In other words, a perfect and ideal operating environment is assumed. Such standards would not be achieved and sustained for any significant period of time, if at all.

Large adverse variances are likely to be a feature of a standard costing system based on ideal standards. They would reflect a deviation not only from an expected level of activity and performance but also from the ideal.

An important feature of any control system is the impact that it has on managerial performance. Standard costing is only a means to an end in that variances and their analysis, as an example of management by exception, should lead management to appropriate action. A manager receiving a variance statement that is evolved from a system based on ideal standards would be unlikely to be motivated to improve performance and act in the best interests of the whole business. On the contrary, such a system might operate in the opposite manner and cause the manager to be demotivated.

2.4 Attainable standards

Standards may also be set at attainable levels which assume efficient levels of operation, but which include allowances for normal loss, waste and machine downtime'. (CIMA, *Official Terminology,* 2000)

Such standards represent what should be achieved with a reasonable level of effort under normal efficient operating conditions. This does not mean that as such they are 'easy' standards. On the contrary, behavioural studies tend to suggest that they should include some element of 'target' in them. Managers at the operating levels in the organisation structure should be encouraged to set standards at the tightest level acceptable by themselves – in other words, at a degree of difficulty that they themselves see as acceptable.

In contrast with ideal standards, attainable standards do include allowances for such occurrences as the normal level of wastage, machine breakdowns and other non-productive time.

If there is any deviation between actual and standard, it is more likely to be such as to give marginally adverse variances rather than favourable. However, such variances are likely to be looked upon by the managers to whose area of responsibility they relate, as an appropriate measure of performance. Expected or currently attainable standards are those most commonly found in organisations operating standard costing systems because they can be seen to serve a range of advantages in terms of planning, control and motivation.

Variances from systems incorporating attainable standards are likely to be most relevant in terms of providing appropriate information to management.

2.5 Current standards

Current standards are based on the current levels of efficiency in terms of allowances for breakdowns, wastage, losses and so on. The major drawback in the use of current standards is that they provide no incentive to improve on the current level of performance.

A system of basing standards either on last period's actuals, or on the average of some previous periods, is not recommended generally. Over time, there could be just a tendency to relax standards in line with actual results rather than an encouragement to management to investigate why variances have arisen and to take the appropriate action. This presupposes adverse variances in the past and a lowering of standards in the future.

Past anomalies or inefficiencies tend to be built into future standards and treated as normal and any potential improvement in efficiency, e.g. due to technological change, may be overlooked. Inefficient use of resources would tend to go unnoticed.

KEY POINT

In the setting of standards, three aspects should be kept in mind:

(a) their value for control

(b) their motivational effect

(c) their usefulness for planning purposes.

2.6 Conclusions on standards

In the setting of standards, three aspects should be kept in mind:

- their value for control

- their motivational effect

- their usefulness for planning purposes.

The types of standard described above may be evaluated against these types of criteria:

3 Preparation of standard costs

3.1 The basic computations

In general, a standard cost will be set for each product, comprising:

- **Direct materials**: standard quantity (kg, litres etc.) × standard price per unit (kg, litre etc.).

- **Direct wages**: standard labour hours × standard hourly rate.

- **Variable overhead**: standard hours (labour or machine) × standard rate per hour.

- **Fixed overhead**: budgeted overhead for the period ÷ budgeted standard hours (labour or machine) for the period.

Standard costs are therefore comprised of two estimates that are multiplied to produce the standard cost of the output unit. These two estimates are:

- a physical measure of the resources required for each unit of output

- the price expected to be paid for each unit of the resource.

It is assumed that an attainable standard is to be used.

3.2 Physical resources

The first step is to identify the resources required for each output unit. This includes:

- each type of different raw material or component
- each grade and skill type of labour
- each type of machine.

For each of these an estimate must then be made of the quantity of materials, number of components, number of hours etc., required for each output unit (allowing for normal losses, wastage, inefficiency).

Sources of information on which to base such estimates would include:

Material usage	– work study techniques will help to identify normal allowances for wastage, losses etc.
	– technical specifications of the material to be used.
Labour times	– technical specifications of the tasks required to manufacture the product or provide the service.
	– work study exercises, from which the standard times to perform required tasks and grades of labour needed could be determined.

3.3 Resource unit prices

For each resource required, an estimate must then be made of the expected cost per unit of the resource (i.e. per kg, per unit, per hour). When making these estimates regard must be given towards the likely level of inflation and price changes expected in the budget period.

Other specific information that may be used includes:

Material price	– quotes/estimates from potential suppliers
	– trend information from past price data
	– bulk discounts available
	– quality of material to be used
	– packaging and carriage inward charges.
Labour rate	– wage rates provided by the personnel department
	– forecasts of likely outcomes of any wage rate negotiations/bonus/incentive scheme in operation.

3.4 Production overhead costs

Earlier, we looked at how predetermined hourly rates were derived for production overhead. These rates represent the standard hourly rates for overhead in each cost centre. They can be applied to standard labour hours or machine hours, etc., for each cost unit.

The overheads will usually be analysed between their fixed and variable elements, to give separate standard rates for fixed and variable production overheads.

Activity 1

Lunches Ltd makes sandwiches for sale to offices and over the counter. Contents of their 'spicy meat special' are as follows:

> 2 slices bread
> 88 grams spicy meat mix
> 44 grams grated cheese
> 20 grams pickle

It is company policy to guarantee the cooked weight of meat mix to be a minimum of 88 grams. There is a 20% loss of mix weight during cooking. Losses due to accidental damage, dropped sandwiches, etc. are estimated to be 5% of completed sandwiches.

Anticipated prices of raw materials for the coming period are:

Bread	54p per loaf of 18 useable slices
Spicy meat mix (uncooked)	£3.20 per kg
Cheese	£3 per kg
Pickle	£1.60 per kg

Prepare the standard ingredients cost of one 'spicy meat special' sandwich.

Feedback to this activity is at the end of the chapter.

Activity 2

The fastest time in which a batch of 20 'spicy meat special' sandwiches has been made was 32 minutes, with no hold-ups. However, work studies have shown that, on average about 8% of the sandwich makers' time is non-productive, and that, in addition to this set-up time (getting ingredients together etc.) is 2 minutes. If the sandwich-makers are paid £4.50 per hour, what is the attainable standard labour cost of one sandwich?

Feedback to this activity is at the end of the chapter.

DEFINITION

A standard hour is the amount of work achievable, at standard efficiency levels, in an hour.

3.5 The standard hour

Output is often measured in terms of standard hours, i.e. the amount of work achievable, at standard efficiency levels, in an hour.

Thus, if 50 articles are estimated to be made in a 'clock' hour, an output of 150 should take three 'clock' hours and would be valued at the standard cost of those three hours, irrespective of the actual time taken to manufacture them.

Example

A factory in week 1 achieved the following activity level:

	Units	*Standard minutes each*
Product F	5,100	6
Product C	2,520	10
Product A	3,150	12

You are required to calculate the number of standard hours produced in week 1.

Solution

Actual standard hours produced were:

		Standard hours
Product F	5,100 × 6/60 =	510
Product C	2,520 ×10/60 =	420
Product A	3,150 × 12/60 =	630
		1,560

Standard hours provide managers with a means of measuring and monitoring output of dissimilar products. For example, suppose that the output for the same factory in week 2 was as follows:

	Units
Product F	1,100
Product C	240
Product A	8,700

Fewer units in total were produced in week 2 than in week 1 (10,040 in week 2 compared with 10,770 in week 1). However we are attempting to add dissimilar units and the comparison is not valid. If we convert the week 2 output to standard hours we will be able to assess whether productivity in week 2 was in fact lower than in week 1.

Standard hours produced in week 2:

		Standard hours
Product F	1,100 × 6/60	110
Product C	240 × 10/60	40
Product A	8,700 × 12/60	1,740
		1,890

A comparison of the number of standard hours produced reveals that productivity in week 2 was actually higher than in week 1.

Summary

This chapter has discussed the basic principles of standard costing, and how standards are set.

Different types of standard may be used – basic, ideal, attainable or current – of which the attainable standard is generally accepted to be of greatest use in planning and control.

Attainable standards will build in allowances for normal levels of loss, wastage, inefficiency, etc.

By the time you have finished this chapter you should be able to:

- explain the principles of standard costing

- prepare the standard cost for a product/service.

Self-test questions

Standard costing

1   What is standard costing? (1.1)

2   What is a standard cost? (1.1)

Types of standards

3   What is a basic standard? (2.2)

4   What is an ideal standard? (2.3)

5   What is an attainable standard? (2.4)

6   What is a current standard? (2.5)

Preparation of standard costs

7   Give three possible sources of information from which a standard materials price may be estimated. (3.3)

8   What is a standard hour? (3.5)

Exam-type questions

Question 1

Performance standards which have remained unchanged over a long period of time are known as:

A   ideal standards

B   current standards

C   basic standards

D   long-term standards.

Question 2

A standard hour is:

A   always equivalent to a clock hour

B   any hour during which no idle time occurs

C   the quantity of work achievable at standard performance in an hour

D   an hour throughout which the same units are made.

Question 3

Attainable standards include no allowances for inefficiencies such as machine downtime, losses, wastage and so on.

True		False	

For the answers to these questions, see the 'Answers' section at the end of the book.

Practice question

Budgets and standards

'Budgets and standards are similar but they are not the same.'

You are required to explain and expand on the above statement, mentioning differences and similarities.

For the answer to this question, see the 'Answers' section at the end of the book.

Feedback to activities

Activity 1

		£
2 slices bread	2/18 × £0.54	0.060
Spicy meat mix	88g cooked weight =	
	88/0.8 uncooked weight @	0.352
	£3.20/kg	
Grated cheese	44g @ £3/kg	0.132
Pickle	20g @ £1.60/kg	0.032
Cost per sandwich started	(95%)	0.576
Allowance due to anticipated losses	(5%)	0.030
Standard ingredients cost	(100%)	0.606

Activity 2

		Per batch of 20
Ideal time	(92%)	32.0 minutes
Non-productive time	(8%)	2.8 minutes
	(100%)	34.8 minutes
Set-up time		2.0 minutes
Total time		36.8 minutes
Total cost @ £4.50/hr		£2.76
Standard labour cost per sandwich (/20)		£0.138

Chapter 15

VARIANCE ANALYSIS: MATERIALS AND LABOUR

Syllabus content

- Variances: materials: total, price and usage; labour: total, rate and efficiency.

Having set the scene in the flexible budgeting and standard costing chapters, we are now ready to look at the detail of variance analysis. This chapter deals with materials and labour, and the next two cover remaining variances and profit reconciliations.

Contents

1 Basic cost variance analysis

2 Direct material cost variances

3 Raw materials stocks

4 Direct labour cost variances

1 Basic cost variance analysis

1.1 Cost variances

A variance is the difference between a planned, budgeted or standard cost and the actual cost incurred. (CIMA, *Official Terminology*).

DEFINITION

A variance is the difference between a planned, budgeted or standard cost and the actual cost incurred. (CIMA Official Terminology).

Cost variances occur when standard costs are compared to actual costs. There is one important feature of standard costing that must be remembered: standard costing carries out variance analysis using the normal, double entry ledger accounts. This is done by recording in the ledgers:

- actual costs as inputs
- standard costs as outputs
- the difference as the variance.

1.2 Calculating variances

It is essential that you do not simply learn formulae for variances without really understanding what they mean and the principles behind their calculation. The examiner may ask you to calculate non-standard variances, which will be testing your understanding rather than your ability to remember formulae.

Therefore, we have considered each variance from a 'common sense' point of view, developing its calculation from basic principles. Make sure you work through this carefully.

2 Direct material cost variances

2.1 Introduction

The purpose of calculating direct material cost variances is to quantify the effect on profit of actual direct material costs differing from standard direct material costs. This total effect is then analysed to quantify how much has been caused by a difference in the price paid for the material and how much by a difference in the quantity of material used.

2.2 Direct material total cost variance

The purpose of this variance is to show the effect on profit for an accounting period of the actual direct material cost being different from the standard direct material cost.

Example

The following standard costs relate to a single unit of product X:

	£
Direct materials	10
Direct labour	8
Production overhead	5
	23

In July, 1,000 units of product X were manufactured, incurring direct material cost of £12,000.

The total direct materials cost variance is:

	£
standard direct material cost = 1,000 units × £10	10,000
actual direct material cost	12,000
direct materials cost variance - adverse	2,000

The variance is adverse because it causes actual profits to be less than expected.

Activity 1

The standard direct material cost of product A is £5. During August 600 units of product A were made, and the actual direct material cost was £3,200. Calculate the direct material total cost variance for the period.

Feedback to this activity is at the end of the chapter.

2.3 Analysing the direct material total cost variance

When a standard material cost is determined for a unit of a product it is made up of two parts. These are estimates of:

- the quantity of material to be used
- the price to be paid per unit of material.

If we return to the earlier example concerning product X, the standard direct material cost per unit was stated to be £10. This was based on using 5 kg of a particular material to make each unit of product X and paying £2/kg for the material.

You should remember that the actual direct material cost incurred in making 1,000 units of product X was £12,000. The invoice for these costs shows:

4,800 kg @ £2.50/kg = £12,000.

It should be noted that this form of analysis corresponds to the two estimates that form the basis of the standard cost. It is this that allows the direct material total cost variance to be analysed.

2.4 Direct material price variance

The purpose of calculating this variance is to identify the extent to which profits will differ from those expected by reason of the actual price paid for direct materials being different from the standard price.

The standard price per kg of material was stated above to be £2/kg. This can be used to calculate the expected cost of the actual materials used to make 1,000 units of product X. On this basis the 4,800 kg of material should have cost:

4,800 kg × £2/kg = £9,600.

The actual cost of these materials was £12,000 that is £2,400 (£12,000 − £9,600) more than expected. Since the actual price was greater than expected this will cause the profit to be lower than expected. This variance, known as the direct material price variance, is adverse.

Activity 2

A raw material, used in the manufacture of product F has a standard price of £1.30 per litre. During May 2,300 litres were bought at a cost of £3,128. Calculate the direct material price variance for May.

Feedback to this activity is at the end of the chapter.

2.5 Direct material usage variance

The purpose of this variance is to quantify the effect on profit of using a different quantity of raw material from that expected for the actual production achieved.

Returning to our example concerning product X, it was stated that each unit of product X had a standard direct material usage of 5 kg. This can be used to calculate the amount of direct material (in kg) that should be used for the actual production achieved.

1,000 units of X @ 5 kg of direct material each = 5,000 kg.

You should remember that the analysis of the actual cost showed that 4,800 kg of direct material were actually used.

Thus a saving of 200 kg (5,000 − 4,800) was achieved.

This saving of materials must be valued to show the effect on profit. If the original standard direct material cost were revised to reflect this saving of material it would become:

4.8 kg (4,800/1,000) @ £2/kg = £9.60.

This is £0.40 per unit of product X less than the original standard and profit would therefore increase by this amount for every unit of product X produced. This has a total value of:

1,000 units × £0.40 = £400.

We achieve the same result by multiplying the saving in quantity by the standard price:

200 kg × £2/kg = £400.

In this case profits will be higher than expected because less material was used than expected in the standard. Therefore the variance is said to be favourable.

We can now check that the two sub-variances total to the total direct material cost variance:

Price variance + usage variance = total material cost variance

£2,400 adverse + £400 favourable = £2,000 adverse

Activity 3

The standard direct material usage per unit of product K is 0.4 tonnes. The standard price of the material is £30/tonne.

During April 500 units of K were made using 223 tonnes of material costing £6,913. Calculate the direct material usage variance, and the direct material price variance.

Feedback to this activity is at the end of the chapter.

3 Raw materials stocks

3.1 Introduction

The earlier example has assumed that the quantity of materials purchased equalled the quantity of materials used by production. Whilst this is possible it is not always certain to occur. Where this does not occur profit will be affected by the change in the level of stock. The extent to which this affects the calculation of direct material variances depends on the methods chosen to value stock.

Stocks may be valued either using:

- the standard price for the material or
- the actual price (as applies from using FIFO, LIFO, etc.).

3.2 Stocks valued at standard price

This is the most common method when using a standard costing system because it eliminates the need to record value based movements of stock on stores ledger cards (since all movements, both receipts and issues, will be valued at the standard price).

The effect of this valuation method is that price variances are calculated based on the quantity purchased rather than the quantity of materials used. This is illustrated by the following example.

Example

Product P requires 4 kg of material Z per unit. The standard price of material Z is £8/kg. During September 16,000 kg of Z were bought for £134,400. There was no opening stock of material Z but at the end of September 1,400 kg of Z remained in stock. Stocks of Z are valued at standard prices.

The price variance is based on the quantity purchased (i.e. 16,000 kg). The standard cost of these materials can be calculated:

	£
16,000 kg × £8/kg	128,000
Actual cost of 16,000 kg	134,400
Direct material price variance – Adverse	6,400

3.3 Stock account

Continuing the above example the issues of material Z of 14,600 kg (16,000 – 1,400) would be valued at the standard price of £8/kg.

The value of the issues debited to work-in-progress would thus be:

14,600 kg × £8/kg = £116,800.

The stock account would appear thus:

Raw material Z

	£		£
Creditor	134,400	Work-in-progress	116,800
		Price variance	6,400
		Bal c/d	11,200
	134,400		134,400

Note that the balance c/d comprises the closing stock of 1,400 kg valued at the standard price of £8/kg.

1,400 kg × £8/kg = £11,200.

The entry representing the price variance is shown as a credit in the raw material account because it is an adverse variance. The corresponding entry is made to a price variance account, the balance of which is transferred to profit and loss at the end of the year. The price variance account is as follows:

Direct material price variance

	£		£
Raw material Z	6,400		

3.4 Stocks valued at actual price

If this stock valuation method is used it means that any price variance is recognised not at the time of purchase but at the time of issue.

When using this method issues are made from stock at actual prices (using FIFO, LIFO, etc.) with the consequence that detailed stores ledger cards must be kept. The price variance is calculated based upon the quantity used.

Example

Using the data concerning material Z above, calculations of the value of closing stock can be made as follows:

$$\text{Actual cost/kg} = \frac{£134,400}{16,000} = £8.40$$

Closing stock value (at actual cost) = 1,400 kg × £8.40
= £11,760.

The direct material price variance based on the issues quantity can be calculated:

	£
Standard cost of 14,600 kg:	
14,600 kg × £8/kg	116,800
Actual cost of 14,600 kg (above)	122,640
Direct material price variance – Adverse	5,840

3.5 Stock account

If stock is valued using actual prices, the stock account will be as follows:

Raw material Z

	£		£
Creditor	134,400	Work-in-progress	116,800
		Direct material price variance	5,840
		Balance c/d	11,760
	134,400		134,400

Note that the closing balance comprises:

	£
1,400 kg × standard price of £8/kg	11,200
Adverse price variance not yet recognised:	
1,400 kg × (£8.40 − £8.00)	560
	11,760

4 Direct labour cost variances

4.1 Introduction

The purpose of calculating direct labour cost variances is to quantify the effect on profit of actual direct labour costs differing from standard direct labour costs.

This total effect is then analysed to quantify how much has been caused by a difference in the wage rate paid to employees and how much by a difference in the number of hours worked.

4.2 Direct labour total cost variance

The purpose of this variance is to show the effect on profit for an accounting period of the actual direct labour cost being different from the standard direct labour cost.

Example

Product Q has a standard labour cost of £12 per unit.

In August, 800 units of product Q were manufactured incurring a direct labour cost of £8,000.

The total direct labour cost variance is:

	£
standard direct labour cost = 800 × £12	9,600
actual direct labour cost	8,000
direct labour cost variance - favourable	1,600

The variance is favourable because it causes actual profits to be more than expected.

Activity 4

The standard direct labour cost of product H is £7. During January 450 units of product H were made, and the actual direct labour cost was £3,450. Calculate the direct labour total cost variance of the period.

Feedback to this activity is at the end of the chapter.

4.3 Analysing the direct labour total cost variance

When a standard labour cost is determined for a unit of a product it is made up of two parts. These are estimates of:

- the number of hours required per unit
- the hourly wage rate.

If we return to the example concerning product Q, the standard direct labour cost per unit was stated to be £12. This was based on 4 direct labour hours being required per unit of Q and paying a wage rate of £3/hour.

You should remember that the actual direct labour cost incurred in making 800 units of product Q was £8,000. An analysis of the payroll records shows:

2,000 hours @ £4/hour = £8,000.

It should be noted that this corresponds to the two estimates that form the basis of the standard cost. It is this that allows the direct labour total cost variance to be analysed.

4.4 Direct labour rate variance

The purpose of calculating this variance is to identify the extent to which profits will differ from those expected by reason of the actual wage rate per hour being different from the standard.

The standard wage rate per hour was stated to be £3. This can be used to calculate the expected cost of the actual hours taken to make 800 units of product Q. On this basis the 2,000 hours should have cost:

2,000 hours × £3/hour = £6,000.

The actual labour cost was £8,000 that is £2,000 (£8,000 − £6,000) more than expected.

Since the actual rate was greater than expected, this will cause the profit to be lower than expected. This variance, known as the direct labour rate variance, is adverse.

4.5 Direct labour efficiency variance

The purpose of this variance is to quantify the effect on profit of using a different number of hours than expected for the actual production achieved.

Continuing with our example concerning product Q, it was stated that each unit of product Q would require 4 direct labour hours. This can be used to calculate the number of direct labour hours that should be required for the actual production achieved.

800 units of Q $\times$ 4 direct labour hours each = 3,200 direct labour hours

You should remember that the analysis of the actual cost showed that only 2,000 hours were used.

Thus a saving of 1,200 direct labour hours (3,200 − 2,000) was achieved.

This saving of labour hours must be valued to show the effect on profit. We do this by multiplying the difference in hours by the standard hourly rate:

1,200 direct labour hours $\times$ £3/hr = £3,600.

In this case profit will be higher than expected because fewer hours were used. Therefore the variance is favourable.

We can now check that the two sub-variances total to the direct labour total cost variance:

rate variance + efficiency variance = total labour cost variance
£2,000 adverse + £3,600 favourable = £1,600 favourable

Activity 5

The following data relates to product C

Actual production of C (units)	700
Standard wage rate/hour	£4.00
Standard time allowance per unit of C (hours)	1.50
Actual hours worked	1,000
Actual wage cost	£4,200

Calculate the direct labour rate and efficiency variances from the above data.

Feedback to this activity is at the end of the chapter.

Summary

This chapter has started your studies of variance analysis, looking at total variances and labour variances, which can be sub-analysed as follows:

Materials – price variance

        – usage variance

Labour – rate variance

        – efficiency variance

By the time you have finished this chapter you should be able to:

- calculate and interpret variances for materials and labour.

Self-test questions

Basic cost variance analysis

1   What is a cost variance? (1.1)

Direct material cost variances

2   What does an adverse materials price variance indicate? (2.4)

3   What would a favourable materials usage variance indicate? (2.5)

Raw material stocks

4   What is the effect on price variance analysis of valuing stocks at standard price? (3.2)

Direct labour cost variances

5   How can a total labour cost variance be further analysed? (4.4, 4.5)

Exam-type questions

Question 1

Q Ltd uses an integrated standard costing system. In October, when 2,400 units of the finished product were made, the actual material cost details were:

Material purchased	5,000 units @ £4.50 each
Material used	4,850 units

The standard cost details are that 2 units of the material should be used for each unit of the completed product, and the standard price of each material unit is £4.70.

The entries made in the variance accounts would be:

	Material price variance a/c		*Material usage variance a/c*	
A	Debit	£970	Debit	£225
B	Debit	£1,000	Debit	£225
C	Credit	£970	Debit	£235
D	Credit	£1,000	Debit	£235

Question 2

S Ltd has extracted the following details from the standard cost card of one of its products:

Direct labour	4.5 hours @ £6.40 per hour

During March, S Ltd produced 2,300 units of the product and incurred direct wages costs of £64,150. The actual hours worked were 11,700.

The direct labour rate and efficiency variances were:

	Rate £	Efficiency £
A	2,090 F	7,402 A
B	2,090 F	8,640 A
C	10,730 F	7,402 A
D	10,730 F	8,640 A

Question 3

The following details have been extracted from a standard cost card of X plc:

PRODUCT X
Direct labour: 4 hours @ £5.40 per hour

During October, the budgeted production was 5,000 units of product X and the actual production was 4,650 units of product X. Actual hours worked were 19,100 and the actual direct labour cost amounted to £98,350.

The labour variances reported were:

	Rate £	Efficiency £
A	9,650 F	4,860 F
B	9,650 F	2,700 A
C	4,790 F	2,575 A
D	4,790 F	2,700 A

Question 4

In a period, 11,280 kilograms of material were used at a total standard cost of £46,248. The material usage variance was £492 adverse.

The standard allowed weight of material for the period was ⬚ kg.

Question 5

During a period 17,500 labour hours were worked at a standard cost of £6.50 per hour. The labour efficiency variance was £7,800 favourable.

The number of standard hours produced was ⬚ .

Question 6

T plc uses a standard costing system, with its material stock account being maintained at standard cost. The following details have been extracted from the standard cost card in respect of direct materials:

8 kg @ £0.80/kg = £6.40 per unit

Budgeted production in April was 850 units.

The following details relate to actual materials purchased and issued to production during April when actual production was 870 units:

Materials purchased	8,200 kg costing £6,888
Materials issued to production	7,150 kg

Which of the following correctly states the material price and usage variance to be reported?

	Price	Usage
A	£286 (A)	£152 (A)
B	£286 (A)	£280 (A)
C	£286 (A)	£294 (A)
D	£328 (A)	£152 (A)

For the answers to these questions, see the 'Answers' section at the end of the book.

Practice question

Company M

The following standard costs apply in Company M that manufactures a single product:

Standard weight of material to produce one unit	12 kg
Standard price per kg	£9
Standard hours to produce one unit	10
Standard rate per hour	£4

Actual production and costs for one accounting period were:

Material used	3,770 kg
Material cost	£35,815
Hours worked	2,755
Wages paid	£11,571

The actual output was 290 units.

You are required:

to calculate relevant material and labour cost variances, and present these in a format suitable for presentation to the management of the company.

For the answer to this question, see the 'Answers' section at the end of the book.

Feedback to activities

Activity 1

	£
Standard direct material cost of 600 units:	
£5 × 600	3,000
Actual direct material cost	3,200
Direct material total cost variance – Adverse	200

Activity 2

	£
Standard cost of 2,300 litres:	
2,300 litres × £1.30/litre	2,990
Actual cost of 2,300 litres	3,128
Direct material price variance – Adverse	138

Activity 3

Standard usage of 500 units of K:

500 × 0.4 tonnes	200 tonnes
Actual usage	223 tonnes
Excess usage	23 tonnes

Valued at standard price of £30/tonne:

Direct material usage variance is:

23 tonnes × £30/tonne = £690 Adverse

	£
Standard price of 223 tonnes (× £30)	6,690
Actual price of 223 tonnes	6,913
Direct material price variance – Adverse	223

Activity 4

	£
Standard direct labour cost of 450 units:	
£7 × 450	3,150
Actual direct labour cost	3,450
Direct labour total cost variance – Adverse	300

Activity 5

	£
Expected cost of actual hours worked:	
1,000 hours × £4/hr	4,000
Actual wage cost	4,200
Direct labour rate variance – Adverse	200
Expected hours for actual production:	
700 units × 1.50 hours/unit	1,050
Actual hours	1,000
A saving (in hours) of	50

These are valued at the standard wage rate/hour.

Direct labour efficiency variance is:

50 hours × £4/hour = £200 Favourable.

Chapter 16

VARIANCE ANALYSIS: OVERHEADS

Syllabus content

- Variances: variable overhead: total, expenditure and efficiency; fixed overhead: total, expenditure and volume (absorption costing); fixed overhead; expenditure (marginal costing).

We continue our studies of variances, looking now at overheads, both fixed and variable.

Contents

1 Overhead variances

1.1 Introduction

In this chapter you will be learning about the analysis of overhead variances. Your syllabus requires you to be able to analyse overhead variances in an absorption costing system and in a marginal costing system.

You need to be able to calculate separate variances for variable overheads and fixed overheads. It should not surprise you that the analysis of variances for variable overhead is unaffected by whether we are using an absorption costing system or a marginal costing system. Both systems apply the same accounting treatment to variable overheads.

You will be seeing that the analysis of fixed overhead variances does differ between the two systems. This is because marginal costing treats fixed overheads as a period cost, whereas absorption costing absorbs fixed production overhead into unit production costs. This differing accounting treatment means that different fixed production overhead variances arise in the two systems.

The analysis of overhead variances requires a sound understanding of the concept of the standard hour. If you have forgotten what this is, return now and reread the relevant section of chapter 14.

2 Variable overhead variances

2.1 Introduction

These variances are very similar to those for material and labour because, like these direct costs, the variable overhead cost also changes when activity changes.

The most common examination question assumes that variable overhead costs vary with labour hours worked. This results in the calculation of two variable overhead variances that are illustrated by the following example.

Example

K Limited has a budgeted variable overhead cost for August of £84,000. Budgeted production is 20,000 units of its finished product and direct labour hours are expected to be 40,000 hours.

During August the actual production was 20,500 units. Actual hours worked were 41,600 hours and the variable overhead cost incurred amounted to £86,700.

2.2 Variable overhead total variance

In order to calculate the total variance it is necessary to calculate the standard variable overhead cost for the actual production achieved.

The budgeted variable overhead cost per hour is calculated by:

$$\frac{\text{Budgeted cost}}{\text{Budgeted hours}} = \frac{£84,000}{40,000} = £2.10 \text{ per hour}$$

Actual production was 20,500 units that is the equivalent of 41,000 standard hours. (According to the budget each unit should require 2 hours, i.e. 40,000 hours/20,000 units.)

	£
The standard cost of 41,000 hours at £2.10 per hour is	86,100
Actual cost	86,700
Variance	600 (A)

The variance is adverse because the actual cost exceeded the standard cost and therefore profits would be lower than expected.

2.3 Variable overhead expenditure variance

This variance measures the effect on profit of the actual variable overhead cost per hour differing from the standard hourly cost.

The actual hours worked were 41,600.

	£
If these had cost £2.10/hour as expected the cost would have been	87,360
This is the standard cost of actual hours.	
The actual cost was	86,700
Variance	660 (F)

This results in a favourable expenditure variance of £660.

2.4 Variable overhead efficiency variance

This variance measures the effect on profit of the actual hours worked differing from the standard hours produced.

Standard hours produced	41,000
Actual hours worked	41,600
Difference	600

This difference in hours is valued at the standard variable overhead cost/hour:

$600 \times £2.10 = £1,260$ (A).

The variance is adverse because actual hours exceeded standard hours.

2.5 Proof of total variance

Note that the sum of these sub-variances, representing expenditure and efficiency equals the total variance:

expenditure variance + efficiency variance = total variance

£660 favourable + £1,260 adverse = £600 adverse

3 Fixed overhead variances

3.1 Introduction

These variances show the effect on profit of differences between actual and expected fixed overhead costs. By definition these costs do not change when there is a change in the level of activity, consequently many of the variances are calculated based upon budgets; however, the effect on profit depends upon whether a marginal or absorption costing system is being used. In the variance calculations that follow firstly an absorption costing system is assumed. These are then compared with the variances that would arise if a marginal costing system were used.

KEY POINT

In an absorption costing system, the fixed overhead total variance is equal to the under or over absorbed fixed production overhead.

3.2 Fixed overhead total variance

Assuming an absorption costing system, this is the effect on profit of there being a difference between the actual cost incurred and the amount absorbed by the use of the absorption rate based on budgeted costs and activity. Therefore the fixed overhead total variance is equal to the under or over absorbed fixed production overhead. This is illustrated by the following example.

Example

Q Limited has completed its budget for October, the following data have been extracted:

Budgeted fixed overhead cost	£100,000
Budgeted production	20,000 units
Budgeted machine hours	25,000

A machine hour absorption rate is used.

The actual fixed overhead cost incurred was £98,500. Actual production was 20,300 units using 25,700 machine hours.

Solution

The absorption rate per machine hour (based upon the budget) is given by:

$$\frac{\text{Budgeted fixed overhead cost}}{\text{Budgeted machine hours}}$$

$$= \frac{£100,000}{25,000} = £4 \text{ per machine hour}$$

This would be used to determine the fixed overhead cost absorbed (i.e. attributed to the actual production achieved).

In a standard costing system the actual production achieved is measured in standard hours, in this case standard machine hours.

According to the budget 20,000 units should require 25,000 machine hours, this is the equivalent of 1.25 machine hours per unit (25,000/20,000).

Thus the actual production of 20,300 units is equivalent to

$20,300 \times 1.25 = 25,375$ standard machine hours.

The amount absorbed is therefore:

25,375 standard machine hours $\times$ £4/machine hour

$= £101,500$

This is the standard cost of the actual production (using absorption costing). It is compared with the actual cost to find the total variance:

	£
Standard cost	101,500
Actual cost	98,500
Variance	3,000 (F)

Since the actual cost is less than the standard cost it is a favourable variance.

3.3 Over/under-absorptions and the total variance

The comparison of actual fixed overhead cost incurred and the amount of fixed overhead cost absorbed is not new, it was used in your earlier studies to determine the extent of any under/over-absorption. Often this is done using a fixed production overhead control account that is shown below based upon the above figures:

Fixed production overhead control a/c

	£		£
Creditors	98,500	Work in progress	101,500
P & L (over absorption)	3,000		
	101,500		101,500

You should note that the over absorption is equal to the total variance.

Activity 1

P has the following data concerning its fixed production overheads:

Budget cost	£44,000
Budget production	8,000 units
Budget labour hours	16,000
Actual cost	£47,500
Actual production	8,450 units
Actual labour hours	16,600

Calculate the fixed overhead total variance assuming an absorption system based upon labour hours.

Feedback to this activity is at the end of the chapter.

3.4 Analysing the total variance

The total variance can be analysed into the causes known as expenditure and volume. The example we used earlier (reproduced below) will be used to show this.

Example

Q Limited has completed its budget for October, the following data have been extracted:

Budgeted fixed overhead cost	£100,000
Budgeted production	20,000 units
Budgeted machine hours	25,000

A machine hour absorption rate is used (calculated in 3.2 at £4 per machine hour).

The actual fixed overhead cost incurred was £98,500. Actual production was 20,300 (standard hours 25,375) units using 25,700 machine hours.

3.5 Fixed overhead expenditure variance

This variance shows the effect on profit of the actual fixed overhead expenditure differing from the budgeted value:

	£
Budgeted expenditure	100,000
Actual expenditure	98,500
Variance	1,500 (F)

The variance is favourable because the actual expenditure is less than that budgeted.

3.6 Fixed overhead volume variance

This variance measures the difference between the amount actually absorbed based upon actual production (in standard hours) compared to the amount expected to be absorbed based upon budgeted production (in standard hours).

Budgeted production (standard machine hours)	25,000
Actual production (standard machine hours)	25,375
Difference	375

This difference of 375 standard machine hours is valued at the absorption rate of £4/hr:

375 hours × £4/hr = £1,500 (F).

This variance is favourable because the actual output exceeded the expected output. Since the cost is fixed, the actual cost/unit is lowered by making greater production and profits will therefore increase or, looking at it another way, production has been overcharged by £1,500 and this will have to be credited back by a favourable variance.

3.7 The total variance and the sub-variances

Note that the sum of the fixed overhead expenditure and volume variances equals the fixed overhead total variance:

expenditure variance + volume variance = total variance

£1,500 (F) + £1,500 (F) = £3,000 (F).

Activity 2

Analyse the total variance you calculated in the previous activity into the fixed overhead expenditure and volume variances.

Feedback to this activity is at the end of the chapter.

KEY POINT

Under marginal costing the total fixed production overhead variance will always equal the fixed production overhead expenditure variance that is calculated in the same way as for absorption costing systems.

3.8 Fixed overhead variances and marginal costing

As was stated earlier, marginal costing does not relate fixed production overhead costs to cost units. The amount shown in the profit and loss account is the cost incurred. Therefore there can be no under or over absorption due to volume changes and the fixed overhead volume variance does not arise in a marginal costing system.

Since the cost is a fixed cost it is not expected to change when activity changes thus the expected cost of any level of production is always the budgeted cost.

The purpose of variance analysis is to calculate the effect on profit of actual performance differing from that expected, consequently, under marginal costing this will be the difference between the actual and budgeted expenditure.

Thus under marginal costing the total fixed production overhead variance will always equal the fixed production overhead expenditure variance which is calculated in the same way as for absorption costing systems.

4 Non-production overheads

4.1 Introduction

Since the purpose of variance analysis is to show the effect on profit of actual results differing from those expected, it is also necessary to compare the costs of non-production overheads such as selling, marketing and administration.

4.2 Non-production overhead variances

These costs are not related to the cost unit (even in an absorption costing system) so the calculation of variances for these items is exactly the same as that for fixed production overheads in a marginal costing system.

In other words the only variance is expenditure that is simply the difference between actual and budgeted expenditure. It is usual for separate variances to be calculated for each function (i.e. selling, marketing, administration).

Summary

This chapter has continued your studies of variance analysis, looking at total variable and fixed production overhead variances, which can be sub-analysed as follows:

Variable overheads	– expenditure variance
	– efficiency variance
Fixed overheads	– expenditure variance
	– volume variance (absorption costing only).

Whilst the variable overhead variances are very similar to the other variable cost variances already studied, the fixed overhead variance is approached from a different angle, due to its nature.

By the time you have finished this chapter you should be able to:

* calculate and interpret variances for variable overheads and fixed overheads.

Self-test questions

Variable overhead variances

1 What does an adverse variable overhead total variance indicate? (2.2)

2 What does the variable overhead efficiency variance reflect? (2.4)

Fixed overhead variances

3 What is the difference between absorption and marginal costing, and how does this affect fixed overhead variance computations? (3.8)

4 How is the fixed overhead volume variance calculated? (3.6)

Exam-type questions

Question 1

The following details relate to product T, which has a selling price of £44.00:

	£/unit
Direct materials	15.00
Direct labour (3 hours)	12.00
Variable overhead	6.00
Fixed overhead	4.00
	37.00

During April, the actual production of T was 800 units, which was 100 units fewer than budgeted. The budget shows an annual production target of 10,800, with fixed costs accruing at a constant rate throughout the year. Actual overhead expenditure totalled £8,500 for April.

The overhead variances for April were:

	Expenditure £	*Volume* £
A	367 A	1,000 A
B	100 A	1,000 A
C	367 A	400 A
D	100 A	400 A

Question 2

F Ltd has the following budget and actual data:

Budget fixed overhead cost	£100,000
Budget production (units)	20,000
Actual fixed overhead cost	£110,000
Actual production (units)	19,500

The fixed overhead volume variance is £ [　　　　　] adverse

The following data relate to questions 3 and 4 below

H Limited operates a standard costing system for its only product. The standard cost card includes:

Fixed overhead:　　　4 hours @ £10 per hour　　　£40.00

Fixed overheads are absorbed on the basis of labour hours. Fixed overhead costs are budgeted at £240,000 per annum and are expected to be incurred in equal amounts in each of the twelve accounting periods during the year.

Production is budgeted to be at an equal number of units in each accounting period.

Actual production during period 6 was 450 units, with actual fixed overhead costs incurred being £19,600 and actual hours worked being 1,970.

Question 3

The fixed overhead expenditure variance for period 6 was:

A　£4,400 (F)

B　£400　(F)

C　£400 (A)

D　£4,400 (A)

Question 4

The fixed overhead volume variance for period 6 was:

A　£300 (A)

B　£1,200 (A)

C　£1,700 (A)

D　£2,000 (A)

Question 5

A company manufactures special electrical equipment. The company employs a standard costing system with separate standards established for each product.

A special transformer is manufactured in the transformer department. Production volume is measured by direct labour hours in this department, and a flexible budget system is used to plan and control departmental overheads.

Standard costs for the special transformer are determined annually. The standard cost of a transformer is shown below:

Direct materials			£
Iron	5 sheets	@ £2	10
Copper	3 spools	@ £3	9
Direct labour	4 hours	@ £7	28
Variable overhead	4 hours	@ £3	12
Fixed overhead	4 hours	@ £2	8
Total			67

Overhead rates were based upon normal and expected monthly capacity, both of which were 4,000 direct labour hours. The variable overhead costs are expected to vary with the number of direct labour hours actually used.

During the month 800 transformers were produced.

The following costs were incurred in the month:

Direct materials

Type	*Quantity purchased*	*Used*
Iron	5,000 sheets @ £2.00 per sheet	3,900 sheets
Copper	2,200 spools @ £3.10 per spool	2,600 spools

Direct labour

    2,000 hours @ £7.00
    1,400 hours @ £7.20

Overheads

    Variable overheads   £10,000
    Fixed overheads   £8,800

(a)   The total material usage variance is £ ⬚ adverse.

(b)   The labour rate variance is £ ⬚ adverse.

(c)   The variable overhead expenditure variance is:

    A   £200 F

    B   £400 A

    C   £600 A

    D   £1,600 A

(d)   The expenditure variance for fixed overhead is:

    A   £2,400 A

    B   Nil

    C   £800 A

    D   £1,000 F

(e)   The fixed overhead volume variance is £ ⬚ adverse.

For the answers to these questions, see the 'Answers' section at the end of the book.

Practice question

Department 7

Shown below is the previous month's overhead expenditure and activity, both budget and actual, for department 7 in a manufacturing company:

	Month's budget	*Month's actual*
Activity:		
Standard hours	8,000	8,400
	£	£
Fixed overheads:		
Salaries	6,750	6,400
Maintenance	3,250	3,315
Variable overheads:		
Power	17,600	20,140
Consumable materials	6,000	5,960
Indirect labour	4,400	4,480
Total overheads	38,000	40,295

The budgeted overheads shown above are based upon the anticipated activity of 8,000 standard hours and it should be assumed that the department's budgeted overhead expenditure and activity occur evenly throughout the year. Variable overheads vary with standard hours produced.

You are required:

(a)   to calculate the following variances incurred by the department during the previous month:

   (i)   fixed overhead volume variance

   (ii)   fixed overhead expenditure variance

   (iii) variable overhead expenditure variance.

(b)   to draft a suitable operating statement which will assist management in controlling the department's overheads.

For the answer to this question, see the 'Answers' section at the end of the book.

Feedback to activities

Activity 1

$$\text{Absorption rate} = \frac{\text{Budgeted cost}}{\text{Budgeted hours}} = \frac{£44,000}{16,000} = £2.75 \text{ per standard labour hour}$$

$$\text{Actual output in standard hours} = 8,450 \times \frac{16,000}{8,000} = \qquad 16,900$$

Amount absorbed = 16,900 × £2.75 =	£46,475
Actual cost =	£47,500
Variance	£ 1,025 (A)

Activity 2

Fixed overhead expenditure variance:

	£
Budget cost	44,000
Actual cost	47,500
	3,500 (A)

Fixed overhead volume variance:

Budget production (labour hours)	16,000
Actual production (standard hours)	16,900
	900

900 hours × £2.75 = £2,475 (F)

Proof of total:

£3,500 (A) + £2,475 (F) = £1,025 (A)

Chapter 17

SALES VARIANCE ANALYSIS AND PROFIT RECONCILIATIONS

Syllabus content

- Variances: sales: total sales margin variance.

In this final chapter on variance analysis, we move away from costs and first look at sales variances.

We are then in a position to see how the variances may be used to reconcile budgeted results to actual results, in the form of a report that management can use as a basis for operational control.

Finally, we look at possible causes of all the variances we have considered in the last three chapters – the examiner requires you to not only be able to calculate variances, but also to interpret them. This may include suggestions as to their cause.

Contents

1   Total sales margin variance

2   Reconciliation of budget and actual results

3   Causes of variances

1 Total sales margin variance

1.1 Introduction

The purpose of calculating a sales variance is to show its effect when a comparison is made between budget and actual profit. Paper C2 syllabus requires a knowledge of only one sales variance: the total sales margin variance.

The cost variances that you have learned to calculate in the last two chapters will have eliminated all of the differences due to variations between actual and standard cost. This means that the calculation of the sales margin variance is based on standard unit costs.

The total sales margin variance measures the total profit difference caused by the following two factors combined.

- The actual selling price being different to standard

- The actual sales volume being different to budget

1.2 Sales margin variance – absorption costing

In an absorption costing system the sales margin variance is calculated by reference to the standard profit per unit, after deduction of absorbed fixed production overheads.

Example

D Limited manufactures and sells a single product for which the following standard data are available.

	£ per unit	£ per unit
Selling price		86
Variable cost	21	
Fixed cost	15	36
Profit		50

Budgeted sales volume for the latest period was 480 units.

Actual sales volume was 420 units, earning a sales revenue of £37,380.

The total sales margin variance is calculated as follows.

		£
Actual margin earned, based on standard unit costs:		
actual sales revenue		37,380
standard cost of actual sales volume	(420 units × £36)	15,120
		22,260
Budgeted margin (480 units × £50)		24,000
Total sales margin variance		1,740 adverse

The variance is adverse because the actual margin earned, at standard cost, was lower than budgeted.

We can see from the example data that the total variance is caused by a combination of two factors.

- The actual selling price was higher than standard (£37,380/420 = £89 compared with a standard selling price of £86 per unit). This would result in a favourable variance

- The sales volume was lower than budgeted (420 units compared with a budget of 480 units). This resulted in an adverse variance which outweighed the favourable impact of the higher selling price

Activity 1

Budgeted sales	500 units
Actual sales	480 units
Budgeted selling price	£100
Actual selling price	£110
Standard variable cost	£50/unit
Budgeted fixed cost	£15/unit

Calculate the total sales margin variance in an absorption costing system.

Feedback to this activity is at the end of the chapter.

The purpose of calculating variances is to identify the different effects of each item of cost/income on profit compared to the expected profit. These variances are summarised in a reconciliation statement.

1.3 Sales margin variance – marginal costing

The sales margin variance under a marginal costing system is calculated in the same way as with an absorption costing system, but instead of the budgeted profit margin the budgeted contribution is used.

Using the data from the previous example the marginal costing sales margin variance would be calculated as follows.

	£
Actual contribution earned, based on standard unit variable costs:	
actual sales revenue	37,380
std variable cost of actual sales volume (420 units × £21)	8,820
	28,560
Budgeted contribution (480 units × £65)	31,200
Total sales contribution variance	2,640

Activity 2

Use the data from activity 1 to calculate the sales margin (contribution) variance in a marginal costing system.

Feedback to this activity is at the end of the chapter.

2 Reconciliation of budget and actual results

2.1 Introduction

The purpose of calculating variances is to identify the different effects of each item of cost/income on profit compared to the expected profit. These variances are summarised in a reconciliation statement.

2.2 The reconciliation statement – absorption costing

The example that follows shows how such a statement reconciles the budget and actual profit of a period, based on absorption costing.

The statement commences with the budgeted profit that is based upon budgeted cost and activity levels.

This is then adjusted by all of the variances to arrive at the actual profit.

Example

Chapel Ltd manufactures a chemical protective called Rustnot. The following standard costs apply for the production of 100 cylinders:

		£
Materials	500 kgs @ 80p per kg	400
Labour	20 hours @ £1.50 per hour	30
Fixed overheads	20 hours @ £1.00 per hour	20
		450

The monthly production/sales budget is 10,000 cylinders. Selling price = £6 per cylinder.

For the month of November the following actual production and sales information is available:

Produced/sold		10,600 cylinders
Sales value		£63,000
Material purchased and used	53,200 kgs	£42,500
Labour	2,040 hours	£3,100
Fixed overheads		£2,200

You are required to prepare an operating statement for November detailing all the variances.

Solution

Operating statement for November

	Adv. £	Fav. £	£
Budgeted profit (10,000 cylinders) (W(a))			15,000
Total sales margin variance (W(f))			300
Less: Cost variances (W(g) – (i)):			
Material price (g)		60	
Wages rate (h)	40		
Fixed overhead expenditure (i)	200		
Material usage (g)	160		
Labour efficiency (h)		120	
Fixed overhead volume (i)		120	
	400	300	
			100
Actual profit (W(b))			15,200

Workings

		£	£
(a)	**Budgeted profit**		
	10,000 cylinders @ £1.50		15,000

		£	£
(b)	**Actual profit**		
	Sales		63,000
	Less: Materials	42,500	
	Labour	3,100	
	Fixed overheads	2,200	
			47,800
			15,200

(d) **Standard hours**

10,600 cylinders × 0.2 hours = 2,120 hours

(e) **Budgeted hours**

10,000 × 0.2 = 2,000 hours

Variances

(f) **Total sales margin variance**

	£	
Actual margin earned, based on standard unit costs:		
actual sales revenue	63,000	
standard cost of actual sales volume	47,700	
	15,300	
Budgeted margin	15,300	
Total sales margin variance	15,000	
	300	favourable

(g) **Raw materials**

The standard price of the raw material is £0.80 per kg. If the actual quantity of 53,200 kg had been bought at the standard price this would have been:

53,200 kg × £0.80/kg = £42,560.

The actual cost was £42,500. This is a price saving, i.e. a favourable price variance of £60.

Each 100 cylinders should use 500 kgs of material. Therefore the 10,600 cylinders produced should use:

10,600 × 500 kg/100 = 53,000 kgs

The actual usage was 53,200 kgs. These additional 200 kgs of material have a value (using standard prices) of:

200 kgs × £0.80 = £160.

This is an adverse material usage variance.

(h) **Labour**

The standard labour rate is £1.50 per hour. The actual labour hours were 2,040 hours, so if they had been paid at the standard rate per hour, the wage cost would have been:

2,040 × £1.50 = £3,060.

The actual wage cost was £3,100. This extra £40 is the adverse wage rate variance.

Each 100 cylinders should take 20 hours to produce. The actual production was 10,600 cylinders so these should have taken:

10,600 × 20/100 = 2,120 hours.

Actual hours were 2,040 hours, a saving of 80 hours. These hours (valued at the standard rate) are worth:

80 × £1.50 = £120.

This is a favourable labour efficiency.

(i) **Fixed overheads**

The standard fixed overhead cost is £20 per 100 cylinders. Monthly production is budgeted at 10,000 cylinders. Therefore the budgeted fixed overhead cost is:

10,000 × £20/100 = £2,000.

The actual cost was £2,200. The extra cost of £200 is an adverse fixed overhead expenditure variance.

But the actual production was 10,600 cylinders, 600 more than budgeted. This extra volume of 600 units (valued at the standard absorption rate of £20/100 units) is:

600 × £20/100 = £120

This is a favourable fixed overhead volume variance.

2.3 Marginal costing reconciliation

The above presentation was based on absorption costing; on a marginal costing basis it would appear as:

			£
Budgeted contribution (10,000 × £(6-4.30))			17,000
Total sales contribution variance (j)			1,020
			———
			17,420
Less: Variable cost variances (W(g)–(i)):	*Adv*	*Fav*	
	£	£	
Material price (g)		60	
Wages rate (h)	40		
Material usage (g)	160		
Labour efficiency (h)		120	
	———	———	
	200	180	
	———	———	
			20
			———
Actual profit (W(b))			17,400
Fixed overhead: budget	2,000		
expenditure variance	200		
	———		
			2,200
			———
Actual profit			15,200
			———

Workings

(a) to (i) are as in the previous example.

(j)

	£
Actual margin earned, based on standard unit variable costs:	
actual sales revenue	63,000
std variable cost of actual sales volume (10,600 × £4.30)	45,580
Budgeted contribution	17,420
Total sales contribution variance	17,000
	420 favourable

3 Causes of variances

3.1 Introduction

The calculation of variances is only the first stage. Management wants information to plan and control operations. It is not sufficient to know that a variance has arisen: we must try to establish why. The figures themselves do not provide the answers, but they point to some of the questions that should be asked.

3.2 Possible causes of cost variances

Possible causes of the individual cost variances are now discussed. In addition to the causes suggested, any of the variances could be due to poor initial standard setting.

(a) **Material price variance**

Possible causes:

- different source of supply

- unexpected general price increase

- alteration in quantity discounts

- substitution of a different grade of material

- standard set at mid-year price so one would expect a favourable price variance in the early months and an adverse variance in the later months of the year.

(b) **Material usage variance**

Possible causes:

- higher/lower incidence of scrap

- alteration to product design

- substitution of a different grade of material.

(c) **Labour rate variance**

Possible causes:

- unexpected national wage award

- overtime/bonus payments different from plan

- substitution of a different grade of labour.

(d) **Labour efficiency variance**

Possible causes:

- improvement in methods or working conditions

- variations in unavoidable idle time

- introduction of incentive scheme

- substitution of a different grade of labour.

(e) **Variable overhead variance**

Possible causes:

- unexpected price changes for overhead items

- labour efficiency variances, (see above).

(f) **Fixed overhead expenditure variance**

Possible causes:

- changes in prices relating to fixed overhead items, e.g. rent increase

- seasonal effects, e.g. heat/light in winter. (This arises where the annual budget is divided into four equal quarters of thirteen equal four-weekly periods without allowances for seasonal factors. Over a whole year the seasonal effects would cancel out.)

(g) **Fixed overhead volume**

Possible causes:

- change in production volume due to change in demand or alterations to stockholding policy

- changes in productivity of labour or machinery

- production lost through strikes, etc.

3.3 Interdependence of variances

The cause of a particular variance may affect another variance in a corresponding or opposite way.

- If supplies of a specified material are not available, this may lead to a favourable price variance (cheaper material used), an adverse usage variance (cheaper material caused more wastage), an adverse fixed overhead volume variance (production delayed while material was unavailable) and an adverse sales margin variance (unable to meet demand due to production difficulties).

- A new improved machine becomes available which causes an adverse fixed overhead expenditure variance (because this machine is more expensive and depreciation is higher) offset by favourable wages efficiency and fixed overhead volume variances (higher productivity).

- Workers trying to improve productivity (favourable labour efficiency variance) might become careless and waste more material (adverse material usage variance).

Summary

This chapter concludes your studies of variance analysis. Our aim is to be able to reconcile budgeted results to actual results, and present the variances in a format that is useful to managers.

We also considered possible causes of variances, and the way in which they can be interdependent.

By the time you have finished this chapter you should be able to:

- calculate and interpret variances for sales

- prepare a report reconciling budget gross profit/contribution with actual profit.

Self-test questions

Sales variances

1   How is the sales margin variance calculated in an absorption costing system? (1.2)

2   How is the sales margin variance calculated under a marginal costing system? (1.3)

Reconciliation of budget and actual results

3   How is a profit/contribution reconciliation statement laid out? (2.2)

Causes of variances

4   Give two possible causes of a materials price variance. (3.2)

5   Give two possible causes of a labour efficiency variance. (3.2)

6   Give two possible causes of a fixed overhead volume variance. (3.2)

Exam-type questions

Question 1

J Ltd operates a standard cost accounting system. The following information has been extracted from its standard cost card and budgets:

Budgeted sales volume	5,000 units
Budgeted selling price	£10.00 per unit
Standard variable cost	£5.60 per unit
Standard total cost	£7.50 per unit

If it used a standard marginal cost accounting system and its actual sales were 4,500 units at a selling price of £12.00, its sales margin (contribution) variance would be

£ [   ]   favourable.

Question 2

P Ltd has the following data relating to its budgeted sales for October:

Budgeted sales	£100,000.00
Budgeted selling price per unit	£8.00
Budgeted contribution per unit	£4.00
Budgeted profit per unit	£2.50

During October, actual sales were 11,000 units for a sales revenue of £99,000.

P Ltd uses an absorption costing system.

The sales margin variance reported for October was £ ⬚ .

The variance was:

adverse ☐

favourable ☐

(tick appropriate box)

Question 3

The following data are available for Scott's production in September:

Budget	
Selling price per unit	£120
Variable cost per unit	£80
Production and sales	18,000 units

Actual for September	
Sales	21,000 units
Fixed costs	£580,000
Fixed costs expenditure variance	£20,000 (F)
Variable cost per unit	£60

The budgeted profit for September was £ ⬚ .

For the answers to these questions, see the 'Answers' section at the end of the book.

Practice question

Gunge

The standard cost per gallon of Gunge, the only product manufactured by Chemit plc, is shown below:

	£
Direct material (4kg @ £3/kg)	12
Direct labour (5 hours @ £4/hour)	20
Variable overhead	5
Fixed overhead	15
Standard cost per gallon	52

The standard selling price of Gunge is £60/gallon and the budgeted quantity to be produced and sold in each period is 10,000 gallons. It may be assumed that variable overheads vary directly with the number of gallons produced.

The actual results achieved during period 4 were:

	£	£
Sales (9,500 gallons)		588,500
Cost of sales:		
Direct material (37,000 kg)	120,000	
Direct labour (49,000 hours)	200,000	
Variable overhead	47,000	
Fixed overhead	145,000	
		512,000
Profit		76,500

There were no stocks of work-in-progress or finished goods at the beginning or end of the period.

You are required:

(a)   to calculate the relevant manufacturing cost variances for period 4

(b)   to calculate the sales margin variance for period 4, and prepare a statement reconciling the budgeted and the actual profit for the period.

For the answer to this question, see the 'Answers' section at the end of the book.

Feedback to activities

Activity 1

	£
Actual margin earned, based on standard unit costs:	
actual sales revenue (480 units × £110)	52,800
standard cost of actual sales volume (480 units × £65)	31,200
	21,600
Budgeted margin (500 units × £(100 − 65))	17,500
Total sales margin variance	4,100 (F)

Activity 2

	£
Actual contribution earned, based on standard unit variable costs:	
actual sales revenue	52,800
std variable cost of actual sales volume (480 units × £50)	24,000
	28,800
Budgeted contribution (500 units × £(100 − 50))	25,000
Total sales contribution variance	3,800 (F)

Chapter 18

JOB AND BATCH COSTING

Syllabus content

- Job, batch costing.

This chapter is the start of the costing and accounting systems part of the syllabus. Marginal and absorption costing are examples of such systems: we have covered these already. Here we start to look at the costing and accounting procedures for specific methods of business – manufacturing in batches, or via a series of processes, or carrying out specific jobs or contracts, or the provision of a service.

Job and batch costing are covered in this chapter, and contract, process and service costing in the following chapters.

Contents

1   Product costing methods

2   Job costing

3   Batch costing

1 Product costing methods

1.1 How are products produced?

So far, we have talked rather loosely about cost units being generated and costs being attributed to them to get a cost per unit. Here, we are going to look a little more closely at how this actually happens.

The production operations of most businesses can be categorised as either being related to specific orders or continuous operations, and have corresponding costing methods.

This covers process costing and service costing.

1.2 Costing methods

There are five costing methods to be considered in two categories:

- Specific order costing is the cost accounting method applicable where work consists of separately identifiable contracts, jobs or batches.

  The distinguishing features are:

  - work is separated as opposed to a continuous flow

  - work can be identified with a particular customer's order or contract.

- Continuous operation costing is applicable where goods or services result from a sequence of continuous or repetitive operations or processes.

Or, more briefly:

Specific order costing – job, batch and contract costing

Continuous operation costing – process and service costing

We will be covering each of these in the following chapters.

2 Job costing

2.1 Introduction to job costing

Job costing is a form of specific order costing in which costs are attributed to individual jobs. (CIMA, *Official Terminology*).

This method of costing is adopted when the factory issues an order to produce one cost unit for a customer. Jobbing firms are engaged in 'one-off' products of a specialist nature such as tools, machines, replacement parts, etc. The firm may meet a demand for products that need to be of a much higher standard than mass-produced equivalents or where the quantity required is so small that the planning and setting up involved for other firms would not be worthwhile.

Jobbing firms normally operate with a variety of machines in order to be able to tackle the majority of operations that will be required in the product. They will handle a wide range of work and are often used as subcontractors to larger firms which have to off-load work where they have not the resources required for particular products or operations. The jobbing firm, therefore, probably has only a small amount of work of a repetitive nature which means that production plans may be prepared for just a few weeks or months ahead, and have to be flexible to meet urgent orders.

Note that job costing can also be applied to services. For example a plumber will use job costing to determine the cost of each individual job.

2.2 Job cost sheet (or card)

The focal point of a job costing system is the cost sheet (or card). Each job will be given a unique job number and a separate sheet will be opened for each job, on which will be recorded:

- materials purchased specifically for the job (from GRNs or suppliers' invoices)

- materials drawn from stock (from requisitions)

- direct wages (from time sheet/job cards)

- direct expenses (from invoices, etc.).

JOB CARD										
Customer:	Green & Co Ltd				Job No:				342	
Description:	Transfer machine				Promised delivery date:				3.11.X1	
Date commenced:	25.9.X1				Actual delivery date:				13.11.X1	
Price quoted:	£2,400				Despatch note no:				7147	
	Materials Estimate £1,250		*Labour Estimate £100*			*Overhead Estimate £176*			*Other charges Estimate £25*	
Date **Ref**						*Hourly rate £11*				
20X1	*Cost £*	*Cum £*	*Hrs*	*Cost £*	*Cum £*	*Cost £*	*Cum £*	*Cost £*	*Cum £*	
b/f		1,200	17		110		187		13	
6 Nov MR 1714	182	1,382								
7 Nov Consultant's test fee								10	23	
8 Nov MR 1937	19	1,401								
9 Nov MRN 213	(26)	1,375								
10 Nov Labour analysis			5	28	138	55	242			

Summary	£	**Comments**
Materials	1,375	
Labour	138	
Overhead	242	
Other charges	23	
	1,778	
Invoice price (invoice number 7147 dated 12.12.X1)	2,400	
Profit	622	

When the job is finished, the job card gives the total direct cost, and overhead can be calculated and entered using one of the accepted methods. If the job is unfinished at the end of an accounting period the total cost recorded to date on the cost sheets will give the work-in-progress figure. The job cost can be compared with the estimate to analyse the difference between actual and estimated cost. Where the product contains a number of components it is advisable to check that the costs of all the components have been recorded.

Documentation in a job costing system

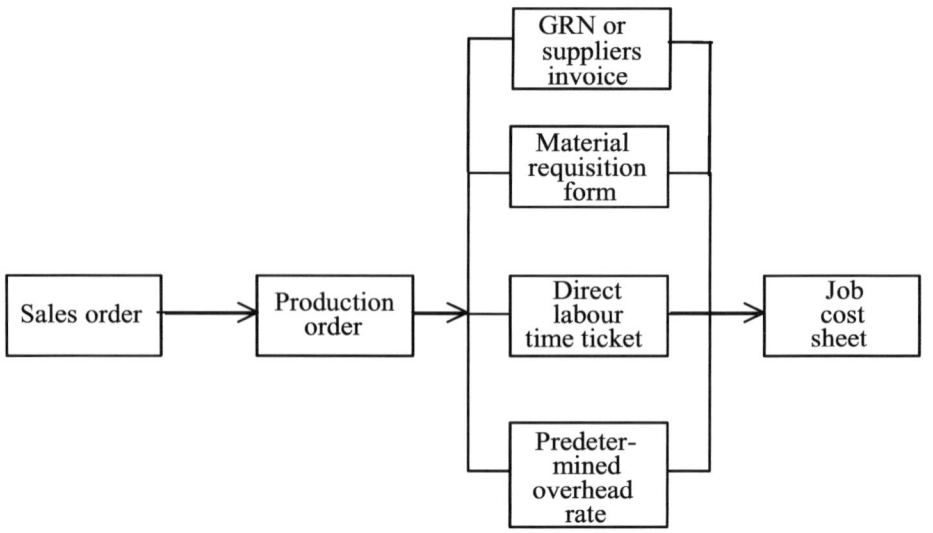

Example of a job cost

Jobbers Ltd undertakes jobbing engineering work. Among the requests for quotations received in December was one from A for a small machine to be manufactured according to the customer's drawings supplied. Jobbers Ltd prepared an estimate of the material and labour content based on the drawings, and amounts were added for overhead and profit. The estimate indicated a price of £900 and this price was quoted to, and accepted by, A.

The work on A's order was started in January on the authority of Production Order No. 1001 signed by the works manager and was completed in that month. The abstract of materials requisitions issued in January showed the following against Production Order No. 1001:

Materials requisition	£
D57	48
D61	24
D70	26
	—
Total	98
	—

Two operatives paid at £4.20 per hour each had been employed in separate cost centres on Production Order No. 1001 during January and their time sheets showed that each had worked for thirty hours on that order. The overhead rates for the cost centres in which the operatives are employed are in one centre £2.00 per direct labour hour and 100% on direct wages in the other. Administration and other overhead are recovered at the rate of 30% on production cost.

Required:

Prepare a statement showing the cost and profitability of the order from A.

Solution

**Statement of cost and profitability – production order number 1001
machine for A per customer's drawing**

	£	£	£
Selling price per estimate			900
Costs:			
Direct materials, per stores abstract		98	
Direct wages, 60 hours @ £4.20		252	
Prime cost		350	
Production overhead:			
30 hours @ £2.00	60		
100% of 30 hours @ £4.20	126		
		186	
Production cost		536	
Administration and other overhead,			
30% of production cost		161	
Total cost of sales			697
Net profit			203

Note: actual and estimated profit on the order would be compared and any
significant difference reported to management. The estimate should have been
compiled on the same lines as the actual cost in the above statement to assist in
locating the particular costs which were not as estimated.

2.3 Effect of inaccurate overhead absorption rates

The above illustration shows that selling prices can reflect estimates and that the
major uncertainty in estimating is calculation of an accurate figure for overhead
recovery. Inaccurate estimating can seriously harm the business because:

- if jobs are over-priced, customers will go elsewhere

- if jobs are under-priced, sales revenue will fail to cover costs and/or
  provide an adequate return.

2.4 Inaccurate estimate of volume

Predetermined overhead rates are based on a volume estimate. If actual volume
is significantly higher or lower than expected, then estimates, and consequently
selling prices, will be inaccurate.

Example

Company A's budget for the year is as follows:

	£
Prime costs	50,000
Overhead	30,000
	80,000
Profit (40% on cost)	32,000
Sales	112,000
Volume	3,000 labour hours

If volume were half budget, i.e. 1,500 hours, actual results would show:

	£
Prime costs (half budget)	25,000
Overhead absorbed	15,000 (1,500 hours $\times \dfrac{£30,000}{3,000}$)
	40,000
Profit (40% on cost)	16,000
Sales	56,000

Actual overhead incurred would not fall to half the budget, however, because of the fixed element. It may fall to, perhaps, £24,000 but job costs would reflect overhead at the predetermined rate of £10 per hour, leaving £9,000 under-absorbed.

Actual profit would therefore be £(16,000 − 9,000) = £7,000.

2.5 Inaccurate absorption basis

Estimated costs should reflect overhead in relation to the way it is incurred, so that selling prices are competitive but profitable.

Example

Company B bases its estimates on the following formulae:

Total cost	=	Prime cost plus 40% for overhead
Selling price	=	Total cost plus 25% for profit

Estimates for two jobs show:

Item	Job X £	Job Y £
Direct materials	200	100
Direct wages @ £5 per hour	200	300
Prime cost	400	400
Overhead absorbed (40%)	160	160
Total cost	560	560
Profit (25%)	140	140
Selling price	700	700

Thus both jobs will be priced the same even though it would appear from the direct wages estimate that Job Y takes 50% more time to complete and therefore uses much more of the factory's resources.

Job X may be over-priced in relation to competitors whereas Job Y is under-priced and the business would lose its Job X customers and get more orders for Job Y.

Consider what would happen if 1,500 hours were available. The factory could produce only 10 of Job Y compared with 15 of Job X, with the resulting lower total contribution.

2.6 Insufficient analysis by cost centre

A similar effect could arise if overhead rates do not recognise use of more or less expensive resources.

Example

Company C uses a 'blanket' overhead rate calculated as follows:

	Overhead cost £	*Labour hours*
Cost centre Y	40,000	4,000
Cost centre Z	80,000	4,000
	120,000	8,000

$$\text{Absorption rate} \quad = \quad \frac{£120,000}{8,000}$$

$$= \quad £15 \text{ per labour hour}$$

Thus a job that takes one hour in Y will be charged the same amount for overhead as a job that takes an hour in Z even though the latter centre costs twice as much per hour to operate.

Once again, estimates would not reflect a realistic charge for the use of resources and over or under-pricing may result.

2.7 Treatment of costs as direct or indirect

Instances may arise when analyses for cost ascertainment can conflict with the analyses required for control.

Example

Jones is paid £6 per hour for a basic week of 40 hours. In one week he worked four hours overtime at time and a half and received £32 under a group bonus scheme. His time sheet for that week shows:

	Hours
Job A	20
Job B	10
Job C	8
Training	6
	44

Jones' gross wage may be allocated in two ways:

(a)   As an average direct wage per hour, i.e.:

	£
Basic 40 × £6	240
Overtime 4 × £9	36
Bonus	32
	308

$$\text{Hourly rate} = \frac{£308}{44 \text{ hours}}$$

$$= £7.00 \text{ per hour}$$

(b) Basic rate used for costing and overtime premium/bonus treated as indirect wages.

Different allocations would result as follows:

		Method (a) £		Method (b) £
Job A	20 × £7.00	140	20 × £6.00	120
Job B	10 × £7.00	70	10 × £6.00	60
Job C	8 × £7.00	56	8 × £6.00	48
		266		228
Overhead:				
Training	6 × £7.00	42	6 × £6.00	36
Overtime		–	4 × £3.00	12
Bonus		–		32
		308		308

Method (a) should give more accurate job costs but the total costs of overtime and bonus will be more difficult to identify for management information purposes.

Activity 1

Discuss how a company manufacturing products on a jobbing basis should deal with the following cost accounting problems.

(a) It employs a draughtsman from whose drawings templates are produced which are used in the production process. These drawings are only made against firm orders. Hitherto the salary and other costs of the draughtsman have been included in factory overhead and absorbed into the cost of the job as part of total factory overhead.

Discuss whether this method of dealing with the draughtsman's costs is satisfactory and suggest what alternative approach might be taken.

(b) The company is at present operating a day and evening shift. It now proposes a night shift whose average wage rate would involve a premium. This night shift would concentrate on one particular contract that would continue over a period of two to three years.

Discuss how the company should deal with the night shift premium in calculating the costs of its products.

(c) One of the major production cost centres involves a chemical process that is very complex. The time required to produce any particular quantity of output depends rather unpredictably on a wide range of factors, some of which are outside the control of the operator.

As a result, a subsidiary smaller machine to do 'touching up' work as and when products require it has been installed in that cost centre.

Discuss the case for treating the wages of the operator of the subsidiary machine as an overhead of the cost centre rather than as direct wages.

Feedback to this activity is at the end of the chapter.

2.8   Cost control

When production is related to a specification or to customers' orders, the costing system will be interlocked with estimating so that the estimate can be used as a standard to locate excessive usage of materials and time.

Control will be assisted by:

(a)   **Detailed production orders or job specifications** – These should be subject to serial number control. The production order is the authority to obtain or allocate specific resources in the form of materials, labour and machines.

(b)   **Excess material requisitions** – Additional requirements for material would be supplied only on presentation of a properly authorised document that would show the reason for the request.

(c)   **Route cards** – Each production order or job can be supported by route cards that specify the sequence of operations and the estimated time for each operation or stage. Actual time would be recorded and causes of excess time noted where appropriate.

(d)   **Regular reports** – The above documents will form the basis of a report to show the incidence of excess usage together with an analysis of main causes. The aim would be to prevent recurrence, where possible by appropriate action, e.g.:

- amendment of existing methods of estimating usages

- change of supplier

- increased labour training

- introduction of incentive payment to all grades of works labour

- improved system of preventive plant maintenance.

3   Batch costing

3.1   Introduction to batch costing

Batch costing is a form of specific order costing in which costs are attributed to batches of products. (CIMA *Official Terminology*).

Businesses that manufacture a variety of products, e.g. household electrical goods, to be held in stock prior to sale, will operate batch costing.

3.2   Collecting the costs of a batch

Batch costing is very similar to job costing. Each batch is a separately identifiable cost unit which is given a batch number in the same way that each job is given a job number.

Costs can then be identified against each batch number. For example materials requisitions will be coded to a batch number to ensure that the cost of materials used is charged to the correct batch.

When the batch is completed the unit cost of individual items in the batch is found by dividing the total batch cost by the number of items in the batch.

$$\text{Cost per unit in batch} = \frac{\text{total production cost of batch}}{\text{number of units in batch}}$$

Summary

This chapter has considered two of the specific order costing methods, job costing and batch costing. You should ensure you are clear when each would be used, but note that the costing principles applied to each are very similar.

By the time you have finished this chapter you should be able to:

- compare and contrast job, batch, contract and process costing systems

- prepare ledger accounts for job and batch costing systems.

Self-test questions

Product costing methods

1   In what circumstances will specific order costing be appropriate? (1.2)

Job costing

2   2   What information will be recorded on a job cost card? (2.2)

3   3   What are the potential problems arising from inaccurate absorption rates? (2.3)

Batch costing

4   4   What is batch costing? (3.1)

Exam-type questions

The following data are to be used for questions 1 and 2 below.

A firm uses job costing and recovers overheads on direct labour.

Three jobs were worked on during a period, the details of which were:

	Job 1 £	Job 2 £	Job 3 £
Opening work-in-progress	8,500	0	46,000
Material in period	17,150	29,025	0
Labour for period	12,500	23,000	4,500

The overheads for the period were exactly as budgeted, £140,000.

Question 1

Jobs 1 and 2 were the only incomplete jobs.

The value of closing work-in-progress was £ [   ]

Question 2

Job 3 was completed during the period and consisted of 2,400 identical circuit boards. The firm adds 50% to total production costs to arrive at a selling price.

The selling price of a circuit board (to the nearest penny) is £ [   ]

Question 3

Which of the following items are contained in a typical job cost? (Tick all that apply)

☐ Actual material cost

☐ Actual manufacturing overheads

☐ Absorbed manufacturing overheads

☐ Actual labour cost

The following data are to be used for questions 4 – 6.

A firm makes special assemblies to customers' orders and uses job costing. The data for a period are:

	Job number AA10 £	Job number BB15 £	Job number CC20 £
Opening WIP	26,800	42,790	0
Material added in period	17,275	0	18,500
Labour for period	14,500	3,500	24,600

The budgeted overheads for the period were £126,000.

Question 4

The overhead to be absorbed by job number CC20 for the period (to the nearest £)

is £ ☐ .

Question 5

Job number BB15 was completed and delivered during the period and the firm wishes to earn 33 $\frac{1}{3}$ % profit on sales.

The selling price of job number BB15 (to the nearest £) is £ ☐ .

Question 6

The approximate value of closing work-in-progress at the end of the period, to the nearest £, is £ ☐ .

For the answers to these questions, see the 'Answers' section at the end of the book.

Practice question

Job number 123

In order to identify the costs incurred in carrying out a range of work to customer specification in its factory, a company has a job costing system. This system identifies costs directly with a job where this is possible and reasonable. In addition, production overhead costs are absorbed into the cost of jobs at the end of each month, at an actual rate per direct labour hour for each of the two production departments.

One of the jobs carried out in the factory during the month just ended was Job No. 123. The following information has been collected relating specifically to this job:

(1) 400 kilos of Material Y were issued from stores to Department A.

(2) 76 direct labour hours were worked in Department A at a basic wage of £4.50 per hour. 6 of these hours were classified as overtime at a premium of 50%.

(3)   300 kilos of Material Z were issued from stores to Department B. Department B returned 35 kilos of Material Z to the storeroom being excess to requirements for the job.

(4)   110 direct labour hours were worked in Department B at a basic wage of £4.00 per hour. 30 of these hours were classified as overtime at a premium of 50%. All overtime worked in Department B in the month is a result of the request of a customer for early completion of another job that had been originally scheduled for completion in the month following.

Overhead costs incurred during the month on all jobs in the two production departments were as follows:

	Dept A £	Dept B £
Indirect labour, at basic wage rate	2,510	2,960
Overtime premium	450	60
Lubricants and cleaning compounds	520	680
Maintenance	720	510
Other	1,200	2,150

Total labour hours worked during the month were:

Department A   2,000 hours
Department B   2,800 hours

Materials are priced at the end of each month on a weighted average basis. Relevant information of material stock movements during the month, for materials Y and Z, is as follows:

	Material Y	Material Z
Opening stock	1,050 kilos (value £529.75)	6,970 kilos (value £9,946.50)
Purchases	600 kilos at £0.50 per kilo	16,000 kilos at £1.46 per kilo
	500 kilos at £0.50 per kilo	
	400 kilos at £0.52 per kilo	

You are required:

(a)   to prepare a list of the costs that should be assigned to Job No. 123. Provide an explanation of your treatment of each item.

(b)   to discuss briefly how information concerning the cost of individual jobs can be used.

For the answer to this question, see the 'Answers' section at the end of the book.

Feedback to activity

Activity 1

(a)   As drawings are only made against firm orders, the cost of producing the drawings may be considered as a direct cost rather than as a production overhead. More accurate information, at little expense, could be obtained by an analysis of time spent by the draughtsman; an hourly rate, including associated costs, could be developed for charging to jobs. The hourly rate could incorporate normal idle time or, alternatively, hours not attributable to a specific order could be charged to drawing office overhead at the rate developed.

(b)   It appears that the night shift will be operated to fulfil the one particular long-term contract. Consequently, there would be no justification for including the night-shift premium in factory overhead as that would unfairly burden jobs completed during the day and evening shift. In fact it could be appropriate to separate this particular contract from the normal costing routine and treat it as a marginal contract by only charging costs directly incurred.

(c)   The alternative methods for dealing with the wages of the operator of the subsidiary machine are:

(i)   **Charge as direct wages** – This method implies that the operator's time can conveniently be analysed between products. In addition, the machine operating costs should be charged in conjunction with the operator's wages, i.e. a composite machine hour rate will be developed.

(ii)   **Charge as overhead of the production cost centre** – Machine operating costs would be charged similarly.

The first method would achieve greater accuracy of product costs and provide useful information on the cost of the 'touching up' machine but would involve additional clerical work analysing the operator's time and developing a machine hour rate.

Chapter 19

CONTRACT AND SERVICE COSTING

Learning objectives

- Contract costing.

- Cost accounting statements for services and service industries.

We conclude our studies of specific order costing by looking at the costing of contracts – which are, basically, large long jobs. Whilst many of the costing principles are identical, the main difference is the recognition of attributable profit part way through the contract.

We then turn to the application of cost accounting techniques where a service is being provided rather than a physical product manufactured. One of the difficulties here is the lack of an obvious cost unit to which costs may be attributed.

Contents

1 Basic contract costing features

1.1 When is contract costing appropriate?

Contract costing is a form of specific order costing in which costs are attributed to individual contracts.

The difference between a contract and a job is one of size and time span. Contract costing is used by businesses undertaking building or other constructional contracts that take months or years to complete. In many cases the work will be done on site and not in the contractor's own works. Each contract is treated as a separate cost unit since management will want to know the profit or loss on each. For major contracts it may be necessary to designate sub-units for each stage of work either to facilitate control or to enable the invoicing of progress claims and the calculation of profit to date.

1.2 Treatment of contract costs

In contract costing each contract is a separately identifiable cost unit, so that costs will be accumulated in a separate ledger account for each contract. The various elements of cost are dealt with as follows:

(a) **Direct materials** – Materials charged to the contract may include both materials purchased specially and materials issued from the contractor's store. The appropriate costs are debited to the contract account. Control of materials at the site can be impaired by the difficulty of organising effective procedures for recording receipts and recording returns from site to store of materials surplus to contract requirements.

(b) **Direct wages** – Labour charges to the contract may include design and drawing office work (involving a time-booking procedure for salaried staff), manufacturing operations in the factory, and work on the site. All labour employed at the site of a contract will be direct. Time sheets may be necessary to disclose the time spent by workers at different sites. All such labour costs are debited to the contract account.

(c) **Direct expenses** – Direct contract costs other than materials and labour are often very significant. The two major items falling within this category are plant and subcontracted work.

   (i) **Plant** – Plant or equipment may be purchased specifically for a contract, in which case the contract account is debited with the cost. Alternatively, plant may be transferred from another contract, in which case it is the written down value that is debited to this contract and credited to the contract from which it has been moved. At the end of each financial period the depreciated value of any plant owned is shown as a credit entry in the contract account (i.e. as a balance carried down on the account to the next period). The net effect of the bookkeeping entries is that depreciation on the plant is automatically debited to the contract. Plant may be hired for use on a particular contract. As the business does not own such plant, the only ledger entries are the hire charges that are debited to the contract account. It is also possible to charge the contract account with a notional hire charge for plant owned by the business, thus treating the plant hire department as a separate entity.

(ii)   **Subcontracted work** – In the case of a large contract or one involving specialist activities, the business may engage subcontractors in certain aspects of the work. The cost of any subcontracted work is a direct expense of a contract and is debited to the contract account.

(d)   **Indirect costs** – Many contractors do not attempt to apportion such costs to specific contracts as they are often negligible compared with direct costs. However, if such apportionment of indirect costs is carried out, the resultant amount is debited to the contract account.

1.3   Architects' certificates and retention monies

For each contract a price is agreed between the business and the client. This is known as the contract price. In the case of large contracts, where the work involved may spread over many months or even years, the contractor will expect interim payments from the client in respect of the contract price. Such payments will be related to the work done so far on the contract. The procedure involved is as follows:

- **Architects' certificates** – As the work on a contract proceeds, the client's architects (or surveyors) will issue certificates indicating that so much of the contract price is now due to the contractor in respect of the work completed. In most cases at this stage the contractor will invoice the contractee with a progress payment.

- **Retention monies** – The contractor normally receives only a proportion of the value shown on the architects' certificates while the contract is still in progress. The amounts held back by the client are known as retention monies. Such retention monies would only be paid over to the contractor some time after the completion of the contract when any faulty work has been rectified.

- **Bookkeeping** – The architects' certificates received by the contractor could be used to make a memorandum record only until the completion of the contract when the contract price would be credited to the contract account. Alternatively, the value of the certificates could be credited to the contract account and debited to the personal account of the client as they are received.

Progress payments received by the contractor from the client are credited to the personal account of the client. Such payments must be deducted from the value placed upon the work performed to date for presentation in the balance sheet.

2   Attributable profit on uncompleted contracts

2.1   SSAP 9

Where a contract extends over a long period SSAP 9 (*Stocks and long-term contracts*) allows the contractor to take credit for part of the profit attributable to the contract in each year's accounts. This percentage of completion method avoids the inconsistency of having a number of years with no profit from a particular contract and then suddenly making a huge profit in the year when it is completed. In deciding to what extent profit can be taken on uncompleted contracts the following matters are important considerations:

- the successful outcome of the contract should be certain before any interim profit is taken

- any profit should only be taken in proportion to the work completed to date on the contract

- any anticipated overall loss on the contract should be provided for as soon as it is recognised.

2.2 Calculation of interim profit

The calculation of the profit to be taken on an uncompleted contract involves five steps.

Step 1

Determine the total sales value of the contract (for a fixed price contract this will be the contract price). Call this (a)

Step 2

Compute the total expected costs to complete the contract. Call this (b). It consists of two elements:

- the actual costs incurred to date on the contract, plus

- the estimated future costs necessary to complete the contract.

Step 3

The expected overall profit on the contract is given by (a) minus (b).

Step 4

The attributable profit to date on the contract should reflect the amount of work that has been completed so far. It can be calculated as follows:

Attributable profit to date =

$$\frac{\text{Value of work certified to date}}{\text{Total sales value of contract}} \times \text{Expected overall profit}$$

It is important to realise that the attributable profit thus calculated is the cumulative figure to date.

Step 5

The profit to be taken this year is the cumulative attributable profit calculated at step 4 less the profit on the contract already recognised in previous years.

Unfortunately, some examination questions do not provide sufficient information to use this approach. If not told the estimated future costs, it is necessary to use the following procedure.

		£	£
Value of work certified			200,000
Less:	Cost to date	80,000	
	Less: Cost of	15,000	
work not yet certified			
			65,000
Profit to date			135,000

Sometimes this figure is reduced by an arbitrary amount (e.g. one-third) to allow for the fact that the contract is incomplete and therefore the outcome is not certain.

The profit to be taken this year is then the profit to date (reduced if necessary) less the profit on the contract already recognised in previous years.

Notes:

1   It is always necessary to calculate profit to ensure that losses are identified and provided for.

2   Attention must be paid to the cost of work not yet certified. This arises where some work has been done but not checked/certified by the architects. Hence the costs will be included in the ledger but the selling price of this work is excluded from the value of work certified. The idea is, therefore, to calculate only profit on work that has been certified.

3   Many different methods may be used to calculate the profit to be taken on an incomplete contract. In an examination you should follow the instructions given to calculate the appropriate profit figure.

3   A worked example

Example

Contract No. 412 commenced during 20X1 and has a fixed contract price of £200,000. The costs incurred during the year 20X1 for materials, wages and subcontractors' charges totalled £90,000. Plant costing £20,000 was purchased during 20X1 specifically for Contract No. 412.

At the end of 20X1:

- the plant was valued at £15,000

- unused materials on the site were valued at £19,000

- architects' certificates had been issued showing that the value of work completed was £100,000.

It is estimated that further costs totalling £74,000 would be incurred in order to complete the contract. The figure includes the appropriate cost of plant and subcontractors in the future.

Retention money representing 20% of the certified value of the work completed has been held back by the client. The balance of the money due has been paid. The contractor credits the contract account with the full value of the architects' certificates as they are received.

You are required to prepare:

(a)   a calculation of the profit to be taken to the profit and loss account for 20X1

(b)   the entries for this year in the contract account and the client (contractee) account.

Solution

(a)   **Profit taken on contract for 20X1**

	£
Actual costs incurred to date:	
Materials, labour and subcontractors' costs	90,000
Less: Materials on site at end of 20X1	19,000
	71,000
Add: Plant depreciation £(20,000 – 15,000)	5,000
Contract costs incurred to end of 20X1	76,000
Projected costs to completion:	
Contract costs incurred to end of 20X1	76,000
Add: Estimated future costs to complete the contract	74,000
Total estimated contract costs	150,000
Contract profit:	
Contract price (fixed)	200,000
Less: Contract costs (as above)	150,000
Contract profit (estimated)	50,000

$$\text{Profit taken in 20X1} = \frac{\text{Work certified}}{\text{Contract price}} \times \text{Estimated contract profit}$$

$$= \frac{£100,000}{£200,000} \times £50,000$$

$$= £25,000$$

Note: as contract number 412 commenced during 20X1, this cumulative attributable profit is all recognised in 20X1. No profit had been taken on this contract in earlier years.

(b)   **Ledger accounts**

Contract number 412

	£		£
Materials, wages and sub contractors' costs	90,000	Client account (certified work)	100,000
Plant (at cost)	20,000	Materials c/d	19,000
Profit and loss account	25,000	Plant c/d	15,000
		Work-in-progress c/d	1,000
	135,000		135,000
Work-in-progress b/d	1,000		
Materials b/d	19,000		
Plant b/d	15,000		

Client (contractee) account

	£		£
Contract account (certified work)	100,000	Cash received (progress payment)	80,000
		Balance c/d	20,000
	100,000		100,000
Balance c/d	20,000		

Activity 1

Watch-It-Go-Up Ltd has a contract for an office and leisure complex. Work is part complete at the year end on 30 June 20X3. The following information is available:

	£'000
Contract price	2,500
Direct materials:	
Issued	680
Returned to suppliers	30
Transferred to other contracts	30
On site at 30 June	40
Direct wages:	
Paid	440
Accrued	20
Direct expenses:	
Paid	50
Accrued	10
Value of work certified to date	1,500
Received from contractee	1,200
Plant installed on site:	
Cost	200
Valuation 30 June	150
Estimated cost to completion	700

Progress payments are based on architects' certificates less 20% retention.

You are required to:

(a)   calculate attributable profit for the year to 30 June 20X3

(b)   prepare the contract and client ledger accounts.

Feedback to this activity is at the end of the chapter.

4   Service costing methods

DEFINITION

Service costing is the cost accounting method that can be applied when the business provides a service, or to a service activity within a manufacturing business. Examples are transport, power generation and hotels.

4.1   Application of service costing

Service costing is the cost accounting method that can be applied when the business provides a service, or to a service activity within a manufacturing business. Examples are transport, power generation and hotels.

Some of the principles explained earlier are appropriate to service costing in that costs are charged to activities and averaged over the units of service provided.

The method is appropriate when the service can be expressed in a standardised unit of measurement, e.g. an accountant in practice would provide an individual service to each client, but the service could be measured in chargeable hours.

4.2   Cost units for service industries

A major problem in service industries is the selection of a suitable unit for measuring the service, i.e. in deciding what service is actually being provided and what measures of performance are most appropriate to the control of costs. Some cost units used in different activities are:

Service	Cost unit
Electricity generation	Kilowatt hours*
Canteens and restaurants	Meals served
Carriers	Miles travelled/ton-miles*
Hospitals	Patient-days*
Passenger transport	Passenger-miles/seat-miles*

* These are examples of composite cost units, where the cost depends not only upon the time or distance over which the service is offered, but also on the level at which the service is operated.

A service undertaking may use several different units to measure the various kinds of service provided, e.g. an hotel may use:

Service	Cost unit
Restaurant	Meals served
Hotel services	Guest-days
Function facilities	Hours

When appropriate cost units have been determined for a particular service, provision will need to be made for the collection of the appropriate statistical data. In a transport organisation this may involve the recording of daily mileages for each vehicle in the fleet. Fuel usage per vehicle and loads or weight carried may be appropriate for the business. Modern technology allows such data to be collected relatively easily.

4.3 Collection, classification and ascertainment of costs

Costs will be classified under appropriate headings for the particular service. This will involve the issue of suitable cost codes to be used in the recording and, therefore, the collection of costs. For a transport undertaking the main cost classification may be based on the following activities:

(a)   operating and running the fleet

(b)   repairs and maintenance

(c)   fixed charges

(d)   administration.

Within each of these there would need to be a sub classification of costs, each with its own code, so that under (c) fixed charges, there might appear the following breakdown:

- road fund licences

- insurances

- depreciation

- vehicle testing fees

- others.

DEFINITION

In service costing it is often important to classify costs into their fixed and variable elements. Many service applications involve high fixed costs and the higher the number of cost units the lower the fixed costs per unit. The variable cost per unit will indicate to management the additional cost involved in the provision of one extra unit of service.

In service costing it is often important to classify costs into their fixed and variable elements. Many service applications involve high fixed costs and the higher the number of cost units the lower the fixed costs per unit. The variable cost per unit will indicate to management the additional cost involved in the provision of one extra unit of service. In the context of a transport undertaking, fixed and variable costs are often referred to as standing and running costs respectively.

4.4 Cost sheets for service industries

At appropriate intervals (usually weekly or monthly) cost sheets will be prepared by the costing department to provide information about the appropriate service to management. A typical cost sheet for a service would incorporate the following for the current period and the cumulative year to date:

(a) cost information over the appropriate expense or activity headings

(b) cost units statistics

(c) cost per unit calculations using the data in (a) and dividing by the data in (b). Different cost units may be used for different elements of costs and the same cost or group of costs may be related to different cost unit bases to provide additional control information to management. In the transport organisation, for example, the operating and running costs may be expressed in per mile and per day terms.

(d) analyses based on the physical cost units.

On a transport cost sheet, the following non-cost statistics may be shown:

(i) average miles covered per day

(ii) average miles per gallon of fuel.

5 Service cost accounting statements

5.1 Introduction

These reports are derived from the cost sheets and other data collected. Usually costs are presented as totals for the period, classified often into fixed and variable costs. The next section illustrates how such statements would be prepared for a number of difference service organisations.

5.2 Power supply industry

Example cost statement

The following figures were taken from the annual accounts of two electricity supply boards working on uniform costing methods.

Meter reading, billing and collection costs:

	Board A £000	Board B £000
Salaries and wages of:		
Meter readers	150	240
Billing and collection staff	300	480
Transport and travelling	30	40
Collection agency charges	–	20
Bad debts	10	10
General charges	100	200
Miscellaneous	10	10
	600	1,000
Units sold (millions)	2,880	9,600
Number of consumers (thousands)	800	1,600
Sales of electricity (millions)	£18	£50
Size of area (square miles)	4,000	4,000

Prepare a comparative cost statement using suitable units of cost. Brief notes should be added, commenting on likely causes for major differences in unit costs so disclosed.

Solution

Electricity Boards A and B
Comparative costs – year ending ....

	Board A £000	% of total	Board B £000	% of total
Salaries and wages:				
Meter reading	150	25.0	240	24.0
Billing and collection	300	50.0	480	48.0
Transport/travelling	30	5.0	40	4.0
Collection agency	–	–	20	2.0
Bad debts	10	1.7	10	1.0
General charges	100	16.6	200	20.0
Miscellaneous	10	1.7	10	1.0
	600	100.0	1,000	100.0

Cost per:	£	£
Millions units sold	208	105
Thousand consumers	750	625
£m of sales	33,333	20,000
Square mile area	150	250

Possible reasons for unit cost differences include:

(a) **Area density**. B covers the same size of area but has double the number of consumers, indicating that B is a more urban territory.

(b) **Industrialisation**. Costs per unit are almost twice as high for A but the pattern is not continued for costs in relation to sales value. B, therefore, probably contains a higher proportion of industrial consumers at cheaper rates.

(c) **Territory covered**. Comparative costs per square mile deviate from the pattern shown by the other measurement units, confirming that the bulk of costs is incurred in relation to consumers and usage.

5.3 Transport operations

Example

Remix Plc makes ready-mixed cement and operates a small fleet of vehicles that delivers the product to customers within its delivery area.

General data

Maintenance records for the previous five years reveal:

Year	Mileage of vehicles	Maintenance cost £
1	170,000	13,500
2	180,000	14,000
3	165,000	13,250
4	160,000	13,000
5	175,000	13,750

Transport statistics reveal:

Vehicle	Number of journeys each day	Average tonnage carried to customers Tonnes	Average distance to customers miles
1	6	4	10
2	4	4	20
3	2	5	40
4	2	6	30
5	1	6	60

There are five vehicles operating a five-day week, for fifty weeks a year.

Inflation can be ignored.

Standard cost data include:

Drivers' wages are £150 each per week.
Supervisor/relief driver's wage is £200 per week.
Depreciation, on a straight-line basis with no residual value.

	Cost	Life
Loading equipment	£100,000	5 years
Vehicles	£30,000 each	5 years

Petrol/oil costs 20p per mile.
Repairs cost 7½p per mile.
Vehicle licences cost £400 pa for each vehicle.
Insurance costs £600 pa for each vehicle.
Tyres cost £3,000 pa in total.
Miscellaneous costs, £2,250 pa in total.

You are required to calculate a standard rate per tonne/mile of operating the vehicles.

Solution

Calculation of standard rate per tonne/mile:

Running costs

	£	£
Maintenance costs (W1)	0.05	
Petrol/oil	0.20	
Repairs cost	0.075	
	0.325	
Total per annum: £0.325 × 170,000 (W2)		55,250
Sundry costs		
Maintenance fixed costs (W1)	5,000	
Drivers' wages: £150 × 52 × 5	39,000	
Supervisor/relief driver: £200 × 52	10,400	
Depreciation of loading equipment: £100,000 ÷ 5	20,000	
Depreciation of vehicles (£30,000 × 5) ÷ 5	30,000	
Vehicle licences £400 × 5	2,000	
Insurance: £600 × 5	3,000	
Tyres	3,000	

Miscellaneous costs	2,250	
		114,650
		169,900

Therefore, standard rate per tonne/mile $= \dfrac{£169,900}{420,000 \, (\text{W3})}$

$= £0.4045$ per tonne/mile

Workings

(W1) Maintenance cost, separation of fixed and variable element using high/low method:

	Mileage	Maintenance cost £
High	180,000	14,000
Low	160,000	13,000
Variable cost	20,000	1,000

Variable/running cost per mile $= \dfrac{£1,000}{20,000} = £0.05$ per mile

Total cost = Total fixed cost + (Variable cost per mile × Number of miles)

£14,000 = Total fixed cost + (£0.05 × 180,000)

Total fixed cost = £14,000 − £9,000 = £5,000

(W2) Distance travelled

Vehicle		miles
1	$6 \times 10 \times 2$	= 120
2	$4 \times 20 \times 2$	= 160
3	$2 \times 40 \times 2$	= 160
4	$2 \times 30 \times 2$	= 120
5	$1 \times 60 \times 2$	= 120

680×5 days $\times 50$ weeks = 170,000 miles

3   Number of tonne/miles

Vehicle		Tonne/miles
1	$6 \times 4 \times 10$	= 240
2	$4 \times 4 \times 20$	= 320
3	$2 \times 5 \times 40$	= 400
4	$2 \times 6 \times 30$	= 360
5	$1 \times 6 \times 60$	= 360

$1,680 \times 5$ days $\times 50$ weeks = 420,000 tonne miles

6 Comparison of manufacturing and service costing

6.1 The nature of a service product

Four key differences can be identified between the products of service industries and those of a manufacturing business.

- **Intangibility** – the output is in the form of performance rather than physical (tangible) goods. As we have seen, this means that it is quite difficult to define a unique cost unit that will serve for cost control purposes.

- **Heterogeneity** – the nature and standard of the output will be variable, due to the high human input. Heterogeneous means 'consisting of elements that are not of the same kind or nature' e.g. you may get a completely different standard of service from two different waiters in the same restaurant (or from the same waiter on different nights). Thus it is difficult to come up with a standard cost that is meaningful for all the units of service.

- **Simultaneous production and consumption** – which precludes advance inspection of the product to ensure it meets a given specification or quality level. Thus a lot more attention must be paid to the quality of the inputs, i.e. staff should be properly trained and customers' requirements should be properly understood.

- **Perishability** – stocks of the product cannot be held to cover periods of unexpectedly high levels of demand; similarly once the opportunity for sale has passed, it may be lost forever. If a cinema seat for a particular film is not sold, for example, that is revenue that is permanently for gone.

6.2 Differences between manufacturing and service cost statements

Looking back at the cost statement for the power supply industry you can see that this is very different to the sort of statement we have been used to dealing with in the manufacturing environment (compare it, for example, with the statement in paragraph 3.1 of chapter 13).

The main difference between manufacturing and service cost statements may be identified as:

- **The lack of a 'flexed budget'** – As it is difficult to define a single cost unit to which costs would be expected to accrue in any clear relationship, it is very difficult to predict 'expected costs'. In most cases, the original, fixed budget, would be used for comparison. Where a predominant activity measure can be identified, however, a flexed budget approach may well be possible – for example in an hotel, where room occupancy rate may be used, or in a restaurant, using meals served as an activity measure.

- **The lack of detailed variance analysis** – Variances, if shown, will generally be of a simple expenditure type, comparing actual total cost with a fixed budget cost. More detailed analysis may be difficult, again due to the lack of a clear cost unit.

- **The lack of stock figures** – Due to the perishability of the service product, no significant stocks will be held. This eliminates the need for stock valuation policies.

- **The inclusion of a variety of performance measures** – A service industry will use a variety of cost control indicators, along the lines of cost ratios using various cost units as a basis. Quality measures, such as customer complaints, new accounts gained or lost, speed of response to customer needs, etc. will also be of particular importance to a service based business.

Summary

This chapter has considered the last of the three specific order-costing methods, contract costing. We considered how costs are attributed to contracts, and how profit may be recognised in the profit and loss account part way through the contract period. We then looked at the particular aspects of service costing, where there is rarely one cost unit that can be used for all planning and control purposes. We contrasted the nature of a service business with that of manufacturing concern, and looked at how this affects the way in which cost information is reported.

By the time you have finished this chapter you should be able to:

- prepare ledger accounts for contract costing systems (in accordance with SSAP 9)

- prepare and contrast cost statements for service and manufacturing organisations.

Self-test questions

Basic contract costing features

1   What is contract costing? (1.1)

2   In the context of contract costing, explain the use of architects' certificates. (1.3)

Attributable profit on uncompleted contracts

3   In the context of contract costing, explain the meaning of 'attributable profit' on uncompleted contracts. (2.1)

4   Why is it necessary to calculate interim profits on uncompleted contracts? (2.1)

5   List the steps required to calculate interim profits on uncompleted contracts. (2.2)

Service costing methods

6   Give two examples of service industries. (4.1)

7   Explain what is meant by a composite cost unit, giving two examples. (4.2)

Comparison of manufacturing and service costing

8   What are the four main differences between the product of a service business and that of a manufacturer? (6.1)

Exam-type questions

Question 1

A construction company has the following data concerning one of its contracts:

Contract price	£2,000,000
Value certified	£1,300,000
Cash received	£1,200,000
Costs incurred	£1,050,000
Cost of work certified	£1,000,000

The company recognises profit on uncompleted contracts according to the formula: notional profit to date × (cash received/value certified).

The profit (to the nearest £1,000) to be attributed to the contract is £ [ ] .

Question 2

Tick the box(es) to indicate which of the following are characteristics of contract costing:

(i)   homogeneous products [ ]

(ii)   customer-driven production [ ]

(iii)   short timescale from commencement to completion of the cost unit. [ ]

Question 3

For operational purposes, for a company operating a fleet of delivery vehicles, which of the following would be most useful?

A   Cost per mile run

B   Cost per driver hour

C   Cost per tonne mile

D   Cost per kilogram carried.

Question 4

Tick the box(es) to indicate which of the following are characteristics of service costing:

(i)   high levels of indirect costs as a proportion of total cost [ ]

(ii)   use of composite cost units [ ]

(iii)   use of equivalent units [ ]

For the answers to these questions, see the 'Answers' section at the end of the book.

Practice question

Jigantic plc

Jigantic plc is a building company engaged in the construction of hospitals and other major public buildings; most of the contracts undertaken extend over a three or four year period.

Shown below are the expenses incurred for the year ended 31 May 20X1, together with other operating details for three of the contracts in which the company is currently engaged:

	Contract A	Contract B	Contract C
	£'000	£'000	£'000
Contract price	4,000	10,200	12,000
Value of work certified by contractees' architects	2,350	7,500	11,000
Cash received from contractees	2,000	6,750	9,900
Costs incurred to 1 June 20X0	–	2,400	5,550
Cost incurred during the year:			
Materials	1,100	1,600	1,050
Labour	700	1,150	975
Other expenses, excluding depreciation	350	475	775
Plant and equipment:			
Written down value at 1 June 20X0	300	800	700
Written down value at 31 May 20X1	600	525	175
Purchases during the year	725	400	125
Cost of work not yet certified	75	–	800

The agreed retention rate is 10% of the value of work certified by the contractees' architects.

Contract C is nearing completion and the site manager estimates that costs of £425,000, in addition to those tabulated above, will be incurred in order to complete the contract. He also considers that the plant and equipment on site will be worthless by the time the contract is complete.

The nature of the work undertaken by Jigantic plc is such that it may be regarded as reasonable for the company to include in its annual accounts a prudent estimate for profit attributable to that part of the work on each contract certified as complete at the end of each accounting year.

Profit of £1,150,000 was taken on Contract C in the accounting periods up to and including 31 May 20X0. No profit had been taken on contract B as, at the 31 May 20X0, work on the project had only recently commenced.

The directors of Jigantic plc propose to incorporate into the company's profit and loss account for the year ended 31 May 20X1, the following amounts of profit/(loss) for each contract:

Contract A	Nil
Contract B	£720,000
Contract C	£2,400,000

Making whatever calculations you consider necessary, you are required to carefully explain whether you agree with the proposed profit/(loss) figures for the above contracts. If you consider any of the proposed amounts are inappropriate suggest, with supporting explanations and calculations, a more suitable figure.

For the answer to this question, see the 'Answers' section at the end of the book.

Feedback to activity

Activity 1

(a) **Costs incurred to date**

		£'000	£'000
Actual costs incurred to date:			
Materials issued			680
Less: Returns		30	
Transfers		30	
On site 30 June		40	
			100
			580
Wages – paid and accrued			460
Direct expenses – paid and accrued			60
Plant depreciation £(200,000 − 150,000)			50
Contract costs incurred to date			1,150

	£'000
Contract costs to completion	
Incurred (above)	1,150
Estimated further costs	700
Total estimated contract costs	1,850
Estimated contract profit	
Fixed contract price	2,500
Total estimated costs	1,850
Estimated profit	650

Attributable profit

Profit taken in year to 30 June 20X3

$$= \frac{\text{Work certified}}{\text{Contract price}} \times \text{Contract profit}$$

$$= \text{£'000} \left(\frac{1,500}{2,500} \times 650\right)$$

$$= \text{£390,000}$$

(b)

Contract account

	£'000		£'000
Material costs	680	Material returns	30
Wages:		Material transfer	30
Cash	440	Client account (work certified)	1,500
Accrued c/d	20	Plant c/d	150
Direct expenses:		Materials c/d	40
Cash	50	Work-in-progress c/d	40
Accrued c/d	10		
Plant	200		
Profit and loss account	390		
	1,790		1,790

Client (contractee) account

	£'000		£'000
Contract account (certified work)	1,500	Cash received (progress payment)	1,200
	———	Balance c/d	300
	1,500		———
	———		1,500
			———

Chapter 20

PROCESS COSTING

Learning objectives

- Process costing.

This chapter is concerned with the method of costing used in situations where the units produced are homogeneous (i.e. all the same), and the operations used to achieve the final product are continuous.

Contents

1   Continuous production

2   Process costing – losses

3   Abnormal losses and gains

4   Partially processed units

5   Opening work-in-process

6   Losses in process – interaction with work-in-process

7   Joint products and by-products

1 Continuous production

1.1 Introduction

In specific order costing costs were directly allocated to a particular job or batch. When standardised goods or services result from a sequence of repetitive and continuous operations, it is useful to work out the cost of each operation. Then, if each unit produced is assumed to have involved the same amount of work, costs for a period are charged to processes or operations, and unit costs are ascertained by dividing process costs by units produced. This is known as process costing.

1.2 Special features of output costing

The basic physical feature of output costing is that only a single operation is required to obtain the final product. Examples of output costing include the extraction of minerals. Output costing applies where such minerals are sold as the final product immediately after extraction; if they are, instead, further processed within the same organisation; then process costing (see below) should be used.

The finished products, such as the minerals extracted, are homogeneous (that is one tonne of mineral extracted is indistinguishable from another). As a consequence it is assumed that each unit of the product will require the same level of resources to acquire as the next unit. It is therefore not necessary to identify the cost of each tonne, (if this were possible, its cost could not be justified). Instead the total cost of a particular time period is divided by the output of the period and an average per unit calculated.

1.3 Calculating the unit cost

Assume that Z Ltd extracts clay from the ground in a single process and sells it to a local pottery.

During June costs incurred amount to £19,500 and output was 6,500 tonnes of clay.

The cost per tonne is:

$$\frac{\text{Cost incurred}}{\text{Output in tonnes}} = \frac{£19,500}{6,500}$$

$$= £3 \text{ per tonne.}$$

This would be used to value stock and prepare profit statements.

Activity 1

Calculate the cost per tonne given that:

Costs incurred	=	£46,740
Output	=	16,400 tonnes

Feedback to this activity is at the end of the chapter.

1.4 Special features of process costing

Process costing applies when goods or services result from a sequence of continuous or repetitive operations or processes, e.g. oil refining, breweries and canned food.

DEFINITION

Process costing applies when goods or services result from a sequence of continuous or repetitive operations or processes, e.g. oil refining, breweries and canned food

The basic physical feature of a processing system is that as products pass from the raw material input stage to becoming finished products they pass through a number of distinct stages or processes of manufacture. In such a situation it is not feasible to link the cost of specific inputs to specific units of output. For example, in the production of paint it would be impossible to isolate one unit of output (a litre can of paint) and determine precisely which inputs have finished up in that particular litre of paint. The nature of a processing business is such that inputs are being added continuously to the manufacturing process, losing their identity, and a continuous output of production is being achieved.

Ascertaining the cost of production involves:

- determination of the costs (direct and indirect) associated with each process

- calculation of the average process unit cost by dividing the appropriate costs by the appropriate number of units of output

- valuation of the units of output transferred from one process to the next and any work-in-process by applying the unit costs

- the cost of output from the first process becomes the cost of input to the second process and so on until output from the final process has accumulated the cost of all processes.

This procedure is complicated by the following factors:

- output units will not equal input units to the extent that losses are sustained during processing

- the existence of partially processed units, i.e. work-in-process, at the end of the period.

Each of these factors will be considered in this chapter.

2 Process costing – losses

2.1 Basic principles

The nature of the processing operation is such that the input volume rarely equals the output volume, the difference, or loss, is analysed between that which is expected (and considered to be unavoidable) and any additional loss (or lack of loss) which actually occurs.

DEFINITION

Normal loss is the amount of loss expected from the operation of a process. This expectation is based on past experience, and this loss is considered to be unavoidable.

2.2 Normal loss

Normal loss is the amount of loss expected from the operation of a process. This expectation is based on past experience, and this loss is considered to be unavoidable.

The normal loss is usually expressed as a percentage of the input volume, and the cost of its production must be borne by the remaining output.

Example

The following data relates to process 1 during March:

Input materials 1,000 kg costing	£9,000
Labour cost	£18,000
Overhead cost	£13,500

A normal loss equal to 10% of input was expected. Actual output was 900 kg.

Method

Step 1

Calculate the number of normal loss units.

Step 2

Calculate the expected number of output units.

Step 3

Total the process costs.

Step 4

Calculate the cost per unit.

Step 5

Write up the process account and normal loss account.

Solution

Step 1

The normal loss equals 10% of 1,000 kg = 100 kg.

Step 2

The expected output units equals the input less the normal loss = 1,000 kg −100 kg = 900 kg.

Step 3

The total process costs = £40,500.

Step 4

The cost per unit equals:

$$\frac{£40,500}{900} = £45 \text{ per kg}$$

Step 5

Process account

	Kg	£		Kg	£/kg	£
Material input	1,000	9,000	Normal loss	100	–	–
Labour		18,000	Output	900	45	40,500
Overhead		13,500				
	1,000	40,500		1,000		40,500

Note:

- that the process account contains columns to record both quantities and values that are both balanced off

- that no value is attributed to the normal loss units in this example (next the effect of scrap and similar values will be shown).

2.3 Normal losses having a scrap sales value

When normal losses have a scrap value, reduce the cost of the process by the income anticipated from the normal loss.

Example

Suppose that the normal loss of 100 kg in the last example could be sold as scrap for £9/kg.

Step 3 is now amended to recognise the reduction in process costs caused by the income anticipated from the normal loss.

Step 3

becomes: The total process cost is:

£40,500 (as before) − (100 kg × £9/kg) (the scrap value of the normal loss).

= £39,600

Step 4

The cost per unit is now:

$$\frac{£39,600}{900} = £44/kg$$

Step 5

Process account

	kg	£		Units	£/kg	£
Material input	1,000	9,000	Normal loss	100	9	900
Labour		18,000	Output	900	44	39,600
Overhead		13,500				
	1,000	40,500		1,000		40,500

Note: the normal loss now has a value equal to its scrap value.

Since the process account is part of the cost bookkeeping system (see later in this text), a corresponding debit entry must be made for the normal loss:

Scrap account

	kg	£		kg	£
Process account	100	900	Cash/bank	100	900

Activity 2

Calculate the cost per tonne from the following data:

Input 5,000 tonnes costing	£15,000
Labour cost	£6,000
Overhead cost	£10,025

Normal loss is 10% of input and has a scrap value of £4/tonne.

Write up the process account and the normal loss account.

Feedback to this activity is at the end of the chapter.

3 Abnormal losses and gains

3.1 Introduction

Often the operation of processes results in the actual loss being different from that expected. The differences are referred to as abnormal losses and gains.

DEFINITION

The extent to which the actual loss exceeds the normal loss is referred to as the abnormal loss. This loss is unexpected and considered to be avoidable consequently the cost of producing abnormal loss units is not treated in the same way as the cost of the normal loss.

3.2 Abnormal losses

The extent to which the actual loss exceeds the normal loss is referred to as the abnormal loss. This loss is unexpected and considered to be avoidable consequently the cost of producing abnormal loss units is not treated in the same way as the cost of the normal loss.

Abnormal losses are valued initially as if they had been good output, the loss (reduced by any scrap value) is then debited to the profit and loss account via the abnormal loss account.

The following example shows how to account for abnormal losses.

Example

The following data relates to one process during April:

Input materials 1,000 kg costing	£9,000
Labour cost	£18,000
Overhead cost	£13,500

A normal loss equal to 10% of input was expected.

Actual output was 850 kg.

Losses are sold as scrap for £9/kg.

Solution

The steps to arrive at cost per unit are the same as in the earlier example.

Step 1

The normal loss equals 10% of 1,000 kg = 100 kg.

Step 2

The expected output units equals the input less the normal loss = 1,000 kg – 100 kg = 900 kg.

Step 3

The process costs equal £40,500 – (100 kg × £9) = £39,600.

Step 4

The cost per unit equals $\dfrac{£39,600}{900} = £44$

Step 5

Process account

	kg	£		kg	£/kg	£
Material input	1,000	9,000	Normal loss	100	9	900
Labour		18,000	Abnormal loss			
Overhead		13,500	(W1)	50	44	2,200
			Output	850	44	37,400
	1,000	40,500		1,000		40,500

Workings

(W1) The abnormal loss units equal the difference between the actual and expected output. These are valued at the cost per unit calculated in step 4.

Scrap account

	kg	£		kg	£
Process account – Normal loss	100	900	Cash/bank (W2)	150	1,350
Abnormal loss account	50	450			
	150	1,350		150	1,350

Abnormal loss

	kg	£		kg	£
Process account – Abnormal loss	50	2,200	Scrap account	50	450
			Profit & Loss		1,750
	50	2,200		50	2,200

(W2) The distinction between normal and abnormal losses is purely an accounting one, all of the loss may be sold as scrap for £9/kg. All of these proceeds are credited to the scrap account.

Note that the transfer to profit and loss shown in the abnormal loss account is the net cost of producing the unexpected loss (after deducting its scrap value). This is used to control the costs of excess losses, i.e. 50 units @ (£44 – 9) = £1,750.

Activity 3

Calculate the net cost of the abnormal loss, to be transferred to the profit and loss account, from the following data:

Input quantity	5,000 kg
Normal loss	5% of input
Process costs	£16,500
Actual output	4,600 kg

Losses are sold for £2.35 per kg.

Feedback to this activity is at the end of the chapter.

DEFINITION

The extent to which the actual loss is less than the normal loss is referred to as an abnormal gain.

3.3 Actual loss is less than normal loss (abnormal gains)

The extent to which the actual loss is less than the normal loss is referred to as an abnormal gain.

The following example shows how to account for abnormal gains.

Example

The following data relates to one process during May:

Input materials 1,000 kg costing	£9,000
Labour cost	£18,000
Overhead cost	£13,500

A normal loss equal to 10% of input was expected.

Actual output was 920 kg.

Losses are sold as scrap for £9/kg.

Solution

Steps 1 to 4 are the same as was shown earlier and cost per kg = £44

Step 5

Process account

	kg	£/kg	£		kg	£/kg	£
Material input	1,000		9,000	Normal loss	100	9	900
Labour			18,000	Output	920	44	40,480
Overhead			13,500				
Abnormal gain	20	44	880				
	1,020		41,380		1,020		41,380

Workings

(W1) The abnormal gain units equal the difference between the actual and expected output. These are then valued at the cost per unit calculated in step four. Note that these entries are made on the debit side of the process account, thus causing it to balance.

Scrap account

	kg	£		kg	£
Process account – Normal loss	100	900	Cash bank	80(W2)	720
			Abnormal gain account	20	180
	100	90		100	
		0			900

Abnormal gain

	kg	£		kg	£
Normal loss account	20	180	Process account –	20	880
Profit and loss (W3)		700	Abnormal gain		
	20	880		20	880

(W2) This is the actual loss being sold at £9/kg.

(W3) This represents the net benefit of producing a lower loss than expected (after deducting the lost income from the anticipated scrap sales), i.e. 20 × (£44 − £9) = £700.

4 Partially processed units

4.1 Introduction

At the end of a period there may be some units that have been started but have not been completed. These are said to be closing work-in-process units.

Assuming at this stage that there is no opening work-in-process, the output for a period will consist of:

- units of production that have been started and fully processed within the period

- units of production that have been started in the period but which are only part-processed at the end of the period; this closing work-in-process will be completed next period when further costs will be incurred in completing it.

4.2 Equivalent units

Costs in a process costing system are allocated to units of production on the basis of equivalent units. The idea behind this concept is that once processing has started on a unit of output, to the extent that it remains in an uncompleted state it can be expressed as a proportion of a completed unit. For example, if 100 units are exactly halfway through the production process in terms of the amount of cost they have absorbed, they are effectively equal to 50 complete units. Therefore, 100 units that are half-complete can be regarded as 50 equivalent units that are complete.

Example

A manufacturer starts processing on 1 March. In the month of March he starts work on 20,000 units of production. At the end of March there are 1,500 units still in process and it is estimated that each is two thirds complete. Costs for the period total £19,500.

Calculate the value of the completed units and the work-in-process at 31 March.

Solution

	Units (a)	Proportion complete (b)	Equivalent units (c)=(a)×(b)
Started and completed	18,500	1	18,500
Work-in-process	1,500	⅔	1,000
			19,500

Cost per equivalent unit $= \dfrac{£19,500}{19,500} = £1$

Valuation

	Equivalent units	Cost £
Finished production	18,500 × £1	18,500
Work-in-process	1,000 × £1	1,000
Total costs for period		19,500

The 1,500 physical units in process at the end of the period have a value (based on 1,000 equivalent units) of £1,000.

4.3 Extension of the equivalent units approach

In practice it is unlikely that all inputs to production will take place at the same time, as was suggested in the example above. For instance, materials are frequently added at the beginning of a process, whereas labour may be applied throughout the process. Thus, work-in-process may be more complete as regards one input or cost element than as regards another. Equivalent units must thus be calculated separately for each input and costs applied on that basis.

Example

As in the example above, except that:

- all materials have been input to the process
- work-in-process is only one-third complete as regards labour
- costs for the period are:

	£
Materials	10,000
Labour	9,500
Total	19,500

Solution

	Units	Materials Proportion complete	Materials Equivalent units	Labour Proportion complete	Labour Equivalent units
Started and Completed	18,500	1	18,500	1	18,500
Work-in-process	1,500	1	1,500	$\frac{1}{3}$	500
Total equivalent units			20,000		19,000
Cost per equivalent unit		$\frac{£10,000}{20,000} = 50p$		$\frac{£9,500}{19,000} = 50p$	

Valuation

	Materials	£	Labour	£	Total £
Cost of finished Production	18,500 × £0.50 =	9,250	18,500 × £0.50 =	9,250	18,500
Cost of work in Process	1,500 × £0.50 =	750	500 × £0.50 =	250	1,000
Total costs for period					19,500

4.4 Six-step method for process costing

The approach used in the last two examples can be summarised into a six-step technique that can be generally used in process costing problems:

Step 1

Trace the physical flow of units so that units input to the production process are reconciled with units output or in process at the end of the period.

Step 2

Convert the physical units determined in Step 1 into equivalent units of production for each factor of production (i.e. materials, labour, etc.).

Step 3

Calculate the total cost for each factor for the period.

Step 4

Divide the total costs by equivalent units to establish a cost per equivalent unit.

Step 5

Multiply equivalent units by the cost per equivalent unit to cost out finished production and work-in-process. Reconcile these values to the total costs for the period as calculated in Step 3.

Step 6

Write up the ledger accounts.

Example

The Excelsior Co Ltd manufactures a single product in two successive processes. The following information is available for the month of July:

Process 1

(a) No opening work-in-process on 1 July.

(b) During the month 815 units costing £2,415 were put into process.

(c) Labour and overhead incurred amounted to £1,600.

(d) During the month 600 units were finished and passed to Process 2.

(e) On 31 July 190 units remained in process, the operations on which were half completed, but the materials for the whole process have been charged to the process.

Process 2

(a) No opening work-in-process on 1 July.

(b) The cost of labour and overhead in this process was £900, and material costing £350 was added at the end of operations.

(c) On 31 July 400 units had been transferred to finished stock.

(d) At that date 180 units remained in process, and it was estimated that one-third of the operations had been completed.

You are required to show the process accounts, treating any process losses as a normal loss.

Solution

Process 1

	Units	£		Units	£
Input	815	2,415	Process 2	600	3,215
Labour and overhead		1,600	Work-in-process c/d	190	800
			Process loss	25	–
	815	4,015			
				815	4,015

Process 2

	Units	£		Units	£
Process 1	600	3,215	Finished stock	400	3,350
Labour and overhead		900	Work-in-process c/d	180	1,115
Material added		350	Process loss	20	–
	600	4,465		600	4,465

Workings

Valuation of work-in-process

Process 1

Step 1

Opening work-in-process	+	Units started	=	Units finished	+	losses	+	Closing work-in-process
0	+	815	=	600	+	losses	+	190

Thus, losses in the period were 815 − (600 + 190) = 25.

Step 2

	Units	Materials Proportion complete	Equivalent units	Labour and overhead Proportion complete	Equivalent units
Started and completed	600	1	600	1	600
Work-in-process	190	1	190	½	95
Total equivalent units			790		695

Step 3

Costs		£2,415	£1,600

Step 4

Cost per unit	$\dfrac{£2,415}{790} =$ £3.057	$\dfrac{£1,600}{695} = £2.302$	£5.359

Step 5

Value of work-in-process	190 × £3.057 = £581	95 × £2.302 = £219	£800
Value of output		600 × £5.359 =	3,215

Process 2

Step 1

Opening work-in-process	+	Units transferred from process 1	=	Units finished	+	losses	+	Closing work-in-process
0	+	600	=	400	+	losses	+	180

Thus, losses in the period were 600 − (400 + 180) = 20.

Step 2

Equivalent units

	Units	Materials from process 1		Labour and overheads		Added materials	
		Proportion complete	Equivalent units	Proportion complete	Equivalent units	Proportion complete	Equivalent units
Started and completed	400	1	400	1	400	1	400
Work-in-process (note 2)	180	1	180	$^1/_3$	60	0	0
Total equivalent units			580		460		400

Step 3

Costs	£3,215	£900	£350

Step 4

Cost per unit $\dfrac{£3,215}{580} = £5.54$ $\dfrac{£900}{460} = £1.96$ $\dfrac{£350}{400} = £0.875$

Step 5

Value of work-in-process $(180 \times £5.54) + (60 \times £1.96) = £1,115$

Value of output $(400 \times £5.54) + (400 \times £1.96) + (400 \times £0.875) =$ £3,350

Notes:

1   The cost of normal losses is borne pro rata by the effective units.

2   As the material costing £350 was added at the end of operations in Process 2, none of it relates to the work-in-process units.

5 Opening work-in-process

5.1 Introduction

In the previous examples it was assumed that there was no opening stock of work-in-process. In reality, of course, this is unlikely to be the case, and changes in levels of work-in-process during the period can give rise to problems. There are basically two methods of accounting for such changes, namely:

• the weighted average (or averaging) method

• the FIFO method.

The examiner has stated that only the first of these need be studied for this syllabus.

5.2 Weighted average (or averaging) method

Under this method the opening stock values are added to the current costs to provide an overall average cost per equivalent unit. No distinction is, therefore, made between units in process at the start of the period and those added during it and the costs associated with them.

Example

FL Manufacturing Co Ltd
Process information for month ended 31 December

Work-in-process, 1 December (15,000 units, two-fifths complete) £10,250 (work-in-process value made up of: materials £9,000 plus conversion costs £1,250).

Units started during December	30,000
Units completed during December	40,000
Work-in-process, 31 December	5,000 (half-completed)
Material cost added in month	£24,750
Conversion cost added in month	£20,000

Materials are wholly added at the start of the process. Conversion takes place evenly throughout the process.

Calculate the values of finished production for December and work-in-process at 31 December, using the weighted average method.

Solution

It is easiest to use the six-step method, proceeding as follows:

Step 1

Physical flows

	Units	Units
Work-in-process at start	15,000	
Added	30,000	
	———	
To be accounted for		45,000
		———
Units completed	40,000	
In process at end	5,000	
	———	
Units accounted for		45,000
		———

Step 2

Equivalent units

	Materials	Conversion
Completed	40,000	40,000
In progress at end (conversion half-complete)	5,000	2,500
	———	———
	45,000	42,500
	———	———

Note: at this point the degree of completion of opening work-in-process is irrelevant under the weighted average method. It would, of course, have been used to value work at 30 November.

Step 3

Costs to be accounted for

	Materials £	Conversion £	Total £
Work-in-process at 1 December	9,000	1,250	10,250
Add: Costs incurred in December	24,750	20,000	44,750
	33,750	21,250	55,000

Step 4

Costs per equivalent unit

$$\frac{£33,750}{45,000} = 75p \qquad \frac{£21,250}{42,500} = 50p$$

Step 5

		£		£	£
Cost of finished work	40,000 × 75p =	30,000	40,000 × 50p =	20,000	50,000
Cost of work-in-process	5,000 × 75p =	3,750	2,500 × 50p =	1,250	5,000
Total costs (agreed with total per Step 3)					55,000

The important feature of this method is that the costs associated with opening work-in-process are added to the costs arising in the current period and then they all become part of an averaging procedure.

Step 6

Process account

	Units	£		Units	£/unit	£
Opening WIP	15,000	10,250	Output	40,000	1.25	50,000
Materials	30,000	24,750	Closing WIP	5,000	1	5,000
Conversion cost		20,000				
	45,000	55,000		45,000		55,000

Do not proceed until you have reworked this example correctly without consulting the solution.

6 Losses in process – interaction with work-in-process

6.1 Introduction

In a process, we may have to deal with both losses and work-in-process.

Example

Input to Process A was 1,000 units costing £4,500. Conversion costs were £3,400. The normal process loss is estimated as 10% of input. At the end of the period 780 units were transferred to Process B and 100 units were in process, 50% complete as regards conversion. There was no opening work-in-process.

Calculate the cost of transfers to process B, abnormal losses and the value of work-in-process.

Process A – unit costs

	Materials units	Conversion equivalent units
Input to Process A	1,000	
Less: Normal loss (10%)	100	
	900	
Transfer to Process B	780	780
Work-in-process	100	50
Abnormal loss	20	20
Total units/equivalent units	900	850

Step 1

Physical flow

Input	=	output	+	losses	+	closing work-in-process
1,000 units	=	780	+	losses	+	100

Thus, losses = 120 units of which normal loss is 10% of input, i.e. $10\% \times 1,000$ = 100 units.

Thus, abnormal losses are 20 units.

Step 2

Equivalent units

	Units	Materials Proportion complete	Materials Equivalent units	Labour Proportion complete	Labour Equivalent units
Started and Completed	780	1	780	1	780
Started and abnormally lost	20	1	20	1	20
Work-in-process	100	1	100	½	50
Total			900		850

Step 3

Cost £	4,500	3,400

Step 4

Cost per unit	£5	£4

Notes:

1 The normal loss of 100 units is excluded from the output units. By doing so the cost of such a loss is absorbed into the unit cost. The unit cost is thus increased.

2 Losses are usually assumed to occur at the end of a process, i.e. when the units involved are fully processed.

Step 5

Valuation

		£	£
Total costs allocated to:			
Transfer to Process B	780 × £9		7,020
Abnormal loss	20 × £9		180
Work-in-process carried down:			
Materials	100 × £5	500	
Conversion	50 × £4	200	
		——	700
Total (agrees with costs incurred)			7,900

6.2 Abnormal gains

If, in the previous example, 820 units had been transferred to Process B, an abnormal gain (i.e. a lower than normal loss) would have arisen. Unit cost would, however, be the same because the normal loss of 100 units is absorbed and the abnormal gain is valued at normal unit cost as a credit to the process.

		£
Input costs (as above)		7,900
Transfer to Process B	820 × £9	7,380
Abnormal gain	−20 × £9	(180)
Work-in-process (as before)		700
		7,900

Note that unit cost always represents $\dfrac{\text{Normal process cost}}{\text{Normal output}}$

6.3 Scrap recovery (normal or abnormal)

Remember that where the losses (normal or abnormal) are in the form of scrap they may be sold to generate revenue.

The treatment of such revenue is consistent with that of losses:

- revenue from normal losses is deducted from process costs

- revenue from abnormal losses (or forgone if there is an abnormal gain) is deducted from the value debited (or credited) to profit and loss account.

Example

Data as per example above but the loss is sold as scrap for £1.80 per unit.

Process A – unit costs

	Materials	*Conversion*
Output in units (as before)	900	850
	£	£
Costs	4,500	3,400
Less: Revenue from scrap sales of normal loss		
(100 × £1.80)	180	–
	4,320	3,400
Cost per unit	4.80	4.00

Note: the recovery is deducted from materials cost since the value of scrap is related to its material content, thus reducing the cost per unit for materials. The cost per unit for conversion remains unchanged.

Process A – cost allocation

		£	£
Input costs net of revenue from scrap sales of normal loss		7,720	
Allocated to:			
Transfer to Process B	780 × £8.80		6,864
Abnormal loss	20 × £8.80		176
Work-in-process:			
Materials	100 × £4.80	480	
Conversion	50 × £4.00	200	
			680
Total (agrees with net costs incurred)			7,720

Revenue from the abnormal loss of 20 units will be credited to the abnormal loss account, so that the net cost of abnormal losses transferred to profit and loss is £176 − (20 × £1.80) = £140.

6.4 Partially completed losses

The example above assumed that losses occurred at the end of the process and, therefore, were completed units. If a question indicates that losses occur part way through the process, the following procedure can be adopted:

Step 1

Calculate the equivalent units for normal and abnormal losses.

Step 2

Divide costs by output units (including losses) to find unit costs by cost element.

Step 3

Multiply normal losses by the unit cost in step 2.

Step 4

Divide step 3 by the total units excluding normal losses.

Step 5

Now step 2 + step 4 = unit cost including normal loss. Step 5 can be used for cost allocation.

Example

Input to Process A was 1,000 units. Process costs for the month were £3,608.

780 units were transferred to Process B in the month and 100 units were in progress at the end of the month (50% complete). Normal loss is estimated as 10% of input and losses occur when the process is 60% complete.

Normal loss is 100 units and abnormal loss is: (1,000 − (780 + 100 + 100)) = 20 units.

Unit costs may be calculated:

	Equivalent units
Transfer to B	780
WIP (50%)	50
Abnormal loss (20 × 60%)	12
	842

	£
Process costs	3,608
Per unit	4.285

Process cost is thus allocated:

		£
Transfer to B	780 units × £4.285	3,342.30
WIP	50 equivalent units × £4.285	214.25
Abnormal loss	12 equivalent units × £4.285	51.42
Rounding-off		0.03
		3,608.00

The rounding would normally be added to the output value, thus increasing it to £3,342.33.

7 Joint products and by-products

7.1 Introduction

It is typical of many manufacturing operations that a process may yield not only the main product desired but also one or more secondary products. This poses the question of how to apportion the process costs to the various products.

The process output will not be separately identifiable unit a certain stage of processing is reached. This is sometimes referred to as the 'split-off point' and the undifferentiated costs incurred up to that point are known as **joint-product costs** or **pre-separation costs**.

It is not possible to determine positively what proportion of pre-separation costs relates to each of the products emerging. It is therefore necessary to use arbitrary methods of apportioning pre-separation costs over the different products. This introduces, to a greater or lesser extent, an element of unreliability as to the accuracy of the costs of each product.

If the saleable value of both products is relatively significant, the outputs are usually called **joint products**. If the secondary product has a small market value relative to that of the principal product, that secondary item is referred to as a **by-product** of the principal item of output; in such cases a decision may be taken not to cost it separately.

7.2 Joint products

Joint products are those resulting from the same process and having substantially equal importance (in value) to the company. For example the joint products resulting from oil refining include petrol, paraffin, etc. After the different products have been separated they may be sold in their (then) existing state or further processed in order to give them a higher sales value. Whereas post-separation costs are usually identifiable with the particular product to which they relate, pre-separation costs can only be apportioned in accordance with one of the recognised bases outline as follows:

(a) According to sales value, which may be:

    (i) the market value at the point of separation

    (ii) the market value after further processing has been carried out, i.e. the final sales value

    (iii) the 'net realisable value', or 'notional sales value' method i.e. the final sales value less the post-separation costs.

(b) According to physical measurement, which may be:

    (i) actual, where there is a common unit of measurement for all products

    (ii) weighted in accordance with some technical estimation which reduces all output to a common basis.

7.3 By-products

By-products are items of relatively low market value that are produced in conjunction with a main product having a significant value. For example the bones left over from meat processing are a by-product. As with joint products, by-products may be sold either in their then current state or after further processing.

Pre-separation costs are not charged to the by-products, but any revenue obtained from the sale of those products is either:

(i) credited to the process account, thereby reducing the pre-separation charge to the main product; or

(ii) credited direct to the profit and loss account.

Summary

This chapter has explained process costing, which is used in organisations whose operations are continuous and are only artificially stopped and restarted by the preparation of monthly cost accounts.

The problems of losses and work-in-process have been illustrated and their solution methods shown.

We have also looked in outline at joint products and by-products and their accounting treatment.

By the time you have finished this chapter you should be able to:

- prepare ledger accounts for process costing systems.

Self-test questions

Continuous production

1   What is output costing? (1.2)

2   What is process costing? (1.4)

Process costing - losses

3   What is a normal loss? (2.2)

Abnormal losses and gains

4   What is an abnormal loss? (3.2)

5   What is an abnormal gain? (3.3)

Partially processed units

6   Explain the concept of equivalent units. (4.2)

Joint products and by-products

7   Distinguish between a joint product and a by-product (7.1)

Exam-type questions

Question 1

A cleaning fluid is produced by a series of processes. The following information relates to the final process

	Litres
Opening work-in-process	2,000
Closing work-in-process	1,500
Input	42,300
Transfer to finished goods stock	40,100
Normal loss	400

The abnormal loss is [   ] Litres.

Question 2

A factory manufactures model cars. During October work commenced on 110,000 new cars. This was in addition to 20,000 that were 50% complete at the start of the month. At the end of October there were 40,000 cars that were 50% complete.

Costs for October were:

	£
Brought forward	11,000
Incurred this period	121,000
	132,000

If this factory chooses the weighted average method of spreading costs, the cost per car for October production was (to the nearest penny) £ [   ] .

Question 3

An error was made in a firm's computation of the percentage of completion of closing work-in-process. The error resulted in assigning a lower percentage of completion than actually was the case.

What was the effect of this error upon the cost per equivalent unit and the cost of goods completed for the period?

	Cost per equivalent unit	*Cost of goods completed*
A	understated	understated
B	understated	overstated
C	overstated	understated
D	overstated	overstated

Question 4

Which one of the following statements is incorrect?

A   Job costs are collected separately, whereas process costs are averages

B   In job costing the progress of a job can be ascertained from the materials requisition notes and job tickets or time sheet

C   In process costing information is needed about work passing through a process and work remaining in each process

D   In process costing, but not job costing, the cost of normal loss will be incorporated into normal product costs

Question 5

The following details relate to the main process of X Ltd, a chemical manufacturer:

Opening work-in-process	2,000 litres, fully complete as to materials and 40% complete as to conversion
Material input	24,000 litres
Normal loss is 10% of input	
Output to process 2	19,500 litres
Closing work-in-process	3,000 litres, fully complete as to materials and 45% complete as to conversion

The numbers of equivalent units to be included in X Ltd's calculation of the cost per equivalent unit, using a weighted average basis of valuation, are:

	Materials	*Conversion*
A	21,400	20,850
B	22,500	21,950
C	22,500	20,850
D	23,600	21,950

For the answers to these questions, see the 'Answers' section at the end of the book.

Practice question

Chemical compound

A chemical compound is made by raw material being processed through two processes. The output of Process A is passed to Process B where further material is added to the mix. The details of the process costs for the financial period number 10 were as shown below:

Process A

Direct material	2,000 kilograms at £5 per kg
Direct labour	£7,200
Process plant time	140 hours at £60 per hour

Process B

Direct material	1,400 kilograms at £12 per kg
Direct labour	£4,200
Process plant time	80 hours at £72.50 per hour

The departmental overhead for Period 10 was £6,840 and is absorbed into the costs of each process on direct labour cost.

	Process A	Process B
Expected output was	80% of input	90% of input
Actual output was	1,400 kgs	2,620 kgs

Assume no finished stock at the beginning of the period and no work-in-process at either the beginning or the end of the period.

Normal loss is contaminated material which is sold as scrap for £0.50 per kg from Process A and £1.825 per kg from Process B, for both of which immediate payment is received.

You are required to prepare the accounts for Period 10, for:

(a) Process A

(b) Process B

(c) Normal loss/gain

(d) Scrap

(e) Finished goods

(f) Profit and loss (extract).

For the answer to this question, see the 'Answers' section at the end of the book.

Feedback to activities

Activity 1

Cost per tonne = £46,740/16,400 = £2.85.

Activity 2

Normal loss = 500 tonnes and has a value of £2,000 (500 × £4)

Process costs　　= £31,025 − £2,000 = £29,025

Cost per tonne　　$= \dfrac{£29,025}{4,500} = £6.45$

Process account

	Tonnes	£		Tonnes	£/ton	£
Materials	5,000	15,000	Normal loss　500		4	2,000
Labour		6,000	Output	4,500	6.45	29,025
Overhead		10,025				
	5,000	31,025		5,000		31,025

Scrap a/c

	Tonnes	£		Tonnes	£
Process a/c	500	2,000	Cash/bank	500	2,000

Activity 3

Step 1

Normal loss = 5% × 5,000 kg = 250 kg

Step 2

Scrap value of normal loss = 250 kg @ £2.35 = £587.50

Step 3

Net process cost = £16,500 − £587.50 = £15,912.50

Step 4

Cost per kg $= \dfrac{£15,912.50}{4,750\,kg} = £3.35$

Step 5

Net cost of abnormal loss/kg = £3.35 − £2.35 = £1.00

Volume of abnormal loss = 4,750 kg − 4,600 kg = 150 kg

Answer: net cost of abnormal loss to be transferred to profit and loss = 150 kg @ £1.00 = £150

Chapter 21

COST BOOKKEEPING

Syllabus content

- Accounting entries for an integrated accounting system.
- Interlocking accounting.

The basic principles of double entry and ledger accounts apply to cost accounting as well as to financial accounting. However the detailed application of these principles differs and the cost accounts must provide more detailed information than is normally required for financial accounts.

In this chapter the basic principles of the two main systems of cost accounting bookkeeping will be examined. These two systems are known as integrated accounts and interlocking accounts (non-integrated accounting systems).

The emphasis in the syllabus is on the first of these, integrated accounting.

Contents

1   Methods of cost bookkeeping

2   Integrated accounting systems

3   Integrated accounting using standard costs

4   Interlocking accounting system

1 Methods of cost bookkeeping

1.1 Definitions

DEFINITION

Integrated accounts are a set of accounting records which provides both financial and cost accounts using a common input of data for all accounting purposes. (CIMA Official Terminology).

Integrated accounts are a set of accounting records which provides both financial and cost accounts using a common input of data for all accounting purposes. (CIMA, *Official Terminology*).

Interlocking accounts are a system in which the cost accounts are distinct from the financial accounts, the two sets of accounts being kept continuously in agreement by the use of control accounts or reconciled by other means. (CIMA, *Official Terminology*).

The syllabus emphasises integrated accounts, and we shall start with these.

2 Integrated accounting systems

DEFINITION

Interlocking accounts are a system in which the cost accounts are distinct from the financial accounts, the two sets of accounts being kept continuously in agreement by the use of control accounts or reconciled by other means. (CIMA Official Terminology).

2.1 Purpose of integration

Integration of the cost and financial accounts into one comprehensive system offers savings in work by avoiding:

- duplication of certain accounting entries. For example, as you will see, in an interlocking system, purchases of raw materials would be posted thus.

Financial account	Dr Purchases	Cr Creditors
Cost account	Dr Stores	Cr Cost Contra

In an integrated system, a single entry would suffice, i.e.

Dr Stores	Cr Creditors

- reconciliation of costing with financial profit. Only one profit and loss account would be prepared and thus only one profit figure, rather than two as in an interlocking system.

More importantly perhaps, integration should improve the usefulness of, and promote the reliance upon, the accounting system as an information base. The overall system will be subject to control by external, internal and management audit. Furthermore, the design of accounting procedures will have to co-ordinate the requirements for management and financial information.

Example of integrated accounting – actual costs

The following transactions are to be recorded as double entry in ledger accounts of an integrated system. Close off to the profit and loss where appropriate.

		£
(1)	Incurred direct wages (gross)	100,000
(2)	Incurred indirect production wages (gross)	41,200
(3)	Administration salaries paid	12,800
(4)	Purchased raw materials	46,500
(5)	Paid business rates	4,000
(6)	Paid creditor for materials	41,400
(7)	Paid wages	98,700
(8)	Paid PAYE creditor	40,900
(9)	Paid bank charges	420
(10)	Sales on credit	480,000
(11)	Production overhead costs (other than business rates) paid	81,400
(12)	Received from debtors	414,600

Notes:

(a) Closing stocks of materials are valued, on a FIFO basis, at £6,300. There is no closing work-in-progress or stock of finished goods.

(b) The amount payable to the PAYE creditor in respect of wages and salaries is £43,400, of which £900 related to administration salaries.

(c) Business rates are to be apportioned: production – 80%; administration – 20%.

(d) Production overhead costs are absorbed into WIP at a rate of 100% of direct wages cost. Any under or over-absorption is carried forward to the end of the year.

Solution

The entries for each transaction/note are numbered as per the question.

Raw material control

	£		£
(4) Creditor	46,500	WIP	40,200
		Bal c/d	6,300 (a)
	46,500		46,500

Creditor

	£		£
(6) Bank	41,400	Raw materials	46,500 (4)
Bal c/d	5,100		
	46,500		46,500

Work-in-progress

	£		£
(1) Wages control	100,000	Finished goods	240,200
Raw material	40,200		
(d) Prod'n Ohd	100,000		
	240,200		240,200

Wages control

	£		£
(7) Bank	98,700	Work in progress	100,000 (1)
(b) PAYE creditor	42,500	Production Ohd	41,200 (2)
	141,200		141,200

Production overhead

	£		£
(2) Wages control	41,200	WIP (d)	100,000
(c) (5) Bank	3,200	Bal c/d	25,800
(11) Bank	81,400		
	125,800		125,800

Administration overhead

	£		£
(3) Bank	12,800	Profit & loss	14,500
(c) (5) Bank	800		
(b) PAYE creditor	900		
	14,500		14,500

Bank

	£		£
(12) Debtors	414,600	Admin Ohd	12,800 (3)
		Admin Ohd	800 (5) (c)
		Production Ohd	3,200 (5) (c)
		Creditor	41,400 (6)
		Wages control	98,700 (7)
		PAYE creditor	40,900 (8)
		Bank charges	420 (9)
		Production Ohd	81,400 (11)

PAYE creditor

	£		£
(8) Bank	40,900	Wages control	42,500 (b)
Bal c/d	2,500	Admin overhead	900 (b)
	43,400		43,400
		Bal b/d	2,500

Cost of sales

	£		£
Finished goods	240,200	Profit & loss	240,200

Bank charges

	£		£
Bank	420	Profit & loss	420

Debtors

	£		£
(10) Sales	480,000	Bank	414,600 (12)
		Bal c/d	65,400
	480,000		480,000
Bal b/d	65,400		

Sales

	£		£
Profit & loss	480,000	Debtors	480,000 (10)

Profit & loss

	£		£
Cost of sales	240,200	Sales	480,000
Admin Ohd	14,500		
Bank charges	420		
Net profit	224,880		
	480,000		480,000

Finished goods

	£		£
WIP	240,200	Cost of sales	240,200

Note the entries required after posting the basic transactions and information in the notes:

- transfer of cost of raw materials used to WIP

- transfer of WIP balance to finished goods, and from there to cost of sales

- closing off admin overhead, cost of sales, bank charges and sales to profit and loss.

3 Integrated accounting using standard costs

3.1 Introduction

The difference here is that variances from standard cost are recognised within the ledger accounts themselves, rather than computed afterwards within an operating statement.

Generally, this means that:

- the price/rate variances studied earlier are extracted within the relevant production cost ledger accounts (materials, labour, overheads), so that the work-in-progress account is charged with standard costs of actual resources used.

- efficiency and usage variances are extracted in the work-in-progress account, so that the finished goods stock account carries stock at standard cost.

- the variances are written off to the profit and loss account.

Example

We shall apply the principles of Chapel Ltd, an example we used earlier, when studying variances (chapter 17). The basic data and the operating statement derived there are reproduced below.

Chapel Ltd manufactures a chemical protective called Rustnot. The following standard costs apply for the production of 100 cylinders:

		£
Materials	500 kgs @ 80p per kg	400
Labour	20 hours @ £1.50 per hour	30
Fixed overheads	20 hours @ £1.00 per hour	20
		450

The monthly production/sales budget is 10,000 cylinders. Selling price = £6 per cylinder.

For the month of November the following actual production and sales information is available:

Produced/sold	10,600 cylinders
Sales value	£63,000
Material purchased and used 53,200 kgs	£42,500
Labour 2,040 hours	£3,100
Fixed overheads	£2,200

The operating statement for November appeared as follows:

	£
Budgeted profit (10,000 cylinders)	15,000
Total sales margin variance	300
	15,300

Less: Cost variances	Adv. £	Fav. £	
Material price		60	
Wages rate	40		
Fixed overhead expenditure	200		
Material usage	160		
Labour efficiency		120	
Fixed overhead volume		120	
	400	300	
			100
Actual profit			15,200

Solution

The entries which would appear in the following selected ledger accounts of Chapel Ltd show how standard cost bookkeeping applies in an integrated accounting system:

Wages control

	£		£
Cash	3,100	Rate variance	40
		Work-in-progress	3,060
	3,100		3,100

Raw material control a/c

	£		£
Creditors	42,500	Work-in-progress	42,560
Raw material price variance	60		
	42,560		42,560

Work-in-progress control a/c

	£		£
Raw material control	42,560	Raw material usage variance	160
Wages control	3,060	Finished goods/Cost of sales	47,700
Labour efficiency variance	120		
Production overhead control	2,120		
	47,860		47,860

Production overhead control a/c

	£		£
Creditor	2,200	Expenditure variance	200
Fixed overhead volume		Work-in-progress	2,120
variance	120		
	2,320		2,320

Profit & Loss

	£		£
Cost of sales	47,700	Sales	63,000
Material usage variance	160	Material price variance	60
Wage rate variance	40	Labour efficiency variance	120
Overhead expenditure variance	200	Fixed overhead volume variance	120
Net profit	15,200		
	63,300		63,300

3.2 Advantages of using standard costs in ledgers

There are three major advantages:

- Bookkeeping is made simpler – the problem of similar stock items having different values is avoided.

- Variances are automatically segregated without further work and without the possibility of discrepancies between financial and cost statements.

- Experience shows that managers take variances more seriously if they are included in the financial accounts.

making only the minimum allowance for inefficiency, may be desirable.

4 Interlocking accounting system

4.1 Introduction

We will now consider the principles of the other cost bookkeeping approach, and contrast it with the integrated system.

Remember, under an interlocking system the cost accounts are kept completely separately from the financial accounts. They will, however, need to be kept in line with each other, by the use of control accounts or other form of reconciliation.

The recording system may be arranged in two ways:

- Separate book records without control account: separate costing records are derived independently from the source documents, but are reconciled periodically with the financial records.

- Separate cost ledger with control account: a separate costing ledger is maintained under the control of the cost accountant, but integrated with the financial books by means of a cost ledger control account through which all cost and revenue information for re-analysis is transferred.

4.2 Cost ledger control account

In an interlocking system the cost accounts will only need to record transactions relating to operating revenue and costs; details of capital, debtors and creditors are part of the financial accounting routine. Frequently, however, such financial accounts are merged into a single account (cost ledger control) solely to maintain the double-entry principle within the cost accounts.

4.3 Control accounts

The cost ledger for a manufacturing business will probably contain control accounts for:

- stores
- work-in-progress
- finished stock
- production overhead
- general administration costs
- marketing costs.

4.4 Subsidiary ledgers

Each control account will be supported by a subsidiary ledger to provide the detail required for financial reporting and/or management information. Analysis will be by:

- item of material
- job number (job costing), product (batch costing) or process (process costing)
- job or production
- cost centres (there will be more than one of these).

4.5 Cost ledger accounts

In addition to the cost ledger control and the control accounts detailed above, separate accounts will be kept as required, particularly:

- sales
- cost of sales
- wages
- profit and loss.

Subsidiary details in the form of a sub-ledger or analysis columns may be necessary.

4.6 Accounting entries

Entries to the cost ledger follow the sequence of transactions in the manufacturing business:

	Transaction	Journal entry		Document
(a)	Purchases	Dr Stores		Invoice/GRN
		Cr	Contra	
(b)	Gross wages	Dr Wages		Payroll
		Cr	Contra	

(c)	Expenses incurred	Dr	Production overhead	Invoices/
		Dr	General admin cost	Petty cash/
		Dr	Marketing cost	Journal
		Cr	Contra	
(d)	Materials issued	Dr	Work-in-progress (direct)	Requisitions
		Dr	Production overhead (indirect)	
		Cr	Stores	
(e)	Analysed wages	Dr	(as (d) above)	Time sheets, etc.
		Cr	Wages	
(f)	Overhead absorbed	Dr	Work-in-progress	Cost journal
		Cr	Production overhead	
(g)	Completed work	Dr	Finished stock	Production order
		Cr	Work-in-progress	
(h)	Goods sold	Dr	Cost of sales/contra	Delivery note/
		Cr	Finished stock/sales	Invoice

Notes:

- (d) and (e) could affect general administration and marketing.

- In a marginal costing system entry (f) would be for variable overhead only.

4.7 Period end procedure

At the end of the reporting period a profit and loss account can be prepared from the cost ledger in the following format:

	£
Sales	X
Less: Cost of sales	(X)
Gross margin	X
Add/Less: Over/under-absorbed overhead	X/(X)
General administration costs	X
Marketing costs	X
Operating profit	X

Balances in stores, work-in-progress and finished stock represent stock valuations at cost. At the end of the financial year the costing profit and loss account will be closed by transfer to cost ledger contra and the balances in stock accounts carried forward with an offsetting credit in cost ledger contra.

4.8 Reconciliation of financial and costing profit

Where the cost accounts are maintained independently in an interlocking system it is necessary to reconcile the financial and costing results.

Activity 1

List examples of differences that you think there might be between the financial and costing profits under the following headings:

(a) Appropriations of profit not dealt with in the costing system.

(b) Income and expenditure of a purely financial nature (i.e. nothing to do with manufacturing).

(c) Items where financial and costing treatments differ.

Feedback to this activity is at the end of the chapter.

4.9 Interlocking systems – advantage

The main advantage of an interlocking system is that it provides more flexibility because it is not constrained (in the cost ledger) by the regulations of financial accounting. However, this flexibility has a cost:

- the administrative burden of recording many transactions twice, once in the cost ledger and once in the financial ledger.

- the need to prepare a statement reconciling the profit shown by the cost and financial ledgers.

4.10 How relevant is all this?

In practice, of course, any organisation large and complex enough to justify a full-blooded costing system would manage it via computer. These days accounting packages are built around relational databases rather than ledgers, even though they may use accounting terminology for the various reports and reconciliations that can be performed.

In effect this means that any kind of analysis of the data you want can be extracted: the integrated/interlocking question is not an issue.

Summary

The information required in cost accounting is often somewhat different to that required in a financial accounting system. The traditional method of dealing with this is to keep two separate sets of ledgers that are not integrated with each other. This is known as an interlocking system. The alternative is to integrate the two systems and this is known as an integrated system.

By the time you have finished this chapter you should be able to:

- prepare accounting entries for an integrated accounting system using standard costs

- explain the difference between integrated and interlocking accounting systems.

Self-test questions

Methods of cost bookkeeping

1 What are integrated accounts? (1.1)

2 What is an interlocking system of accounts? (1.1)

COST BOOKKEEPING : **CHAPTER 21**

Integrated accounting systems

3   What are the two main benefits of an integrated system of accounting? (2.1)

4   In an integrated system what would be the double entry for purchase of raw materials? (2.1)

Interlocking accounting system

5   What is the name of the account used in the cost ledger of an interlocking system in order to maintain the double entry? (4.2)

6   What types of control accounts are likely to be kept in an interlocking system? (4.3)

7   What accounts, other than control accounts and the cost ledger contra, are likely to be kept in an interlocking system? (4.5)

8   What type of appropriations of profit might there be that are not dealt with in a costing system? (Activity 1)

9   What types of items might be treated differently in financial and costing accounts? (Activity 1)

Exam-type questions

Question 1

A firm operates an integrated cost and financial accounting system.

The accounting entries for an issue of Direct Materials to Production would be:

A   Dr Work-in-progress control account   Cr Stores control account

B   Dr Finished goods account   Cr Stores control account

C   Dr Stores control account   Cr Work-in-progress control account

D   Dr Cost of sales account   Cr Work-in-progress control account

Question 2

In an integrated cost and financial accounting system, the accounting entries for factory overhead absorbed would be:

A   Dr Work-in-progress control account Cr Overhead control account

B   Dr Overhead control account   Cr Work-in-progress control account

C   Dr Overhead control account   Cr Cost of sales account

D   Dr Cost of sales account   Cr Overhead control account

Question 3

The bookkeeping entries in a standard cost system when the actual price for raw materials is less than the standard price are:

A   Dr   Raw materials control account   Cr   Raw material price variance account

B   Dr   WIP control account   Cr   Raw materials control account

C   Dr   Raw material price variance account   Cr   Raw materials control account

D   Dr   WIP control account   Cr   Raw material price variance account

For the answers to these questions, see the 'Answers' section at the end of the book.

Practice question

Integrated process

A processing organisation operates an integrated accounting system.

From the following information **you are required:**

(a)   to write up the accounts in the cost ledger for June

(b)   to extract a trial balance as at 30 June.

The trial balance of the cost ledger as at 31 May was as follows:

	£	£	£
Stores control		90,400	
Work-in-progress, Process 1:			
Direct materials	8,200		
Direct wages	6,400		
Production overhead	22,400		
		37,000	
Work-in-progress, Process 2:			
Direct materials	31,200		
Direct wages	8,800		
Production overhead	22,000		
		62,000	
Finished goods		89,000	
Production overhead, under/over-absorbed			4,800
Sales			680,000
Cost of sales		529,200	
General ledger control			131,800
Abnormal loss		9,000	
		816,600	816,600

During June the following transactions took place:

	£
Materials returned to suppliers	1,560
Actual cost of materials purchased	42,500
Materials issued to:	
Process 1	21,200
Process 2	10,400
Materials issued to production maintenance department	1,280
Direct wages incurred in:	
Process 1	16,800
Process 2	21,600
Indirect wages and salaries incurred	48,200
Production indirect expenses incurred	72,000
Sales	300,000

Production reports include the following:

	Direct materials £	Direct wages £
Abnormal loss in:		
Process 1	480	400
Process 2	1,400	280
Transfer from:		
Process 1	24,600	19,600
Process 2	110,000	20,520

The value of finished goods in stock at 30 June was £98,200.

Overhead is absorbed by means of direct wages percentage rates.

Production transferred from Process 1 to Process 2 is treated as an item of materials cost in Process 2 accounts.

For the answer to this question, see the 'Answers' section at the end of the book.

Feedback to activity

Activity 1

(a) **Appropriations of profit not dealt with in the costing system**

  (i) corporation tax

  (ii) transfers to reserves

  (iii) dividends paid and proposed

  (iv) amounts written off intangibles such as goodwill, discount on issue of debentures, expenses of capital issues, etc.

(b) **Income and expenditure of a purely financial nature** (i.e. outside the scope of manufacture)

  (i) interest and dividends received

  (ii) profits and losses on the sale of fixed assets and investments

      (iii)   interest on bank loans, mortgages and debentures

      (iv)   damages payable at law, fines and penalties.

(c)   **Items where financial and costing treatments differ**

      (i)   Differences in the valuation of stocks and work-in-progress. Stocks may, for costing purposes, be valued at LIFO, whereas FIFO may be employed in the financial accounts.

      (ii)   Depreciation. In the financial accounts this charge is normally based solely upon the passage of time, whereas in the cost accounts it may be a variable charge based upon machine/man hours worked.

      (iii)   Abnormal losses in production and storage. In the financial accounts, materials and wages will include any abnormal losses of material or time. In the cost accounts such losses may be excluded to avoid misleading comparisons.

      (iv)   Interest on capital. Notional interest on capital employed in production is sometimes included in the cost accounts to reflect the nominal cost of employing the capital rather than investing it outside the business.

      (v)   Charge in lieu of rent. Again a notional amount for rent may be included in costs in order to compare costs of production with costs of another business that occupies a rented or leasehold factory.

Chapter 22

ANSWERS TO EXAM-TYPE AND PRACTICE QUESTIONS

Chapter 1

EXAM-TYPE QUESTIONS

Question 1

B Prime cost is defined in the CIMA Official Terminology as 'the total cost of direct material, direct labour and direct expenses'.

Question 2

C A notional cost is a cost used in performance measurement etc to represent the cost of using resources which have no conventional 'actual cost'.

Question 3

B The stores function in a factory is an indirect activity. Any costs of the stores function are therefore classified as indirect.

Question 4

C Item B describes costs of an activity or cost centre. Item A describes cost units. Item D describes budget centres. A cost centre is defined in the CIMA *Official Terminology* as 'a production or service location, function, activity or item of equipment for which costs are accumulated'.

Question 5

A Direct costs are those attributable to a cost unit, which can be economically identified with the unit.

Question 6

Suitable cost units might be a full time student and a lecture hour. A lecture room and the personnel department would be more suitable as cost centres. Lecturer fees are an actual cost incurred, rather than a part of the cost accounting system.

PRACTICE QUESTION

Classify

Cost number	Classification number
1	iv
2	vii
3	ii
4	vii

5	viii
6	iv
7	vi
8	iv
9	i or iv
10	iii

Chapter 2

EXAM-TYPE QUESTIONS

Question 1

C   C = 1,000 + 250P

Costs depend on production

Fixed costs = £1,000

Variable costs per unit = £250

Question 2

The amount of fixed overheads per period is £187,000.

Workings

	£
Total cost of 17,000 hours	246,500
Less variable cost of 17,000 hours (× £3.50)	59,500
Balance = fixed costs	187,000

Question 3

B   X is clearly fixed. To test for strict variability dividing total cost by total units at each activity should produce the same cost per unit, there being no fixed element to cloud the issue.

	Cost per unit @ 100	*Cost per unit @ 140*
W	£80	£75.40
Y	£65	£65.00
Z	£67	£61.30

Thus Y is variable and W and Z are semi-variable with a decreasing fixed cost element per unit as activity level increases.

Question 4

The estimated overhead cost if 16,200 square metres are to be cleaned is £88,095.

Workings

	Sq metres	*Overheads £*
	12,750	73,950
	15,100	83,585
Difference	2,350	9,635

Variable cost is $\dfrac{£9,635}{2,350}$, i.e. £4.10 per square metre.

Fixed costs can be found by substitution:

$$(12,750 \times £4.10) + F = 73,950$$
$$\Rightarrow F = 21,675$$

So for 16,200 square metres:

overheads   =   £21,675 + (16,200 × £4.10)
                  =   £88,095

Question 5

The graph depicts the cost of direct labour, where increased hourly rates are paid for achieving higher levels of output. This cost is a curvilinear variable cost, which has a steeper gradient as activity increases due to the higher hourly rate paid.

The cost of direct materials as described would be a curvilinear variable cost where the gradient becomes less steep as activity increases.

The cost of salaried supervisors as described would be a step cost which increases in fixed steps as each additional supervisor is employed.

PRACTICE QUESTION

D & E Ltd

(a)   **Scatter graph of electricity cost against production**

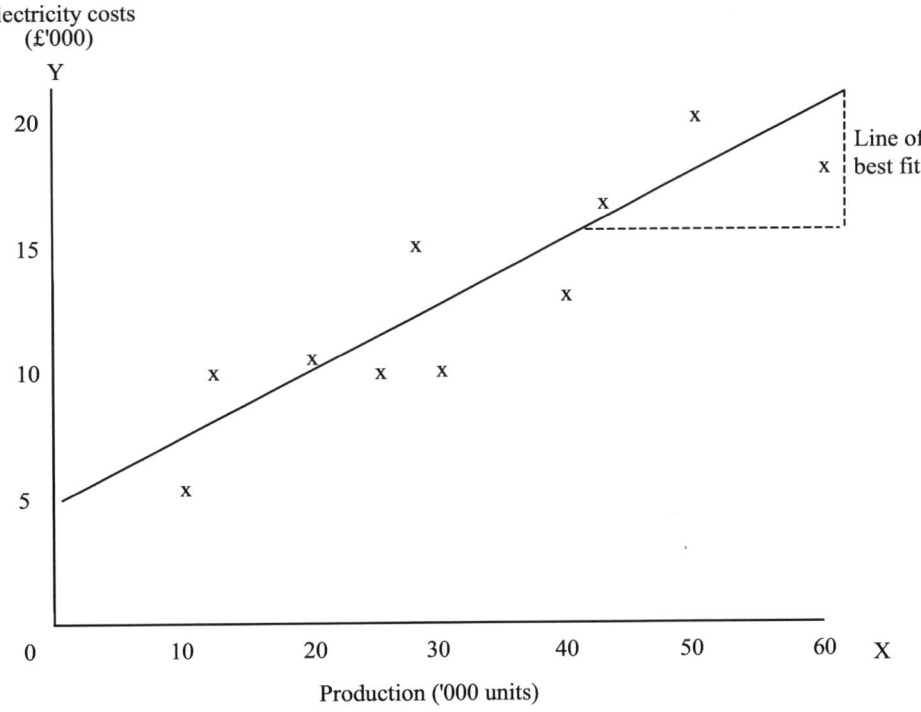

(b)   The line of best fit cuts the vertical axis at approximately £5,000. This is the estimated fixed cost.

The variable cost is estimated by determining the gradient of the line of best fit.

Variable cost per unit $= \dfrac{£(20,000 - 15,000)}{(60,000 - 40,000)\text{units}}$

(c)   Forecast electricity costs = fixed cost + variable cost (£0.25 × units produced)

Quarter 11 forecast = £5,000 + £(0.25 × 15,000 units) = £8,750

Quarter 12 forecast = £5,000 +£(0.25 × 55,000 units) = £18,750

(d)   There are two main sources of error in the forecasts:

     (i)   The assumed relationship between electricity costs and production.

         The scatter graph shows that there can be fairly wide variations in electricity cost for a given level of production. Also the forecast assumes that the same conditions will prevail over the next two quarters as in the last ten quarters.

     (ii)   The line of best fit is drawn by eye. The inherent inaccuracy in this method will affect the reliability of any forecasts based on the analysis.

Chapter 3

EXAM-TYPE QUESTIONS

Question 1

(a)   Overheads for the period were under-absorbed.

(b)   The amount of the under absorption was £146,085.

Workings

Predetermined overhead absorption rate = £349,780/87,445 = £4 per machine hour

Overhead absorbed by actual activity = 72,785 hours × £4 = £291,140

Under-absorbed overhead = £291,140 - £437,225 = £146,085

The overhead is under-absorbed because the actual overhead incurred was greater than the overhead absorbed.

Question 2

The budgeted overhead absorption rate was £15 per direct labour hour.

Workings

Overhead absorbed during period = £330,000 - £15,000 under-absorbed = £315,000

Overhead absorbed = actual hours × overhead absorption rate

Therefore, overhead absorption rate = £315,000/21,000 hours = £15 per hour.

Question 3

D   The repeated distribution method takes account of reciprocal servicing between any number of service cost centres.

The company's overhead rates are based on estimates (option A) but this would apply even if the company did not use the repeated distribution method.

The repeated distribution method may be used when there are two or more service cost centres, regardless of the number of production cost centres. Therefore option B is not correct.

The repeated distribution method will not necessarily help the company to avoid under or over absorption of overheads (option C).

Question 4

B   Absorption relates to cost units, allocation to costs relating to one cost centre only, analysis is the classification of overheads.

Question 5

C   A relates to allocation and apportionment, B is addition, and absorption does not control overheads thus D is not correct.

PRACTICE QUESTION

Fibrex Ltd

Note: Overheads are indirect costs so take care to ensure that the direct materials and wages are not included in the overhead calculations.

(a)   The first step is to allocate and apportion total overheads to the cost centres:

Overhead item	*Basis of apportionment*	*Weaving dept*	*Proofing dept*	*Finishing dept*	*Personnel dept*	*Maint-enance*	*Total*
		£	£	£	£	£	£
Indirect materials and wages	Given	1,100	900	300	1,500	3,800	7,600
Power	Given	5,200	1,000	200	100	800	7,300
Rent and rates	Floor area	1,600	3,600	800	1,600	400	8,000
Factory admin & supervision	Number of employees	2,400	4,000	1,600	400	1,600	10,000
Machine insurance	Gross book value	1,600	400	400	–	–	2,400
		11,900	9,900	3,300	3,600	6,600	35,300
Reapportionments: Personnel	(see Tutorial note) Number of employees 6:10:4:4	900	1,500	600	(3,600)	600	
					–	7,200	
Equipment maintenance	Gross book value (or machine hours) 4:1:1	4,800	1,200	1,200		(7,200)	
		17,600	12,600	5,100			

Overhead absorption rate

		Weaving dept	*Proofing dept*	*Finishing dept*
	=	Budgeted overhead	Budgeted overhead	Budgeted overhead
		Budgeted machine hours	Budgeted labour hours	Budgeted wage cost $\times$ 100

$$\frac{£17,600,000}{1,600,000} \qquad \frac{£12,600,000}{1,800,000} \qquad \frac{£5,100,000}{3,000,000} \times 100$$

$$\begin{array}{ccc} £11 \text{ per} & £7 \text{ per direct} & 170\% \text{ of direct} \\ \text{machine hour} & \text{labour hour} & \text{wage cost} \end{array}$$

Tutorial note:

Reapportionment of service cost centres

As personnel provides a service to another service department (equipment maintenance) it is important to reapportion first the service cost centre which services other service cost centres, i.e. in this case personnel. Then the total of the equipment maintenance costs, including a charge from personnel, can be reapportioned to the production cost centres.

(b)   The circumstances under which a blanket overhead rate may be suitable include the following:

(i)   Where the company offers only a single product or service that must therefore absorb all overheads irrespective of where they are incurred. This does not obviate the need for charging overheads to functional cost centres for cost control purposes.

(ii)   Where all products are similar in nature and use approximately the same amount of the services provided by each department.

(iii)   Where overhead costs are relatively insignificant and the costs of calculating more detailed absorption rates would exceed the benefits resulting from the exercise.

Chapter 4

EXAM-TYPE QUESTIONS

Question 1

B   Fixed overheads = $\frac{1}{4} \times 16$ = £4 per unit

Difference between marginal costing and absorption costing profit is:

(closing stock – opening stock) × fixed OAR

= (2,500 – 0) × £4 = £10,000

As stock has increased, absorption costing profit will be bigger.

Question 2

B   Profit: When stocks increase, some fixed production costs incurred are carried through to next period in an absorption costing system. This means that the profit will be higher under absorption costing.

Closing stock: The absorption costing valuation of closing stock includes fixed production cost, which the marginal costing system excludes, hence the valuation will be higher in the absorption costing system.

Question 3

(a) The profit reported under an absorption costing system is £47,000.

Workings

Absorption costing

	Units	£	£	£
Sales	9,000	20		180,000
Production	11,000	12	132,000	
Closing stock	2,000	12	-24,000	
				108,000
				72,000
Over-absorbed	1,000	4		4,000
				76,000
Variable selling	9,000	1	9,000	
Fixed selling cost	10,000	2	20,000	
				29,000
				47,000

(b) The profit reported under a marginal costing system is £39,000.

Workings

Marginal costing

	Units	£	£	£
Sales	9,000	20		180,000
Production	11,000	8	88,000	
Closing stock	2,000	8	-16,000	
				72,000
				108,000
Fixed production overhead	1,000		40,000	
Variable selling	9,000	1	9,000	
Fixed selling cost	10,000	2	20,000	
				69,000
				39,000

Question 4

A Under or over absorption is determined by comparing what was actually spent with what has been absorbed using the standard absorption rate.

PRACTICE QUESTION

Rayners plc

(a) **Operating statement**

	Year 1 £000	Year 1 £000	Year 2 £000	Year 2 £000	Year 3 £000	Year 3 £000
Marginal costing						
Sales		1,080		1,320		1,140
Opening stock @ £5	Nil		50		50	
Add: Production cost @ £5	500		550		450	
	500		600		500	
Less: Closing stock @ £5	50		50		25	
Cost of sales		(450)		(550)		(475)

	Year 1		Year 2		Year 3	
	£000	£000	£000	£000	£000	£000
Contribution		630		770		665
Less: Fixed costs:						
Production overhead	270		270		270	
Administration overhead	20		20		20	
		(290)		(290)		(290)
Profit		340		480		375

Absorption costing

	Year 1		Year 2		Year 3	
Sales		1,080		1,320		1,140
Opening stock @ £8	Nil		80		80	
Add: Production cost @ £8	800		880		720	
	800		960		800	
Less: Closing stock @ £8	80		80		40	
Cost of sales		(720)		(880)		(760)
		360		440		380
Over absorption (see working)		30		60		Nil
Administration overhead		(20)		(20)		(20)
Profit		370		480		360

Working

	Year 1 £000	Year 2 £000	Year 3 £000
Fixed production overhead absorbed:			
100,000 units × £3	300		
110,000 units × £3		330	
90,000 units × £3			270
Fixed production overhead incurred:			
90,000 units × £3	270	270	270
Over absorption	30	60	-

(b)   The difference in profit arises because of the difference in the amount of fixed production overhead included in stock under the absorption costing system.

When the opening and closing stock includes the same amount of fixed overheads (i.e. here when the volume of opening and closing stock is the same, in year 2) profit is the same under both techniques. Where volume of stock has gone up (year 1) and the amount of fixed production overhead in stock has increased then profit is higher under absorption costing and *vice versa*.

This may be summarised as follows:

	Year 1 £000	Year 2 £000	Year 3 £000
Profit per marginal costing	340	480	375
Add: Increase in fixed overhead included in stock under absorption costing: 10,000 units @ £3	30	–	–
Less: Decrease in fixed overhead included in stock under absorption costing: 5,000 units @ £3	–	–	(15)
Profit per absorption costing	370	480	360

Chapter 5

EXAM-TYPE QUESTIONS

Question 1

(a) Closing stock values with the LIFO method, compared with the FIFO method, will be lower. This is because the LIFO method values issues at the latest prices and values the remaining stock at the older, lower prices.

(b) Reported profits with the LIFO method, compared with the FIFO method, will be lower. The latest, higher prices are charged to cost of sales, therefore profit will be lower than with FIFO.

Question 2

(a) The stock valuation at 31 August on FIFO basis would be £22,200.

Working

Closing stock = 4,000 + 1,200 + 2,800 – 3,900 – 1,100 = 3,000 kg

FIFO valuation = 2,800 × £7.50 + 200 × £6 = £22,200.

(b) The stock valuation at 31 August on a weighted average cost basis would be £22,185.

Working

	kg		£/Kg	£
Received	4,000	@	5.000	20,000
Issued	3,900	@	5.000	19,500
	100			500
Received	1,200	@	6.000	7,200
	1,300	@	5.923	7,700
Issued	1,100	@	5.923	6,515
	200			1,185
Received	2,800	@	7.500	21,000
	3,000			22,185

Question 3

(a) $200 \times £7 = £1,400$

(b)   Purchase cost – stock value = $£6,550 - (100 \times £5 + 100 \times £6) = £5,450$

Question 4

A   FIFO means that the value of closing stock reflects the most recent prices paid. Since there is a high stock turnover these will be close to current prices.

Question 5

Goods received note	3
Purchase requisition	1
Materials requisition	4
Purchase order	2
Materials returned note	5

PRACTICE QUESTION

Material X

(a)   (i)   Continuous stocktaking refers to a system whereby stocktaking is carried out on an ongoing rota basis throughout the year, so that every stock item is checked at least once. Items of greater value or importance may be counted several times during the year. As a result, stocktaking effort can be directed so as to maximise control and minimise costs. In contrast to periodic stocktaking it also avoids disruption to production.

(ii)   Perpetual inventory is a system of entering details of all stock receipts and issues for each individual raw material/finished product onto a record card, thus enabling the stock quantity on hand to be known at any time. The stock quantity provides the necessary information for stock re-ordering and for verifying/reconciling physical stock counts.

(b)

	£/kg		£
3,040 kg	0.765/kg	=	2,325.60
1,400 kg	0.780/kg	=	1,092.00
4,440 kg	0.770/kg (TN 1)	=	3,417.60
(1,700) kg	0.770/kg	=	(1,309.00)
2,740 kg			2,108.60
60 kg	0.770/kg (TN 2)	=	46.20
(220) kg	0.780/kg (TN 2)	=	(171.60)
1,630 kg	———		1,268.14
4,210 kg			3,251.34
(1,250) kg	0.772/kg	=	(965.00)
2,960 kg			£2,286.34

Tutorial note:

1   The weighted average price is calculated after each purchase, by dividing the total value of the stock at that time by the total volume. So the weighted average after the purchase on Day 1 is calculated as:

$$\frac{£(2,325.60+1,092.00)}{(3,040+1,400)\text{kg}} = £0.76973 = £0.770 \text{ to 3 dp.}$$

2   Note here there are returns to stock and to the supplier. You should treat these as reversals of part of the original transactions to which they relate – so stock returns are brought back in at the price at which they were issued, and supplier returns recorded at the price at which they were bought.

Chapter 6

EXAM-TYPE QUESTIONS

Question 1

Free stock = physical stock + stock ordered – stock scheduled

13,000 = physical stock + 27,500 – 16,250

Physical stock = 1,750 units

Question 2

Re-order level = maximum usage – maximum lead time

$\qquad$ = 175 per day × 16 days

$\qquad$ = 2,800 tyres

Question 3

Maximum level = re-order level + re-order quantity – (minimum usage × minimum lead time)

$\qquad$ = 2,800 (from qu. 2) + 3,000 – (90×10)

$\qquad$ = 4,900 tyres

Question 4

Maximum stock $\quad$ = $\quad$ re-order level + re-order quantity – (minimum usage × minimum lead time)

$\qquad$ = $\qquad$ 6,300 + 6,500 – (180 × 11)

$\qquad$ = $\qquad$ 10,820 units

Question 5

Minimum stock $\quad$ = $\quad$ re-order level – (average usage × average lead time)

$\qquad$ = $\qquad$ 6,300 – (350 × 13)

$\qquad$ = $\qquad$ 1,750 units

Question 6

C   The EOQ formula derives the exact quantity to be ordered each time to minimise the total annual cost of ordering and storing stock.

PRACTICE QUESTION

Computer bureau order quantity

(a)   **Calculation of cost associated with particular order quantities**

Order Quantity	Delivery cost $\dfrac{1,000}{x}\times 15$	Storage cost $\dfrac{x}{2}\times 2.70$	Ordering cost Delivery + Storage cost cost
	£	£	£
50	$\dfrac{1,000}{50}\times 15 = 300$	$\dfrac{50}{2}\times 2.70 = 67.50$	367.50
100	$\dfrac{1,000}{100}\times 15 = 150$	$\dfrac{100}{2}\times 2.70 = 135.00$	285.00
150	$\dfrac{1,000}{150}\times 15 = 100$	$\dfrac{150}{2}\times 2.70 = 202.50$	302.50
200	$\dfrac{1,000}{200}\times 15 = 75$	$\dfrac{200}{2}\times 2.70 = 270.00$	345.00
250	$\dfrac{1,000}{250}\times 15 = 60$	$\dfrac{250}{2}\times 2.70 = 337.50$	397.50

(b)   From the figures calculated in (a) we can see that the order quantity of approximately 100 units results in the lowest cost.

(c)   EOQ = $\sqrt{\dfrac{2\times £15 \times 1,00}{£2.70}}$

        =   105 units

Chapter 7

EXAM-TYPE QUESTIONS

Question 1

The budgeted labour cost of the job is £30,000.

Actual labour hours are 2,400 but $100/80 \times 2,400$ hours will have to be paid, because of the idle time.

Question 2

B   Unless the overtime can be traced to a specific product or job, it will be treated as an indirect production cost and absorbed into units using the normal absorption basis.

Question 3

D   The wages are a guaranteed amount, even at zero output. Beyond a certain output the total wages rise in a linear fashion, which represents the piecework payment beyond the guaranteed.

PRACTICE QUESTION

Components A, B and C

(a)   **Calculation of total payroll cost**

		Grade of labour			
		I	II	III	IV	Total
		£	£	£	£	£
Basic pay:						
I	$6 \times £6.00 \times 40$	1,440.00				
II	$18 \times £5.00 \times 42$		3,780.00			
III	$4 \times £4.80 \times 40$			768.00		
IV	$1 \times £4.80 \times 44$				211.20	
		1,440.00	3,780.00	768.00	211.20	6,199.20
Overtime premium:						
I	$6 \times £3.00 \times (40 - 38)$	36.00				
II	$18 \times £2.50 \times (42 - 38)$		180.00			
III	$4 \times £2.40 \times (40 - 38)$			19.20		
IV	$1 \times £2.40 \times (44 - 38)$				14.40	
		36.00	180.00	19.20	14.40	249.60
Bonus payable (see working):						
I	$\dfrac{6 \times 40}{1,200} \times 360 \times (75\% \times £6)$	324.00				
II	$\dfrac{18 \times 42}{1,200} \times 360 \times (75\% \times £5.00)$		850.50			
III	$\dfrac{4 \times 40}{1,200} \times 360 \times (75\% \times £4.80)$			172.80		
IV	$\dfrac{1 \times 44}{1,200} \times 360 \times (75\% \times £4.80)$				47.52	
		324.00	850.50	172.80	47.52	1394.82
Total (gross pay)		1,800.00	4,810.50	960.00	273.12	7,843.62

Working

Standard time for actual output:

Component		Std hrs
A	$444 \times 0.5 =$	222
B	$900 \times 0.9 =$	810
C	$480 \times 1.1 =$	528
Total standard hours		1,560

Actual time:

Grade		Hours
I	6×40	240
II	18×42	756
III	4×40	160
IV	1×44	44
Total actual hours		1,200
Total hours saved		360

(b) **Journal**

	Dr £	Cr £
Wages	7,843.62	
National insurance (paid by company):		
5% × £7,843.62	392.18	
Income tax payable		884.00
National insurance payable		
£392.18 + (6% × £7,843.62)		862.80
Social club (12 × £0.25)		3.00
Bank		6,486.00
	8,235.80	8,235.80

Being the payroll with deductions and national insurance for Week 26.

(c) Advantages of a group incentive scheme:

(i) Emphasises the need for worker co-operation to achieve required targets for the company.

(ii) Applicable when a production line exists or when operatives work in crews or gangs.

Disadvantages of a group incentive scheme:

(i) The more conscientious members of the group create the benefit that has to be shared with the less efficient members of the group. This can have a demotivational effect on the former.

(ii) Where there are different degrees of skill required by members of the group it might be difficult to recognise this easily and objectively in allocating the bonus between the group members.

Chapter 8

EXAM-TYPE QUESTIONS

Question 1

C   Current costs may be relevant but only if they are indicative of future costs.

Question 2

B   A is future expenditure, C is nonsense, D refers to fixed costs.

Question 3

B   The original cost is irrelevant. The material could be sold now for scrap for £12,500. If reworked, it could be sold for a net £10,000. The incremental effect of reworking is therefore a loss of £2,500.

Question 4

The relevant cost of the material R to be included in the quotation is £6,000.

Since material R is in regular use and is readily available in the market, its relevant cost is the replacement price of £6/kg.

So 1,000 kg × £6/kg = £6,000

Question 5

The relevant labour cost of the contract is £115,000.

The relevant cost is the lower of the relevant costs of each option.

		£
Recruitment:	4 employees @ £40,000 =	160,000
Manager (no change)		Nil
		160,000
Retrain and replace:	Training	15,000
	Replacement	100,000
		115,000

PRACTICE QUESTION

Civil engineering

(a)

Note		Northeast £	Northeast £	South coast £	South coast £
	Contract price		288,000		352,000
1	Material X: stock	19,440			
2	Material X: firm orders	27,360			
3	Material X: not yet ordered	60,000			
4	Material Y			49,600	
5	Material Z			71,200	
6	Labour	86,000		110,000	
8	Staff accommodation and travel	6,800		5,600	
9	Penalty clause			28,000	
10	Loss of plant hire income			6,000	
			199,600		270,400
	Profit		88,400		81,600

The company should undertake the northeast contract. It is better than the south coast contract by £6,800 (£88,400 − £81,600).

(b) *Notes*:

1   Material X can be used in place of another material that the company uses. The relevant cost of material X for this purpose is $90\% \times$ £21,600 = £19,440. If the company undertakes the northeast contract it will not be able to obtain this saving. This is an opportunity cost.

2   Although the material has not been received yet the company is committed to the purchase. Its treatment is the same therefore as if it was already in stock. The relevant cost is $90\% \times$ £30,400 = £27,360.

3   The future cost of material X not yet ordered is relevant.

4   The original cost of material Y is a sunk cost and is therefore not relevant. If the material was to be sold now its value would be £24,800 $\times 2 \times 85\%$ = £42,160, i.e. twice the purchase price less 15%, however, if the material is kept it can be used on other contracts, thus saving the company from future purchases. The second option is the better. The relevant cost of material Y is $2 \times$ £24,800 = £49,600. If the company uses material Y on the south coast contract, it will eventually have to buy an extra £49,600 of Y for use on other contracts.

5   The future cost of material Z is an incremental cost and is relevant.

6   As the labour is to be subcontracted it is a variable cost and is relevant.

7   Site management is a fixed cost and will be incurred whichever contract is undertaken (and indeed if neither is undertaken), and is therefore not relevant.

8   It is assumed that the staff accommodation and travel is specific to the contracts and will only be incurred if the contracts are undertaken.

9   If the south coast contract is undertaken the company has to pay a £28,000 penalty for withdrawing from the northeast contract. This is a relevant cost with regard to the south coast contract.

10   The depreciation on plant is not a cash flow. It is therefore not relevant. The opportunity cost of lost plant hire is relevant, however.

11   It is assumed that the notional interest has no cash flow implications.

12   It is assumed that the HQ costs are not specific to particular contracts.

Chapter 9

EXAM-TYPE QUESTIONS

Question 1

$$\text{B/E point} = \frac{1,000 \times (£4.60 + 5.80)}{£24.90 - (£5.60 + 3.40)} = 654 \text{ units}$$

Question 2

C   Break even number of units $= \dfrac{\text{Fixed costs}}{\text{Contribution per unit}}$

If selling price per unit and variable cost per unit rise by 10%, then contribution per unit rises by 10%.

$\therefore$ Break even number of units will decrease

(assuming a positive contribution in the first place!)

Question 3

	£ per unit
Selling price	40
Variable cost	32
Contribution	8

Increase in fixed cost = £8,000

∴ Increase in B/E point = £8,000 ÷ 8 = 1,000 units

Question 4

The budgeted break even sales value (to the nearest £1,000) is £253,000.

Weighted average c/s ratio equals

$$\frac{(1 \times 40\%) + (3 \times 50\%)}{4} = 47.5\%$$

$$\text{Break even point} = \frac{\text{Fixed costs}}{\text{c / s ratio}} = \frac{£120,000}{0.475} = 252,632$$

Question 5

The margin of safety was 2,000 units.

$$\text{Break even point} = \text{Fixed costs} \times \frac{1}{\text{c / s ratio}} = £48,000 \times \frac{1}{40\%} = £120,000$$

If actual sales = £140,000, then the margin of safety is £20,000 (£140,000 − £120,000)

Since the selling price is £10 per unit this is equivalent to 2,000 units.

Question 6

If a sales value of £100 per unit is assumed then the original and revised situations will be:

	Original £ per unit	Revised £ per unit
Selling price	100	110
Variable cost	60	60
Contribution	40	50

Fixed costs do not affect contribution and if sales volume is unchanged then the overall change in contribution can be measured using the contribution per unit:

$$\frac{(50 - 40)}{40} = 25\%$$

PRACTICE QUESTION

Shoe shop

(a) $\text{Break even point} = \dfrac{\text{Total fixed costs}}{\text{Contribution per pair}}$

     Contribution per pair = Selling price − Variable cost = £40 − £25 = £15

     $\text{Break even point} = \dfrac{£(100,000 + 40,000 + 100,000)}{£15}$

                      = <u>16,000 pairs</u>

Margin of safety $\quad$ = Current level of sales − Break even sales

$\qquad\qquad\qquad\qquad$ = 25,000 − 16,000

$\qquad\qquad\qquad\qquad$ = <u>9,000 pairs</u>

(b) Net income from sale of 20,000 pairs:

	£
Contribution: 20,000 × £15	300,000
Less: Fixed costs	240,000
Net profit	60,000

(c) Sales volume for a required profit

$$= \frac{\text{Total fixed cost} + \text{Required profit}}{\text{Contribution per pair}}$$

$$= \frac{£240,000 + £10,000}{£(15 - 2)}$$

Sales volume for a net income of £10,000

$$= \quad 19,231 \text{ pairs}$$

Note: Because of the need for a whole number answer, actual net income will be $((19,231 \times £13 - £240,000))$, i.e. £10,003.

(d) Breakeven point $= \dfrac{£240,000 + £20,000}{£\left(15 + \left(40 \times \dfrac{12}{100}\right)\right)}$

Break even point $= \dfrac{£260,000}{£19.80} \quad = \quad \underline{13,131 \text{ pairs}}$

Note: again this whole number answer results in just below break even point being achieved, i.e.:

	£
Contribution: 13,131 × £19.80 =	259,993.80
Less: Fixed costs	260,000.00
Net loss	6.20

Chapter 10

EXAM-TYPE QUESTIONS

Question 1

Finishing process hours required for production to meet maximum demand

	Units	*Hours/unit*	*Hours*
X	4,500	45/60	3,375
Y	4,500	36/60	2,700
Z	4,500	25/60	1,875
			7,950

$\therefore$ Hours are a limiting factor

	X	*Y*	*Z*
Contribution/unit (£)	10	9	6
Hours/unit	0.750	0.600	0.417
Contribution/hr (£)	13.333	15.000	14.400
Ranking	3rd	1st	2nd

Optimal plan

Product	*Units*	*Hours*
Y	4,500	2,700
Z	4,500	1,875
		4,575
X	1,900	1,425 (Bal fig)
		6,000

Question 2

D   Only buy those components where the buying price is less than the variable manufacturing cost. This applies only to component T.

Question 3

Scarce resource – 7,000 labour hours

	A	*B*	*C*
Labour hours per unit	2.5	6	7.5
Contribution per unit	£6.50	£6.80	£15
Contribution per labour hour	£2.60	£1.13	£2
Ranking	1	3	2

Production plan

		Hours
Maximum demand for		
A	1,000 units × 2.5 hours	2,500
C	200 units × 7.5 hours	1,500
B	500 units × 6 hours	3,000 (balance)
		7,000

Question 4

C

	Kilts	Skirts	Dresses	Total
Material per unit (sq. metres)	1.0	0.5	2.0	
Material for 1,000 units (sq. metres)	1,000	500	2,000	3,500
Labour per unit (hours)	3.0	1.0	1.0	
Labour for 1,000 units (hours)	3,000	1,000	1,000	5,000

Labour hours are a limiting factor. Only one product can be manufactured since only 1,000 labour hours are available.

	Kilts £	Skirts £	Dresses £
Contribution per unit	12.00	5.50	7.00
Contribution per labour hour	4.00	5.50	7.00

Dresses therefore earn the highest contribution from the limiting factor.

PRACTICE QUESTION

Barford bakery

(a)

	Barford £	Wilden £	Roxton £	Total £
Sales	112	183	174	469
Labour	40	75	75	190
Flour	32	45	48	125
Other ingredients	8	15	18	41
	80	135	141	356
Contribution	32	48	33	113
Fixed overheads				38
Profit				75

(b)   Barford   32/112 =   28.57%

       Wilden   48/183 =   26.23%

       Roxton   33/174 =   18.97%

(c)   Cost increases are:

	Barford £	Wilden £	Roxton £
Labour (10%)	4	7.5	7.5
Other variable costs (5%)	2	3.0	3.3
Increase in sales value required	£6	£10.5	£10.8
Percentage increase (e.g. 6/112)	5.4%	5.7%	6.2%

(d)

	Barford £	Wilden £	Roxton £
Selling price	0.28	0.61	0.29
Variable costs per loaf (W1)	0.20	0.45	0.235
Contribution/loaf	0.08	0.16	0.055
Labour hours/loaf	0.04	0.1	0.05
Contribution per labour hour	£2	£1.60	£1.10
Ranking	1st	2nd	3rd

Produce 400 Barford loaves requiring 0.04 hours each	=	16 hours
Produce 300 Wilden loaves requiring 0.1 hours each	=	30 hours
Produce 280 Roxton loaves requiring 0.05 hours each	=	14 hours
		60 hours

The profit that will result from this plan is:

					£
Barford	400	loaves	×	£0.08 contribution	32.0
Wilden	300	loaves	×	£0.16 contribution	48.0
Roxton	280	loaves	×	£0.055 contribution	15.4
					95.4
Less fixed costs					38.0
Profit					57.4

Workings

$$(W1) \quad \frac{(\text{Labour} + \text{Flour} + \text{Other Ingredients})}{5}$$

Chapter 11

EXAM-TYPE QUESTIONS

Question 1

The budgeted labour cost is £11,200.

$$\text{Actual expected total time} = \frac{2,520}{0.9} = 2,800 \text{ hours}$$

∴ Budgeted labour cost = 2,800 × £4 = £11,200.

Question 2

B   The scale of operations may be limited by various factors, e.g. sales, labour, material, cash or machinery.

The limiting factor must be identified at the first stage of the budgeting process, since it will determine all the other budgets. In this context the limiting factor is referred to as the principal budget factor.

Question 3

B   The quantity of goods available for sale comprises the sales quantity plus the required closing stock. Some of these are provided from the opening stock.

Question 4

The production budget for month 1 will be 6,600 units.

	Units
40% produced in month of sale = 40% × 6,000 =	2,400
60% of next month's sales = 60% × 7,000 =	4,200
	6,600

PRACTICE QUESTION

S Ltd

Production budget

	Product A '000 units	Product C '000 units	Product E '000 units
Sales (W1)	140	190	420
Stock increase/(decrease)	(5)	2	(40)
Production required	135	192	380
Add: Excess to cover normal loss (W4)	15	48	20
Production budget	150	240	400

Workings

1   Sales units = $\dfrac{\text{Budgeted sales value}}{\text{Expected selling price}}$

2   Expected selling price = Expected unit cost plus expected profit, i.e.:

Product A   £24 × $^{100}\!/_{80}$ =   £30

Product C   £15 × $^{100}\!/_{75}$ =   £20

Product E   £20 × $^{100}\!/_{83\frac{1}{3}}$ =   £24

3   Stock units = $\dfrac{\text{Budgeted stock values}}{\text{Expected unit costs}}$

4   Additional requirements to cover normal loss of production:

Required production × $\dfrac{\text{Loss percentage}}{\text{Normal production percentage}}$

i.e.   Product A   135 × $^{10}\!/_{90}$ =   15

Product C   192 × $^{20}\!/_{80}$ =   48

Product E   380 × $^{5}\!/_{95}$ =   20

Chapter 12

EXAM-TYPE QUESTIONS

Question 1

A   Depreciation is not a cash flow, so would not be included in the cash budget.

Question 2

D   60% of August sales less 2% discount:

	£
£60,000 × 60% × 98% =	35,280
25% of July sales:	
£40,000 × 25%	10,000
12% of June sales:	
£35,000 × 12%	4,200
	49,480

Question 3

Repayment of a bank loan and proceeds from the sale of a fixed asset are both cash flows and so would be included in the cash budget, but not in the budgeted profit and loss account.

The bad debts write off is not a cash flow and would not be included in the cash budget.

PRACTICE QUESTION

(a)   **Cash budget: January – March**

	January £	February £	March £
Receipts of cash			
Current month sales	120,000	160,000	240,000
Less discounts given	(4,800)	(6,400)	(9,600)
Previous month's sales	25,000	30,000	40,000
	140,200	183,600	270,400
Cash payments			
Purchases	100,000	150,000	280,000
Less discounts received	(10,000)	(15,000)	(28,000)
Expenses (W1)	19,200	24,200	29,200
Dividend	1,000		
Interest (W2)			1,500
	110,200	159,200	282,700
Net cashflow for month	30,000	24,400	(12,300)
Opening balance	(9,000)[1]	21,000	45,400
Closing balance	21,000	45,400	33,100

[1]   From balance sheet

Workings

W1   Monthly depreciation = 12% × 80,000 × 1/12 = £800

   Deduct this from the monthly expense figures to obtain the cash flow

W2   Loan interest per annum = 15% × £40,000 = £6,000

   Loan interest per quarter = $\frac{1}{4}$ × £6,000 = £1,500

(b) **Budgeted Profit and Loss account for January - March**

	£	£
Sales		650,000
Cost of sales (= purchases since stock constant)		530,000
Gross profit		120,000
Add: discount received		53,000
		173,000
Less:		
Expenses (including depreciation)	75,000	
Interest	1,500	
Discounts allowed	20,800	
		(97,300)
Net Profit		75,700

Chapter 13

EXAM-TYPE QUESTIONS

Question 1

A B, C (and possibly D) are true of fixed costs.

Question 2

	£
Actual expenditure for 18,000 units	98,000
Less: Fixed overheads over budget	(11,000)
Standard expenditure for 18,000 units	87,000
Less: Standard variable element (18,000 × £2.75)	(49,500)
Budgeted fixed cost	37,500

Question 3

Raw material content £4 after 6,000 units = £3.80/unit

$(5,000 \times (4 + VC)) + FC = 76,500$

$(8,000 \times (3.8 + VC)) + FC = 106,400$

$20,000 + 5,000 VC + FC = 76,500$

$30,400 + 8,000VC + FC = 106,400$

$10,400 + 3,000VC = 29,900$

$3,000VC = 19,500$

$VC = £6.50/unit$

$FC = £24,000$

Total cost after 6,000 units = (Units × £10.30) + £24,000

At 7,000 units, total cost = (7,000 × £10.30) + £24,000 = £96,100

Question 4

Variable production cost per unit = (£12,600 - £8,700)/(7,000 − 4,000) = £1.30

Fixed cost = £12,600 − (7,000 × £1.30) = £3,500

Flexible budget cost allowance for 5,200 units = £3,500 + (5,200 × £1.30) = £10,260

Question 5

C   A flexible budget is a budget that recognises which costs remain constant and which change when the level of activity changes. From this analysis a budget is prepared which shows the total costs expected at different levels of activity.

PRACTICE QUESTION

C Ltd

Note: this is very much a thinking question where the student has to apply knowledge of budgetary control and some common sense to identify the 'deliberate mistakes' made by the examiner.

The following changes ought to be made to the report:

- The budgeted cost figures should be adjusted/flexed to allow for the effect on costs of the 100 unit increase in the activity level before variances are calculated. This will have the effect of increasing the budgeted variable costs to reflect the increase in the activity level. It would be easier for this purpose to separate costs into fixed and variable.

- It would be helpful to provide a breakdown of the overhead allocated and sundries figures to obtain a clearer idea of which cost items have changed. It would also be useful to indicate where possible which costs are controllable by the cost centre manager.

- There should be space on the report for the department supervisor to be able to explain why variances have occurred. It should not be assumed they are as a result of 'considerable inefficiency'. The current approach is rather insensitive to the feelings/opinions of the supervisor.

- Budget and actual figures for the year to date would be useful.

- It may be more relevant from the point of view of cost behaviour to measure the activity level for some of the costs in labour/machine hours.

Chapter 14

EXAM-TYPE QUESTIONS

Question 1

C   Basic standards may provide the basis for developing current standards. The show the trend of costs over time.

Question 2

C   For example, if it is expected that 50 widgets will be produced in an hour, 200 widgets represents 4 standard hours (regardless of actual clock hours spent)

Question 3

False   Attainable standards assume efficient levels of production, but include allowances for normal loss, waste and machine downtime. This statement describes an ideal standard.

PRACTICE QUESTION

Budgets and standards

A budget is a quantitative or financial plan relating to the future. A standard is a predetermined measurable quantity set in defined conditions.

Similarities

- Both budgets and standards relate to the future.

- Both budgets and standards must be quantified.

- Both are used in planning.

- Both are used in controlling the activities of the business. Actual results are compared against the budget or standard and if a significant difference occurs, the reasons behind the difference are investigated and if possible and desirable, corrective action taken.

- Both may be used as a basis for evaluating performance. Managers and workers may be judged on their performance compared with the expected result.

- Neither budgets nor standards should be prepared as just 'cold' mathematical exercises, the computational/numerate aspects should be considered in conjunction with motivational effects of budgets and standards used as targets.

- Both budgets and standards can be designed to show purely the expected results for a forthcoming period or may be designed to provide a more difficult target in order to motivate managers/workers.

Differences

- The biggest difference between budgets and standards is that standards tend to be expressed per unit, whereas budgets are for much bigger entities such as departments, functions or resources.

- Standards are most often set for materials and labour (but can be set for variable overheads and fixed overheads). Budgets cover a much greater variety of costs and entities, such as cash, fixed assets, research and development, etc.

- Standards are often set up in order to prepare the budget.

Chapter 15

EXAM-TYPE QUESTIONS

Question 1

D   **Material price variance:**

Calculated based on purchases because an integrated standard costing system is in use:

Cost saving per unit = £0.20 (£4.50 − £4.70)

Total saving = 5,000 × £0.20 = £1,000

This is a favourable variance and will be credited to the variance account.

2,400 units of the finished product should use 4,800 units of material (2,400 × 2).

Actual usage was 50 units more (4,850 − 4,800), so the usage variance is:

50 × £4.70 (standard price) = £235 (A)

This will be debited to the variance account.

Question 2

D   Rate variance

	£
11,700 hours should cost £6.40/hour	74,880
Actual cost	64,150
Price variance	10,730 F

Efficiency variance

	Hours
2,300 units should use 4.5 hours each	10,350
Actual hours	11,700
An extra	1,350 hours

1,350 hours @ £6.40/hour (standard rate) = £8,640 A

Question 3

D   £

	£
Actual cost was	98,350
19,100 hours should cost:	
19,100 × £5.40	103,140
Rate variance	4,790 (F)

	Hours
Actual hours	19,100
4,650 units should require:	
4,650 × 4 hours	18,600
An extra	500
500 hours × £5.40 (standard rate)	£2,700 (A)

Question 4

$$\text{Standard price/kg} = \frac{\text{Standard cost}}{\text{Actual usage}}$$

$$= \text{£46,248/11,280}$$
$$= \text{£4.10}$$

The usage variance is adverse so the actual usage exceeded the standard allowed weight. The excess usage is:

£492/£4.10   = 120 kg

Standard allowed weight = Actual usage − Excess usage

= 11,280 kg − 120 kg

= 11,160 kg

Question 5

An efficiency variance of £7,800 equates to 1,200 standard hours (1,200 × £6.50 = £7,800). Since the variance is favourable, this amount must be added to the actual hours worked: 17,500 + 1,200 = 18,700 standard hours.

Question 6

D Since stock is valued at standard cost, the price variance is extracted at the time of purchase.

Price variance:	£
8,200 kg should cost £0.80/kg =	6,560
Actual cost	6,888
	328 (A)

Usage variance:	
870 units should use 8 kg/unit =	6,960 kg
Actual usage	7,150 kg
	190 kg

190 kg @ £0.80/kg = £152 (A)

PRACTICE QUESTION

Company M

Tutorial note: The question asks for a 'format suitable for presentation to management'. It is therefore recommended that the first part of the solution is a summary of the variances and the detailed workings are shown separately.

Summary of variances for one accounting period

(F = Favourable; A = Adverse)

	£
Materials:	
Price	1,885 (A)
Usage	2,610 (A)
Cost	4,495 (A)
Labour:	
Rate:	551 (A)
Efficiency	580 (F)
Cost	29 (F)

Workings

	£			£	

Direct materials

	£			£	
Actual cost	35,815		Price variance	1,885	(A)
Actual quantity purchased/ used at 3,770 × £9	33,930		Usage variance	2,610	(A)
Standard quantity for actual production at standard price 290 × 12 × £9	31,320			4,495	(A)
Cost variance					

Labour

	£			£	
Actual cost	11,571		Rate variance	551	(A)
Actual hours paid/worked at standard rate 2,755 × £4	11,020		Efficiency variance	580	(F)
Standard hours for actual production at standard rate 290 × 10 × £4	11,600			29	(F)
Cost variance					

Assumptions

1 Quantity of material purchased = Quantity used.

2 Actual hours paid for = Actual hours worked.

Chapter 16

EXAM-TYPE QUESTIONS

Question 1

D **Expenditure variance**

Monthly budgeted production (10,800/12)	900 units		
		£	
Monthly budgeted expenditure			
900 × £4		3,600	Fixed
800 (flexed budget) × £6		4,800	Variable
		8,400	
Actual expenditure		8,500	
Expenditure variance		100	(A)

Volume variance

This only applies to fixed overhead costs:

Difference in volume = 100 units

100 units × £4 per unit = £400 (A)

Question 2

Absorption rate $= \dfrac{£100,000}{20,000} = £5/\text{unit}$

Difference in volume	=	20,000 − 19,500	
	=	500 units	
Volume variance	=	500 units × £5/unit	
	=	£2,500 (A)	

It is adverse because actual volume is less than that budgeted.

Question 3

B   Budgeted cost $\dfrac{£240,000}{12 \text{ months}}$ =   £20,000

Actual cost   =   £19,600

£400 (F)

Question 4

D   Budgeted volume/period is:

$\dfrac{\text{Budgeted cost/period}}{\text{Absorption rate/unit}} = \dfrac{£20,000}{£40}$ =   500

Actual units   =   450

Shortfall   50 units

50 units × £40/unit = £2,000 (A)

Question 5

(a)   Iron $= 2 \times (800 \times 5 - 3,900) =$ £200 (F)
      Copper $= 3 \times (800 \times 3 - 2,600) =$ £600 (A)

Total material usage variance   £400 (A)

(b)   Labour rate variance = $(3,400 \times £7 - (2,000 \times £7 + 1,400 \times £7.20)) = £280$ (A)

(c)   **A**   Variable overhead expenditure = $3,400 \times 3 - 10,000$ $= £200$ (F)

(d)   **C**   Fixed overhead expenditure = $(£2 \times 4,000) - £8,800$ $= £800$ (A)

(e)   Fixed overhead volume = $£8 \times (800 - (4,000 \div 4))$ $= £1,600$ (A)

PRACTICE QUESTION

Department 7

(a)   Calculation of variance

(F = Favourable; A = Adverse)

Fixed overhead volume variance

Budget		Actual	Variance
8,000	–	8,400	$= 400 \text{ hours} \times \dfrac{£6,750 + £3,250}{8,000}$

$$= 400 \times £1.25 = £500 \text{ (F)}$$

Fixed overhead expenditure variance

Flexed budget	Actual	Variance
£	£	£
6,750	6,400	
3,250	3,315	
10,000	9,715	£285 (F)

Variable overhead expenditure variance

Original budget	Flexed budget	Actual £	Variance
17,600		20,140	
6,000		5,960	
4,400		4,480	
$28,000 \times \dfrac{8,400}{8,000} = £29,400$		30,580	£1,180 (A)

(b)   Operating statement for control of department overheads

	Flexed budget	Actual	Variance
	£	£	£
Fixed overhead:			
Salaries	6,750	6,400	350 (F)
Maintenance	3,250	3,315	65 (A)
Total	10,000	9,715	285 (F)
Variable overhead:			
Power $£17,600 \times \dfrac{8,400}{8,000} =$	18,480	20,140	1,660 (A)
Consumable materials $£6,000 \times \dfrac{8,400}{8,000} =$	6,300	5,960	340 (F)
Indirect labour $£4,400 \times \dfrac{8,400}{8,000} =$	4,620	4,480	140 (F)
Total	29,400	30,580	1,180 (A)
Overall total	39,400	40,295	895 (A)

Strictly an 'operating statement' should include information relating to sales and to prime costs but information was not provided by the examiner.

A further point is that in practice variances would normally be stated for the previous month and for the budget period to date.

Chapter 17

EXAM-TYPE QUESTIONS

Question 1

	£	
Actual contribution earned, based on standard unit costs:		
actual sales revenue	54,000	
std variable cost of actual sales volume (4,500 × £5.60)	25,200	
	28,800	
Budgeted contribution (5,000 × £(10.00 − 5.60))	22,000	
Total sales contribution variance	6,800	(F)

Question 2

Budgeted sales units = £100,000/£8 = 12,500 units

	£	
Actual margin earned, based on standard unit costs:		
actual sales revenue	99,000	
std cost of actual sales volume(11,000 × £(8.00 − 2.50))	60,500	
	38,500	
Budgeted margin (12,500 units × £2.50)	31,250	
Total sales margin variance	7,250	(F)

Question 3

Budgeted contribution	= 18,000 × £40 = £720,000
Budgeted fixed costs	= £580,000 + £20,000 = £600,000
Budgeted profit	= £720,000 − £600,000 = £120,000

PRACTICE QUESTION

Gunge

(a) **Direct material**

	£	
Actual quantity at actual price	120,000	Price variance
Actual quantity at standard price		£9,000 (A)
37,000 kg @ £3/kg	111,000	Usage variance
Standard quantity at standard price		£3,000 (F)
(9,500 × 4) @ £3/kg	114,000	

Direct labour

	£	
Actual hours at actual rate	200,000	Rate variance
Actual hours at standard rate		£4,000 (A)
49,000 hours @ £4/hour	196,000	Efficiency
Standard hours at standard rate		variance
(9,500 × 5) @ £4/hour	190,000	£6,000 (A)

Variable overhead

	£	
Actual hours at actual rate	47,000	Expenditure
Actual hours at standard rate		variance
49,000 hours @ £1/hour	49,000	£2,000 (F)
Standard hours at standard rate		Efficiency
(9,500 × 5) @ £1/hour	47,500	variance
		£1,500 (A)

Fixed overhead

	£	
Actual cost	145,000	Expenditure
Budgeted cost: 10,000 galls. @ £15/gall.		variance
		£5,000 (F)
Standard cost (overhead absorbed)	150,000	Volume
9,500 galls. @ £15/gall.	142,500	variance
		£7,500 (A)

(b) **Sales margin variance**

		£
Actual margin earned, based on standard unit costs:		
actual sales revenue		588,500
standard cost of actual sales volume	(9,500 × £52)	494,000
		94,500
Budgeted margin	(10,000 × £(60 − 52))	80,000
Total sales margin variance		14,500 (F)

Profit reconciliation statement
Period 4

		£	£
Budgeted profit			80,000
Sales margin variance			14,500 (F)
			94,500
Cost variances:	Materials	6,000 (A)	
	Labour	10,000 (A)	
	Variable overhead	500 (F)	
	Fixed overhead	2,500 (A)	
			18,000 (A)
Actual profit			76,500

Chapter 18

EXAM-TYPE QUESTIONS

Question 1

The value of closing work in progress was £214,425

	Job 1 £	Job 2 £	Total £
Opening WIP	8,500	0	8,500
Material in period	17,150	29,025	46,175
Labour for period	12,500	23,000	35,500
Overheads (see working)	43,750	80,500	124,250
Closing WIP	81,900	132,525	214,425

Working

Total labour for period = £(12,500 + 23,000 + 4,500) = £40,000

$\therefore$ Overhead absorption rate = $\dfrac{£140,000}{£40,000}$ = 350% of direct wages

Question 2

The selling price of a circuit board is £41.41

	Job 3 £
Opening WIP	46,000
Labour for period	4,500
Overheads (3.5 × £4,500)	15,750
Total production costs	66,250
Profit (50%)	33,125
Selling price of 2,400 boards	99,375

$\therefore$ Selling price of one board = £41.41

Question 3

Of the four items listed, only the actual manufacturing overheads would not be contained in a typical job cost. Overheads are absorbed into the cost of jobs using a predetermined absorption rate; the actual overhead cost for each job is not known.

Question 4

The overhead to be absorbed by job number CC20 is £72,761.

Assuming overhead is absorbed based on labour cost:

$$\frac{£24,600}{£(24,600 + 14,500 + 3,500)} \times £126,000 = £72,761$$

Question 5

The selling price of job number BB15 is £56,642	£
WIP	42,790
Material	–
Labour	3,500
Overhead $\dfrac{£3,500}{£(24,600+14,500+3,500)} \times £126,000$	10,352
	56,642

$$\Rightarrow \text{sales price} = \frac{£56,642}{66\frac{2}{3}} \times 100 = £84,963$$

Question 6

The approximate value of closing work in progress is £217,323.

	AA10 £	CC20 £	Total £
Opening WIP	26,800	0	
Materials	17,275	18,500	
Labour	14,500	24,600	
Overhead	42,887	72,761	
Total	101,462	115,861	217,323

(Exclude BB15 as it was completed and delivered during the period, per question 5.)

PRACTICE QUESTION

Job number 123

Notes:

1 One point to note is that overhead is absorbed at an actual rate. The normal approach is to use a predetermined rate.

2 The information is presented in three sections:

- quantities specifically related to Job 123, labelled as items (1) to (4)

- actual overhead costs of Departments A and B

- information concerning Materials Y and Z.

The approach in answering is to go through items (1) to (4) one at a time and select the relevant information from the other parts of the question as needed.

3 The weighted average used here is a periodic average, i.e. calculated monthly as opposed to continuously valuing each issue as it occurs during the month. The latter approach is normally used in problems concerning valuation of issues.

(a) **List of costs that should be assigned to job number 123**

(1)

	Kilos	£
Material Y:		
Opening stock	1,050	529.75
Purchases	600	300.00
	500	250.00
	400	208.00
	2,550	1,287.75

$$\text{Weighted average price} = \frac{£1,287.75}{2,550} = £0.505$$

Value of material issued to this job: 400 kilos @ £0.505 = £202.00

(2) Department A labour: 76 hours @ £4.50 = £342.00

It is assumed that the overtime is not worked at the specific request of the customer for Job 123 and hence the premium has been excluded from direct cost and therefore included in production overhead.

(3)

	Kilos	Value £
Material Z	6,970	9,946.50
	16,000	23,360.00
	22,970	33,306.50

$$\text{Weighted average price} = \frac{£33,306.50}{22,970} = £1.45$$

Value of material issued to this job: $(300 - 35) \times £1.45$ = £384.25

(4) Department B labour: 110 hours @ £4 = £440.00

The cost of the overtime premium should be charged as a direct cost to the other customer's jobs.

Carried forward	£1,368.25
Brought forward	£1,368.25

(5) Production overhead:

	Dept A £	Dept B £
Amount incurred:		
Indirect labour	2,510	2,960
Overtime premium*	450	–
Lubricants and cleaning compounds	520	680
Maintenance	720	510
Other	1,200	2,150
	5,400	6,300

* Overtime premium in department B is a direct cost of a specific job.

Overhead recovery rate:

$$\frac{\text{Actual overhead}}{\text{Actual labour hours}} = \quad \frac{£5,400}{2,000} \qquad \frac{£6,300}{2,800}$$

$$= £2.70 \text{ per} \quad = £2.25 \text{ per}$$
$$\text{labour hour} \quad \text{labour hour}$$

Production overhead absorbed by Job number 123:

Department A: 76 hours @ £2.70	£205.20
Department B: 110 hours @ £2.25	£247.50
Cost of Job No. 123	£1,820.95

(b) The cost of individual jobs may be used in the following ways:

(i) The estimated cost can be calculated in advance in order to provide a basis for fixing the selling price. In this case it would be necessary to use a predetermined overhead absorption rate.

(ii) The estimated budgeted cost can be used as a guideline while the work is being carried out so as to try to ensure that actual costs are kept within the original estimate.

(iii) The actual cost of jobs can be used for valuing work-in-progress stock if the job is on hand at the end of the accounting period.

(iv) Actual cost can be compared with the estimated cost in order to identify variances on individual cost items. This should help to control costs and to improve the quality of future estimates.

(v) Actual cost can be compared with the selling price of the job in order to assess profitability of the job.

Chapter 19

EXAM-TYPE QUESTIONS

Question 1

	£
Value certified	1,300,000
Cost of work certified	1,000,000
Notional profit to date	300,000

$$£300,000 \times \frac{\text{Cash received}}{\text{Value certified}}$$

$$= £300,000 \times \frac{£1,200,000}{£1,300,000}$$

$$= £276,923$$

Question 2

Contract costing is used when the work is usually unique, customer specific, and takes a long time to complete (usually more than one year).

Thus only (ii) is correct.

Question 3

C   Costs would be affected by the quantity delivered and the distance travelled. Cost per tonne mile gives a measure of both quantity and distance.

Question 4

Service industries use composite cost units, e.g. passenger miles, because it is difficult to measure their output activity using a single measure. Therefore (ii) is correct. It is difficult to identify costs with cost units for the same reason. Therefore there is a high level of indirect cost and (i) is correct. Equivalent units are used in connection with work-in-progress stocks, which does not apply in service costing, therefore (iii) is incorrect.

PRACTICE QUESTION

Jigantic plc

Note: the key to dealing with the profit calculation is to try to use the SSAP 9 approach by calculating total profit (contract price – [costs to date + estimated costs to completion]).

If there is insufficient information (i.e. estimated costs to completion not given), then calculate profit to date based on value of work certified, i.e. profit should always be calculated so as to identify any losses – in this case on Contract A.

It is then necessary to consider whether the contracts are sufficiently far advanced for it to be 'prudent' to recognise profit.

For Contract B the contract is, based on 'sale value' (7,500/10,200 × 100%), approximately 75% completed.

It is therefore assumed reasonable to take profit.

It is also reasonable to take profit on Contract C as it is 'nearing completion'.

(a)   **Cost of contracts as at 31 May 20X1**

	Contract A £'000	Contract B £'000	Contract C £'000
Cost to 1 June 20X0		2,400	5,550
Costs incurred during the year:			
Materials	1,100	1,600	1,050
Labour	700	1,150	975
Other expenses	350	475	775
Depreciation (b)	425	675	650
Total cost to 31 May 20X1	2,575	6,300	9,000

(b)   **Depreciation of plant and equipment**

	Contract A £'000	Contract B £'000	Contract C £'000
Written down value, 1 June 20X0	300	800	700
Purchases	725	400	125
	1,025	1,200	825
Written down value, 31 May 20X1	600	525	175
Depreciation for the year	425	675	650

Contract A

	£'000	£'000
Value of work certified		2,350
Cost as at 31 May 20X1 (a)	2,575	
Less: Cost of work not yet certified	75	
		2,500
Loss to date		(150)

To include a 'nil' profit in the accounts would be inappropriate since clearly the contract has incurred a loss of £150,000 to date. In accordance with the requirements of SSAP 9 relating to long-term contract work-in-progress, this loss should be incorporated into the year's accounts. Strictly speaking the loss expected to arise on the whole of the contract should be provided for but insufficient information has been given to do this (i.e. estimated completion costs not given).

Contract B

	£'000
Value of work certified	7,500
Cost as at 31 May 20X1 (a)	6,300
Profit to date	1,200

The proposed profit figure of £720,000 is well below the profit that has been earned to date. However, because of the uncertainty surrounding long-term contracts, considerable caution should be exercised when allocating profits over the life of a contract. Hence a figure lower than £1,200,000 presumably reduced in accordance with the accounting policy of the company, is acceptable.

Note: it would appear that the examiner used the following formula for estimating the amount of profit to incorporate into the profit and loss account:

$$\frac{2}{3} \times \frac{\text{Cash received}}{\text{Value of work certified}} \times \text{Profit to date} = \frac{2}{3} \times \frac{6,750}{7,500} \times 1,200 = 720$$

This formula is recognised in many textbooks but represents only one possible way of prudently reducing profits to take account of the uncertainty surrounding uncompleted contracts.

Contract C

	£'000	£'000
Contract price		12,000
Cost as at May 20X1 (a)	9,000	
Estimated completion costs (425 + 175)	600	
		9,600
Estimated total profit		2,400

The proposal to incorporate a profit of £2,400,000 in the profit and loss account for the year ended 31 May 20X1 is not allowable for three reasons:

- an estimated profit of £1,150,000 for Contract C has already been included in previous years' accounts
- some provision should be made for expenses which have not been anticipated but which may well arise, for example, the cost of rectification work

- part of the work is yet to be carried out. Profit should only prudently be taken on work completed by the end of the accounting period.

Hence the figure of £2,400,000 needs to be reduced in two respects: firstly to reflect the work done to date – by using the formula:

$$\text{Total profit } \times \frac{\text{Value of work certified}}{\text{Contract price}}$$

and secondly by the profit incorporated in previous years' profit and loss accounts.

	£'000
Profit on contract to date $2{,}400 \times \dfrac{11{,}000}{12{,}000}$	2,200
Less: Profit already taken	1,150
Profit applicable to this year's accounts	1,050

Chapter 20

EXAM-TYPE QUESTIONS

Question 1

The abnormal loss is 2,300 litres

$2{,}000 + 42{,}300 - (1{,}500 + 40{,}100 + 400) = 2{,}300$

Question 2

The cost per car was £1.20

Opening work-in-progress	+	Started	=	Finished	+	Closing work-in-progress
= 20,000	+	110,000	=	90,000	+	40,000

$$\text{Cost per car} = \frac{£132{,}000}{90{,}000 + (0.5 \times 40{,}000)} = £1.20$$

Question 3

D   If the number of equivalent unit is down, then cost per unit is up and cost of finished goods is up.

Question 4

D   Statement A is correct. Job costs are identified with a particular job, whereas process costs (of units produced and work-in-process) are averages, based on equivalent units of production.

Statement B is also correct. The direct cost of a job to date, excluding any direct expenses, can be ascertained from materials requisition notes and job tickets or time sheets.

Statement C is correct, because without data about units completed and units still in process, losses and equivalent units of production cannot be calculated.

Statement D is incorrect, because the cost of normal loss will usually be incorporated into job costs as well as into process costs. In process costing this is commonly done by giving normal loss no cost, leaving costs to be shared between output, closing stocks and abnormal loss/gain. In job costing it can be done by adjusting direct materials costs to allow for normal wastage, and direct labour costs for normal reworking of items or normal spoilage.

Question 5

D

Process account (units only)

	Units		Units
Opening WIP	2,000	Normal loss	2,400
Input	24,000	Output	19,500
		Closing WIP	3,000
		Abnormal loss (balance)	1,100
	———		———
	26,000		26,000
	———		———

Equivalents units table

	Materials		Conversion	
	%	eu	%	eu
Output	100	19,500	100	19,500
Abnormal loss	100	1,100	100	1,100
Closing WIP	100	3,000	45	1,350
		———		———
		23,600		21,950
		———		———

PRACTICE QUESTION

Chemical Compound

(a)   **Process A**

$$\text{Cost/kg} = \frac{\text{Total costs - scrap value of normal loss}}{\text{Expected output}}$$

Total costs

	£
Direct material (2,000kg @ £5/kg)	10,000
Direct labour	7,200
Process plant time (140hrs @ £60/hr)	8,400
Departmental overhead (60% × £7,200) (W1)	4,320
	———
	29,920
Scrap value of normal loss (20% × 2,000kg × £0.50/kg)	200
	———
	29,720
	———

$$\text{Cost/kg} = \frac{£29,720}{2,000\text{kg} \times 80\%} = £18.575\text{/kg}$$

Process A

	Kg	£		Kg	£
Direct material	2,000	10,000	Normal loss	400	200
Direct labour		7,200	Process B	1,400	26,005
Process plant time		8,400	Abnormal loss	200	3,715
Departmental overhead		4,320			
				2,000	29,920
	2,000	29,920			

(b) **Process B**

Total costs

	£
Transfer from process A	26,005
Direct material (1,400kg @ £12/kg)	16,800
Direct labour	4,200
Process plant time (80hrs @ £72.50/hr)	5,800
Departmental overhead (60% × £4,200)	2,520
	55,325
Scrap value of normal loss (2,800kg × 10% × £1.825)	(511)
	54,814

$$\text{Cost/kg} = \frac{£54,814}{2,800\text{kg} \times 90\%} = £21.751587$$

Process B

	Kg	£		Kg	£
Process A	1,400	26,005	Normal loss	280	511
Direct material	1,400	16,800	Finished goods	2,620	56,989
Direct labour		4,200			
Process plant time		5,800			
Departmental overhead		2,520			
Abnormal gain	100	2,175			
	2,900	57,500		2,900	57,500

(c)

Scrap

	Kg	£		Kg	£
Process A – normal loss	400	200	Scrap	100	182.5
Abnormal loss – A	200	100	Bank (Bal)	780	628.5
Process B – normal loss	280	511			
	880	811		880	811.0

(d)

Abnormal loss/gain

	Kg	£		Kg	£
Process A	200	3,715	Scrap	200	100
Scrap	100	182.5	Process B	100	2,175
			P&L a/c (Bal fig)		1,622.5
	300	3,897.5		300	3,897.5

(e)

Finished goods

	£		£
Process B	56,989		

(f)

Profit and Loss account (Extract)

	£		£
Abnormal loss/gain	1,622.5		

Workings

(W1) Departmental overhead absorption rate

$$= \frac{£6,840}{£7,200 + £4,200} = 60\% \text{ of direct labour cost}$$

Chapter 21

EXAM-TYPE QUESTIONS

Question 1

A This transaction increases the asset 'work-in-progress', so debit work-in-progress; it decreases the asset 'materials stock', so credit stores control.

Question 2

A The others are incorrect.

Question 3

A Materials price variances are conventionally extracted when materials are bought (via the materials control account) rather than after having been transferred to the WIP account.

PRACTICE QUESTION

Integrated process

(a) **Initial working**

Overhead absorption rates, using data for opening work in progress:

$$\text{Process 1} = \frac{£22,400}{£6,400} \times 100\% = 350\% \text{ of direct wages}$$

$$\text{Process 2} = \frac{£22,000}{£8,800} \times 100\% = 250\% \text{ of direct wages}$$

Stores control

	£		£
Balance, 31 May	90,400	Returns	1,560
Purchases	42,500	Process 1	21,200
		Process 2	10,400
		Production overhead	1,280
		Balance, 30 June	98,460
	132,900		132,900

Work-in-progress – Process 1

	Material £	Wages £	Overhead £	Total £		Material £	Wages £	Overhead £	Total £
Balance, 31 May	8,200	6,400	22,400	37,000	Abnormal loss	480	400	1,400	2,280
Direct materials	21,200	–	–	21,200	Transfers to				
Direct wages	–	16,800	–	16,800	Process 2	24,600	19,600	68,600	112,800
Production					Balance 30 June	4,320	3,200	11,200	18,720
overhead	–	–	58,800	58,800					
						29,400	23,200	81,200	133,800
	29,400	23,200	81,200	133,800					

Work-in-progress – Process 2

	Material £	Wages £	Overhead £	Total £		Material £	Wages £	Overhead £	Total £
Balance, 31 May	31,200	8,800	22,000	62,000	Abnormal loss	1,400	280	700	2,380
Transfers in					Transfers to				
(Process 1)	112,800	–	–	112,800	finished goods	110,000	20,520	51,300	181,820
Direct materials	10,400	–	–	10,400	Balance, 30 June	43,000	9,600	24,000	76,600
Direct wages	–	21,600	–	21,600					
Production									
overhead	–	–	54,000	54,000		154,400	30,400	76,000	260,800
	154,400	30,400	76,000	260,800					

Finished goods

	£		£
Balance, 31 May	89,000	Cost of sales (bal. fig.)	172,620
Process 2	181,820	Balance, 30 June	98,200
	270,820		270,820

Production overhead control

	£		£
Indirect wages and salaries	48,200	Balance, 31 May	4,800
Production indirect expenses	72,000	WIP, Process 1	58,800
Maintenance materials	1,280	WIP, Process 2	54,000
		Balance, 30 June	3,880
	121,480		121,480

Sales

	£		£
Balance, 30 June	980,000	Balance, 31 May	680,000
		General ledger control	300,000
	980,000		980,000

Cost of sales

	£		£
Balance, 31 May	529,200	Balance, 30 June	701,820
Finished goods	172,620		
	701,820		701,820

General ledger control

	£		£
Returns	1,560	Balance, 30 May	131,800
Sales	300,000	Purchases	42,500
Balance, 30 June	31,340	Direct wages – wages control	38,400
		Indirect wages and salaries	
		– wages control	48,200
		Production indirect expenses	72,000
	332,900		332,900

Abnormal loss

	£		£
Balance, 31 May	9,000	Balance, 30 June	13,660
Process 1	2,280		
Process 2	2,380		
	13,660		13,660

Wages control

	£		£
Direct wages	38,000	Work in process 1	16,800
Indirect wages	48,200	Work in process 2	21,600
		Production overhead control	48,200
	86,600		86,600

(b) Trial balance as at 30 June

	£	£	£
Stores control		98,460	
Work-in-progress, Process 1:			
Direct materials	4,320		
Direct wages	3,200		
Production overhead	11,200		
		18,720	
Work-in-progress, Process 2:			
Direct materials	43,000		
Direct wages	9,600		
Production overhead	24,000		
		76,600	
Finished goods		98,200	
Production overhead, under/over-absorbed		3,880	
Sales			980,000
Cost of sales		701,820	
General ledger control			31,340
Abnormal loss		13,660	
		1,011,340	1,011,340

Index